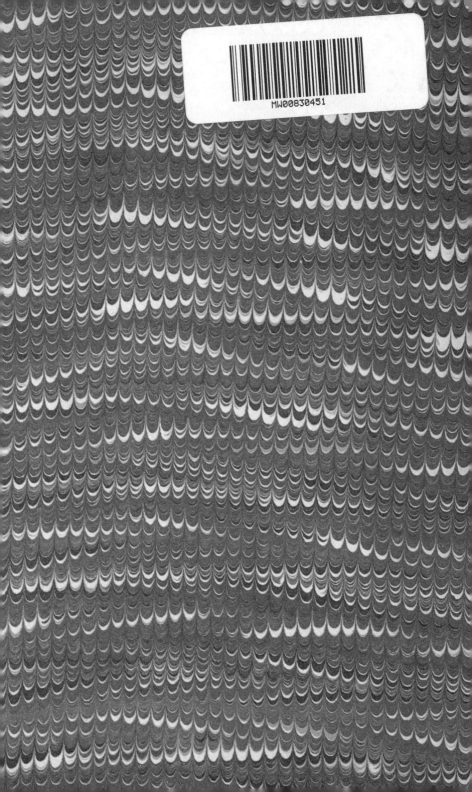

Reprinted 1984 from the 1910 edition.
Cover design © 1981 Time-Life Books Inc.
Library of Congress CIP data following page 362.

This volume is bound in leather.

A SOLDIER'S RECOLLECTIONS

BELVIDERE, BALTIMORE, MD.

The Author's boyhood home

A SOLDIER'S RECOLLECTIONS

LEAVES FROM THE DIARY OF A YOUNG CONFEDERATE

WITH AN ORATION ON THE MOTIVES AND AIMS OF THE SOLDIERS OF THE SOUTH

BY

RANDOLPH H. McKIM

LATE 1ST LIEUTENANT AND A. D. C., 3D BRIGADE, JOHNSTON'S
DIVISION, ARMY OF NORTHERN VIRGINIA

"QUAEQUE IPSE . . . VIDI"

LONGMANS, GREEN, AND CO.
FOURTH AVENUE & 30TH STREET, NEW YORK
LONDON, BOMBAY, AND CALCUTTA
1910

THE · PLIMPTON · PRESS
[W · D · O]
NORWOOD · MASS · U · S · A

𝕿𝖔

THE PRIVATE SOLDIERS OF THE
CONFEDERATE ARMIES

FOREWORD

I HAVE set down in the pages that follow some of my experiences and observations during my service with the Army of Northern Virginia, first as a private soldier, then as a staff officer, and finally as a chaplain in the field. I served in the ranks under Gen. Jos. E. Johnston and Gen. Thos. J. Jackson; as a staff officer under Brigadier-Gen. Geo. H. Steuart in the army of Gen. R. E. Lee; and as a chaplain in the Second Virginia Cavalry under Col. Thos. T. Munford, in the brigade of Gen. Fitzhugh Lee.

It has not been my purpose to write a history of the campaigns in which I took so humble a part, but simply to present a few pen and ink sketches of the life and experience of a Confederate soldier, in the hope that I may thereby contribute in some small degree to a better understanding of the spirit of the epoch — both of the soldiers who fought the battles, and of the people on whose behalf they dared and suffered what they did.

In telling this plain and unvarnished story I have been aided by the diary, or rather the diaries, which I kept during the war, and from which I have freely quoted, just as they were written, without recasting the sentences, or improving the style, or toning down the sentiments they contain. The thoughts and the opinions expressed, and the often crude form in which

they are cast, are just those of a young soldier, jotted
down on the march, or by the camp-fire, or in the quies-
cent intervals of battle, without any thought that
they would ever be put into print. This I have done,
believing that I would thus best attain my object,
— to show the mind and the life of the Confederate
soldier as they were while the struggle was going on.
But there was a hiatus in my material. My diary
for the larger part of one of the four years of the war
was lost, and therefore I have omitted those months
from my narrative.

I have also tried to give the point of view of the
young men of the South in espousing the cause of the
Confederacy, and to remove some misapprehensions
still entertained in regard to the motives which animated the men who followed the banner of the Southern Cross.

In connection with the Gettysburg campaign, I
have undertaken to discuss the much mooted question of the action of Gen. J. E. B. Stuart, with the cavalry under his command. This I have felt constrained
to do because of the view (erroneous, as I believe)
presented by Col. John S. Mosby in his recent book
on the subject.

I have also reproduced an article written many years
ago by request, and published in the Southern Historical Society Magazine, telling the story of the part
taken at Gettysburg by the Third Brigade of Johnson's Division, Ewell's Corps. And in the Appendix
I have placed an Oration upon the Motives and Aims
of the Soldiers of the South, delivered in 1904 before
the United Confederate Veterans.

Fully sensible how much I stand in need of the

reader's indulgent good-will as he follows me in this simple story of an obscure soldier's life in the Army of Northern Virginia, I still hope that what I have recorded may, here and there, throw a side-light on the conditions under which the Confederate soldier lived and fought those four stern, fateful years, and give fresh emphasis to his purity of motive and his heroic constancy in danger and adversity.

One closing word as to the spirit in which I have undertaken this modest contribution to the literature of the Civil War. I am not, in these pages, brooding over the ashes of the past. The soldiers of the Southern Cross have long ago bowed to the decree of Almighty God in the issue of the great conflict. His will is wiser and better than ours. We thank God that to-day the sun shines on a truly reunited country. We love our Southland; we are Southern men; but we are glad that sectionalism is dead and buried, and we claim our full part in working out the great destiny that lies before the American people. We may not forget — we veterans of the Civil War — that the best of our life and work lies behind us: *morituri salutamus.* But whatever of life remains to us we have long ago dedicated to the service of our common country. We joyfully accept our share in the responsibilities, the opportunities, the strenuous conflicts, of the future, against foes within and without, for the moral and material glory of our country. We are Americans in every fibre; and nothing that pertains to the honor, to the welfare, to the glory, of America is foreign to us.

CONTENTS

LIST OF ILLUSTRATIONS

A SOLDIER'S RECOLLECTIONS

CHAPTER I

ON THE BRINK OF THE MAELSTROM

ON a bright morning in the month of April, 1861, there is a sudden explosion of excitement at the University of Virginia. Shouts and cheers are heard from the various precincts where the students lodge. Evidently something unusual has occurred. The explanation is soon found as one observes all eyes turned to the dome of the rotunda from whose summit the Secession flag is seen waving. It has been placed there during the night by persons then unknown. Of course it has no right there, for the University is a State institution and the State has not seceded; on the contrary the Constitutional Convention has given only a few days before a strong vote for the Union.

But it is evident the foreign flag is a welcome intruder in the precincts of Jefferson's University, for a great throng of students is presently assembled on the lawn in front of the lofty flight of steps leading up to the rotunda, and one after another of the leaders of the young men mounts the steps and harangues the crowd in favor of the Southern Confederacy and the Southern flag waving proudly up there. Among the speakers I recall Wm. Randolph Berkeley, the recently elected orator of the Jefferson Society.

So general was the sympathy with the Southern cause

that not a voice was raised in condemnation of the
rebellious and burglarious act of the students who
must have been guilty of raising the Southern flag.
Not so general was the approval of the professors;
some of these were strong Union men, among them one
who was deservedly revered by the whole student
body, Prof. John B. Minor, the head of the Law Department. Walking up under the arcades to his lecture room, he was shocked at the sight that met his
eyes, and (so a wag afterwards reported) broke forth
into rhyme as follows:

> "Flag of my country, can it be
> That that rag's up there instead of thee!"

Meantime the excitement waxed greater and greater,
so much so that the students forsook their lecture
rooms to attend the mass-meeting on the lawn. In
vain did Prof. Schele de Vere endeavor to fix the
attention of his class by the swelling periods of his
famous lecture on Joan of Arc. The proceedings
outside on the lawn interested them much more than
the tragic fate of the Maid of Orleans, and one after
another they rose and stalked out of the lecture room
to join in the overture to another and more tremendous tragedy then unfolding itself to the world, until
the baffled professor of modern languages gave up the
attempt and abruptly closed his lecture.

At this juncture the burly form of Dr. Albert Taylor
Bledsoe, professor of mathematics, was seen mount-
ing the steps of the rotunda, his great head as usual
far in advance of the rest of his body. At once there
was silence in the throng. To him the students gave
a respectful attention, such as, I fear, in their then

mood, they would not have given to Professor Minor. For Dr. Bledsoe was an enthusiastic advocate of Secession, to such an extent that he would not infrequently interlard his demonstration of some difficult problem in differential or integral calculus — for example, the *lemniscata* of Bernouilli—with some vigorous remarks in the doctrine of States' rights.

At this juncture, however, the big-brained professor spoke to the young men in a somewhat different strain. He began by saying he had no doubt the students who had put up that flag were "the very nicest fellows in the University," but, inasmuch as the State of Virginia had not yet seceded, the Secession flag did not really belong on that rotunda, and he hoped the students themselves would take it down, — "but," he said, "young gentlemen, do it very tenderly."

The facts of the case were these. A group of seven students (of whom I was one) bought the bunting and had the flag made, seven stars and three bars, by some young lady friends who were bound to secrecy, and then, having supplied themselves with augers and small saws, they went to work after midnight and sawed their way through five doors to gain access to the roof of the rotunda, where, in their stocking feet, they at length succeeded, not without risk of a fatal fall, in giving the "Stars and Bars" to the breeze, just as the first faint streaks of dawn appeared on the eastern hills. They then scattered and betook themselves to bed, and were the last men in the University to hear the news that the Secession flag was floating over the rotunda!

It was not many days after this occurrence that Mr. Lincoln issued his proclamation calling upon Virginia to furnish her quota of troops to coerce the seceded States back into the Union, and thereby instantly transformed the old Commonwealth from a Union State into a seceded State. All differences now disappeared among her statesmen and her people, and Virginia with entire unanimity threw in her lot with her Southern sisters "for better, for worse, for weal or for woe."

It was the *threat of invasion* that revolutionized the position of the State of Virginia. In illustration of this I refer to the case of a talented young man from Richmond who had been an extreme and uncompromising "Union man" — the most extreme among all the students at the University. He was also bold and aggressive in the advocacy of his opinions, so much so that he became very unpopular, and his friends feared "serious trouble and even bloody collision." The morning President Lincoln's proclamation appeared he had gone down town on personal business before breakfast, and while there happened to glance at a paper. He returned at once to the University, but not to breakfast; spoke not a word to any human being; packed his trunk with his belongings; left a note for the chairman of the faculty explaining his conduct; boarded the first train for Richmond, and joined a military company before going to his father's house or taking so much as a morsel of food. What was the overwhelming force which thus in a moment transformed this splendid youth? Was it not the God-implanted instinct which impels a man to *defend his own hearthstone ?* [1]

[1] The story is told by Major Robert Stiles in his "Four Years under Marse Robert."

The visitor to the University to-day will see on the rotunda porch two large bronze tablets on the right and left of the central door, on which are graven the names of the alumni who laid down their lives in the Civil War for the independence of the South.   There are just five hundred and three names.

The number itself is significant.   If five hundred died, there must have been more than two thousand five hundred, perhaps as many as three thousand, on the rolls of the Confederate armies, who called this University mother.   We have no accurate register of the number of alumni who were living in 1861 and fit for military service.   But we do know that of the six hundred and twenty-five who were students here when the tocsin of war sounded, five hundred and thirty hailed from the seceding States, and about five hundred and fifteen went to the front.   Two of the professors followed their students, — our illustrious professor of Greek, Basil L. Gildersleeve, who was wounded fighting with Gordon in the valley of Virginia — he still lives, thank God! to adorn American scholarship — and Lewis Minor Coleman, our right royal professor of Latin, who fell gloriously while commanding a battalion of artillery at Fredericksburg.

These numbers are significant.   They bear eloquent witness, not only to the gallantry of our brother alumni, but to the unanimity of the Southern people in that great struggle, and they afford convincing proof of the falsity of the theory, held by some historians of the Civil War, that the uprising of the Southern people was the result of a conspiracy of a few ambitious leaders.   When we see five hundred and fifteen out of

six hundred and twenty-five students,[1] representing
the flower of the intellect and culture of the South —
its yeomen as well as its aristocracy — spring to arms
at the first sound of the long roll, we realize that the
resistance offered to coercion in 1861 was in no sense
artificial, but free and spontaneous, and that it was
the act of the people, not of the politicians.

This conclusion may be fortified by a comparison
with the record of a great New England university.
The memorial tablets at Harvard contain the names
of one hundred and seventeen of her alumni who gave
their lives to the cause of the Union, while the whole
number who entered the Union army and navy was nine
hundred and thirty-eight. If the same proportion of
loss held among the men of our Alma Mater, then there
would have been four thousand students and alumni
of the University of Virginia in the army and navy of
the Confederate States. But the proportion of killed
in action was greater on our side, so that this total
must be much reduced. We know from the records
that not less than two thousand five hundred of the
men who followed the battle flag of the Southern Cross
were sons of this Virginia University. The actual
number was probably considerably larger. Thus
though her students and alumni of military age were
less numerous than those of Harvard, in something
like the proportion of four to seven, yet there were more
than three times as many of them serving with the
colors in the great conflict; and while one hundred and
seventeen men of the Cambridge university laid down

---

[1] This number represents all the students from all the States, North
as well as South. Not a few came from localities which were not in
sympathy with the South.

their lives for the Union, five hundred and three of the men of the University of Virginia died for the Southern cause — more than four times as many.

As I think of some of these brave young fellows, I recall the scene that used to be presented many an afternoon on the slope of the hill directly to the south of the University lawn — D'Alphonse, the stalwart professor of gymnastics, leading his numerous pupils in singing the "Marsellaise," or "Les Girondins." The clear fresh voices of those fine young fellows come back to me as I write, — the fine tenor of Robert Falligant rising above the rest, — singing:

> "Par la voix du cannon d'alarme,
> La France appelle ses enfants,
> Allons, dit le soldat, aux armes,
> C'est ma mère, je la defends.

> *Chorus,* "Mourir pour la patrie,
> Mourir pour la patrie,
> C'est le sort le plus beau
> Le plus digne d'envie!"

Alas! how soon and how unexpectedly were those words to be exemplified on the field of battle, in the gallant deaths of many who sang them then, with little realization of their possible significance for them.

There were two military companies organized at the University the autumn before the fateful cloud of Civil War burst upon the land. These were in no way connected with the organization of the institution, but were purely private and voluntary. One called itself "The Sons of Liberty," the other took the name of "The Southern Guard." To the latter I belonged, and when Virginia joined the Confederacy, these two companies of boys were ordered to Winchester, Va., to join in the movement of Gen. Thomas J. Jackson against Harper's Ferry.

I remember that after a long railway ride in box cars (which sadly tarnished our uniforms) we were detrained at Strasburg, and marched to Winchester, eighteen miles distant, beating handsomely in the march the regular companies of State militia that formed part of the expedition.

The two University companies remained several weeks at Harper's Ferry, and were then very properly ordered back to their studies. I did not tarry so long, but made my way to Baltimore, where stirring scenes had been witnessed on the 19th of April, when the Massachusetts troops en route to Washington were attacked by the populace.

Arrived there I very soon found "nothing would be doing," — advices from Confederate headquarters in Virginia discouraging any attempt in that quarter, and so after about a week's sojourn, I returned to the University, promising my mother to stay till the end of the session.

While in Baltimore at dear old "Belvidere," the beautiful home of my childhood and boyhood, I had to endure the pain of my father's displeasure, because of my espousal of the Southern cause. He himself had been in warm personal sympathy with the South, but through the strong intellectual influence of a near relative his political sympathy had been turned to the North. His heart was with my mother's people, but his head turned him to the side of the Union. I mention it because this difference was, by reason of our great mutual attachment, very painful to us both.

In an interview between us, when he had expressed himself in severe condemnation of my course, I turned and said with much feeling, "Well, father, I comfort myself with the promise, 'When my father and my mother forsake me, then the Lord will take me up.'" And so we parted never to meet again, for he died in January, 1865. A noble and high-minded man he was, and particularly devoted to me. Nothing but the strongest conviction of duty could have led me to act contrary to his wishes. During the whole war I constantly sent him messages of love, and sometimes wrote to him. When my marriage took place, February 26, 1863, he sent my bride a beautiful present with his likeness. My first child was named for him, "John," to which I added "Duncan" for my much-loved cousin. When my ordination was approaching, in April, 1864, I wrote him as follows:

"My father, I ask to be remembered at the family altar, that God may prepare me for the responsible office which I am about tremblingly to undertake after seven months' study."

No picture of this crucial epoch is a true one which suppresses these most painful divisions of sentiment which often occurred in devoted families.

When I returned to the University I had lost, first and last, six weeks at a critical part of my course. My "tickets," this my second year, were French, German, moral philosophy, and senior mathematics. I determined to drop German and concentrate on the other three schools. And then, finding the "math." examination coming on in ten days, I gave my whole time to preparation for that severe test. Such was the excitement among the students, many of whom were already leaving to join the Army, that study was very difficult, so I betook myself to a little one-room structure at the foot of Carr's Hill on the north side, isolated from other buildings, and there studied the differential and integral calculus from twelve to four-teen hours a day for the ten days before examination, Sunday excepted, with the result that on the day of the test I soon developed a severe headache, which nearly cost me my diploma. However, I passed, and later passed also in my other tickets, and received the three diplomas on Commencement day, much to my satisfaction.

These, with diplomas in Latin and Greek taken the previous year, made the path clear to the coveted and difficult honor of M.A. the third year.[1] But that "third year" never came. It was "knocked out" by four years in the school of war under Stonewall Jackson and Lee. And when these were passed, I had entered on the active duties of life.

I wrote to my mother, June 20th, as follows: "I stand moral philosophy on Tuesday next. To-morrow and next day I am to read two essays in the Moral class, — one on two of Butler's sermons, one on a chapter in the Analogy. I got through French exam-ination very well, I believe, but I am scared about my last math. examination. I find that I mistook one of the questions."

[1] On an average not more than a dozen students made the "M.A." in a year.

CHAPTER II

SOMETHING may here be appropriately said, before proceeding with my narrative, upon the constitutional question involved in the action taken by Virginia in seceding from the Union, and the action of these young men at the University in obeying her summons and rallying to the standard of the Southern Confederacy.

Virginia loved the Union which her illustrious sons had done so much to establish. She refused to secede from the Union until she was called upon to assist in the work of coercing the already seceded States back into the Union. This she refused to do. She would not raise her arm to strike down her Southern sisters. She would not be a party to the coercion of a sovereign State by the general government. That, she had been taught by the fathers of the Constitution, Washington, Madison, Jefferson, and Hamilton, was an unconstitutional act. Alexander Hamilton had denounced the proposal to coerce a State as a mad project. Edmund Randolph said it meant "civil war." So the project was abandoned in the Constitutional Convention. Her people believed that the several States possessed the inalienable right of dissolving the compact with their sister States whenever they became

11

convinced that their sacred rights were no longer safe in the Union.

All acknowledge that the right of Secession does not exist to-day. The fourteenth amendment has changed the character of the Federal Constitution. The surrender at Appomattox, moreover, involved the surrender of the right of Secession. Since the 9th of April, 1865, the Union has been indissoluble. That is universally acknowledged in the South to-day. But it was not so in 1861. Logically and historically the weight of evidence is clearly on the side of those who hold that the right of withdrawing from the Union existed from the foundation of the government.

Mr. Madison, the "father of the Constitution," held that, in adopting the Constitution, "they were making a government of a Federal nature, consisting of many co-equal sovereignties." Washington held that the Union then formed was "a compact." In a letter to Madison, Aug. 3, 1788, he uses this language, "till the States begin to act under the new compact." John Marshall said in the debate on the adoption of the Constitution: "It is a maxim that those who give may take away. It is the people that give power, and can take it back. Who shall restrain them? They are the masters who give it." This was said in discussing Virginia's right "to resume her powers if abused." Whatever he may have held late in life, this was his opinion in 1788 in the great debate on the Constitution. He was then in his thirty-third year. See Elliott's Debates, III, p. 227. It is an historical fact that the Constitution was regarded as a compact between the States by the leaders of opinion in New England for at least forty years after its adoption. In the same quarter the sovereignty of the States was broadly affirmed, and also the right of a State to resume, if need be, the powers granted or delegated under the Constitution. When Samuel Adams objected to the preamble because it expressed the idea of "a National Government instead of a Federal Union of sovereign States," Governor Hancock brought in the tenth amendment reserving to the States all the powers not expressly delegated to the General Government.

Webster and Story apostatized from the New England interpretation of the Constitution. I may here recall the fact that the first threat of Secession came from the men of New England. Four times before the Secession of South Carolina, Secession was threatened in the North, — in 1802–1803, in 1811–1812, in 1814, and in 1844–1845. The first time it came from Col. Timothy Pickering, of Massachusetts, a friend of Washington and a member of his Cabinet; the second time from Josiah Quincy, another distinguished citizen of Massachusetts; the third time from the Hartford Convention of 1814; and the fourth time from the Legislature of Massachusetts. Josiah Quincy in the debate on the admission of Louisiana, Jan. 14, 1811, declared his "deliberate opinion that, if the bill passes, the bonds of this Union are virtually dissolved, . . . as it will be the right of all [the States], so it will be the duty of some, to prepare definitely for a separation, — amicably if they can, violently if they must." In 1812 pulpit, press, and rostrum in New England advocated Secession. In 1839 John Quincy Adams declared "the people of each State have a right to secede from the Confederated Union."

In 1844 and again in 1845 the Legislature of Massachusetts avowed the right to secede and threatened to exercise the right if Texas should be admitted to the Union. This was its language:

"The Commonwealth of Massachusetts, faithful to the compact between the people of the United States, according to the plain meaning and intent in which it was understood by them, is sincerely anxious for its preservation, but it is determined, as it doubts not the other States are, to submit to undelegated powers in no body of men on earth."

This expresses exactly the attitude of the seceding States in 1861. Thus the North and the South at these two epochs (only a dozen years apart) held the same view of the right of withdrawal from the Union. And the ground of their apprehension was very similar. New England believed that the admission of Louisiana and Texas would give the South a preponderance of power in the Union, and hence that her rights within the Union would no longer be secure. The cotton States believed that the election of a sectional President by a party pledged to the abolition of slavery gave the North a preponderance of power in the Union and left their rights insecure. And when Virginia beheld the newly elected President preparing to coerce the seceding States by force of arms, she believed that the Constitution was being violated, and that her place was now with her Southern sisters.

It is a fact full of significance that even Alexander Hamilton, strong Federalist as he was, could threaten Jefferson with the Secession of New England, "unless the debts of the States were assumed by the General Government." And Madison spoke of the thirteen

States as "thirteen sovereignties," and again he said, "Each State, in ratifying the Constitution, is considered as a sovereign body."

Daniel Webster, in 1830 and again in 1833, argued that the Constitution was not a "compact," not a "confederacy," and that the acts of ratification were not "acts of accession." These terms, he said, *would imply the right of Secession*, but they were terms unknown to the fathers; they formed a "new vocabulary," invented to uphold the theory of State sovereignty. But in this Mr. Webster was wholly mistaken. Those terms we now know were in familiar use in the great debates on the Constitution. In 1787 Mr. Gerry, of Massachusetts, said, "If nine out of thirteen States can dissolve the compact (*i.e.*, the Articles of Confederation), six out of nine will be just as able to dissolve the new one." (It had been agreed that the consent of nine out of the thirteen States should be sufficient to establish the new government.) Gouverneur Morris, Alexander Hamilton, Washington all spoke of the Constitution as a "Compact," and of the new government as a "Confederacy." Both Massachusetts and New Hampshire, in their acts of ratification, refer to the Constitution as a "solemn Compact." We have then the authority of Webster himself for the opinion that these terms implied the right of Secession.

Nor is this all. Virginia, New York, and Rhode Island all declared in their acts of ratification that the powers granted by them to the General Government "may be resumed by them." Thus the right of Secession was solemnly asserted in the very acts by which these States ratified the Constitution. That assertion was part of the ratification. The ratification was conditioned by it. And the acceptance of these States as members of the Union carried with it the acceptance of the Constitution and the recognition of the right of Secession.

This was recognized by Webster in his maturer years. See his speech at Capon Springs, W. Va., in 1851.

I have thought it just to my comrades of whom I am to write in these pages to give at the outset this defence of the course they took in 1861. They followed that interpretation of the Constitution which they received from their fathers — from Jefferson and Madison and Washington — rather than that which can claim no older or greater names than those of Story and Webster.

These arguments appeared to us convincing then. They are no less convincing to-day from the standpoint of things as they were in 1861. And we appeal to the candid judgment of history to decide whether, believing *as* we did, we were not justified in doing *what* we did. The most recent, and one of the ablest, of Northern historians acknowledges that "a large majority of the people of the South believed in the constitutional right of Secession," and as a consequence believed that the war on the part of the National Government was "a war of subjugation." But surely it is an act of patriotism to resist a war of subjugation, spoliation, and conquest, and by that standard the soldiers of the Confederate Armies must go down to history not as traitors, but as patriots. Our argument for the constitutional right of withdrawing from the Union may, or may not, appear conclusive, but at least the right of revolution, asserted by our sires in 1776, cannot be denied to their descendants of 1861.

On that ground I claim the assent even of those who still stoutly deny the right of Secession to the assertion that the armies of the South were composed not of traitors, but of patriots.

There was a time, during those dark days of Reconstruction, when public opinion in the North demanded that we, who had fought under the Southern flag, should prove the sincerity of our acceptance of the results of the war by acknowledging the unrighteousness of our cause and by expressing contrition for the course we pursued.

But could we acknowledge our cause to be unrighteous when we believed it just? Could we repent of an act done in obedience to the dictates of conscience? Our late antagonists — now, thank God, our friends — may claim that our judgment was at fault; that our action was not justified by sound reasoning; that the fears that goaded us to withdraw from the Union were not well grounded; but, so long as it is acknowledged that we followed duty as we understood it, they cannot ask us to repent. We could not repent of obeying the dictates of conscience in the face of hardship, danger, and death!

And now I turn to the consideration of a grievous reproach often directed against the men who fought in the armies of the South in the Civil War. When we claim for them the crown of patriotism, when we aver that they drew their swords in what they believed to be the cause of liberty and self-government, it is answered that the corner-stone of the Southern Confederacy was slavery, and that the soldiers who fought under the banner of the Southern Cross were fighting for the perpetuation of the institution of slavery.

That is a statement which I wish to repudiate with all the earnestness of which I am capable. It does a grievous injustice to half a million patriot soldiers who were animated by as pure a love of liberty as ever throbbed in the bosom of man, and who made as splendid an exhibition of self-sacrifice on her behalf as any soldiers who ever fought on any field since history began.

In the first place, I ask, If slavery was the cornerstone of the Southern Confederacy, what are we to say of the Constitution of the United States? That instrument as originally adopted by the thirteen colonies contained three sections which recognized slavery. (Art. 1, Sec. 2 and 9, and Art. 4, Sec. 2.) And whereas the Constitution of the Southern Confederacy prohibited the slave trade, the Constitution of the United States prohibited the *abolition* of the slave trade for twenty years (1789–1808)! And if the men of the South are reproached for denying liberty to three and a half millions of human beings, at the same time that they professed to be waging a great war for their own liberty, what are we to say of the revolting colonies of 1776 who rebelled against the British crown to achieve their liberty while slavery existed in every one of the thirteen colonies undisturbed? Cannot those historians who deny that the South fought for liberty, because they held the blacks in bondage, see that upon the same principle they must impugn the sincerity of the signers of the Declaration of Independence? We ask the candid historian to answer this question: If the colonists of 1776 were freemen fighting for liberty, though holding the blacks in slavery in every one of the thirteen colonies, why is the title of soldiers of liberty denied the Southern men of 1861, because they too held the blacks in bondage? Slavery was an inheritance which the people of the South received from the fathers, and if the States of the North, within fifty years after the Revolution, abolished the institution, it cannot be claimed that the abolition was dictated by moral considerations, but by differences of climate, soil, and industrial interests.

Let me here state a fact of capital importance in this connection: the sentiment in favor of emancipation was rapidly spreading in the South in the first quarter of the nineteenth century. Wilson acknowledges that "there was no avowed advocate of slavery" in Virginia at that time. In the year 1826 there were one hundred and forty-three emancipation societies in the United States, and of these, one hundred and three were in the South. So strong was the sentiment in Virginia for emancipation that, in the year 1832, one branch of her Legislature came near passing a law for the gradual abolition of slavery; and I was assured in 1860 by Col. Thomas Jefferson Randolph, who was himself a member of the Legislature that year, that emancipation would certainly have been carried at the next session but for the reaction created by the fanatical agitation of the subject by the Abolitionists, led by Wm. Lloyd Garrison. Though emancipation was defeated at that time by a small vote, yet the Legislature passed a resolution postponing the consideration of the subject till public opinion had further developed. The *Richmond Whig* of March 6, 1832, said: "The great mass of Virginia herself rejoices that the slavery question has been taken up by the Legislature, that her legislators are grappling with the monster," etc.   A Massachusetts writer, George Lunt, says: "The States of Virginia, Kentucky, and Tennessee were engaged in practical movements for the gradual emancipation of their slaves.   This movement continued until it was arrested by the aggressions of the Abolitionists."

These facts are beyond dispute: 1. That from 1789 down to 1837 slavery was almost universally considered in the South a great evil; 2. That public opinion there underwent a revolution on this subject in the decade 1832–1842.   What produced this fateful change of sentiment?   Not the invention of the cotton gin, for that took place in 1793.   No, but the abolition crusade launched by Wm. Lloyd Garrison, Jan. 1, 1831.   Its violence and virulence produced the result that might have been expected.   It angered the South. It stifled discussion.   It checked the movement toward emancipation.   It forced a more stringent policy toward the slave.   The publication of Garrison's "Liberator" was followed, seven months later, by Nat Turner's negro insurrection in which sixty-one persons — men, women, and children — were murdered in the night. President Jackson, in his message of 1835, called attention to the transmission through the mails "of inflammatory appeals addressed to the passions of the slaves, in prints and various sorts of publications, calculated to stimulate them to insurrection, and to produce all the horrors of a servile war."

The conclusion is irresistible that but for that violent and fanatical movement slavery would have been peaceably abolished in Virginia, and then in other Southern States.

Before leaving the subject I would like to recall

one or two historical facts. Not the Southern people, but the Government of Great Britain, must be held responsible for American slavery. The colony of Virginia protested again, and again, and again to the British King against sending slaves to her shores — but her protest was in vain. In 1760 South Carolina passed an act prohibiting the further importation of slaves, but England rejected it with indignation. Let it be remembered, too, that Virginia was the first of all the States, North and South, to prohibit the slave trade, and Georgia was the first to incorporate such a prohibition in her Constitution. Virginia was in fact in advance of the whole world on this subject. She abolished the slave trade in 1778, nearly thirty years before England did the same, and the same length of time before New England was willing to consent to its abolition.

But I am chiefly concerned to show that my comrades and brothers, of whom I write in these pages, did not draw their swords in defence of the institution of slavery. They were not thinking of their slaves when they cast all in the balance — their lives, their fortunes, their sacred honor — and went forth to endure the hardships of the camp and the march and the perils of the battle field. They did not suffer, they did not fight, they did not die, for the privilege of holding their fellow men in bondage!

No, it was for the sacred right of self-government that they fought. It was in defence of their homes and their firesides. It was to repel the invader, to resist a war of subjugation. It was in vindication of the principle enunciated in the Declaration of Independence that "governments derive their just powers from the consent of the governed."

Only a very small minority of the men who fought in the Southern armies — not one in ten — were financially interested in the institution of slavery. We cared little or nothing about it. To establish our independence we would at any time have gladly surrendered it. If any three men may be supposed to have known the object for which the war was waged, they were these: Abraham Lincoln, Jefferson Davis, and Robert E. Lee. Their decision agrees with what I have stated. Mr. Lincoln consistently held and declared that the object of the war was the restoration of the Union, not the emancipation of the slaves. Mr. Davis as positively declared that the South was fighting for independence, not for slavery. And Robert E. Lee expressed his opinion by setting all his slaves free Jan. 8, 1863, and then going on with the war for more than two years longer. In February, 1861, Mr. Davis wrote to his wife in these words, "In any case our slave property will eventually be lost." Thus the political head of the Confederacy entered on the war foreseeing the eventual loss of his slaves, and the military head of the Confederacy actually set his slaves free before the war was half over. Yet both, they say, were fighting for slavery!

CHAPTER III

NOW at length I had redeemed my promise to my mother, in leaving Baltimore, that I would not enter the army, at any rate till the end of the session of the University. But I had made another promise. On June 20th I had written her: "You know that of course I will join no company without papa's consent. Though I did do it once, I shall not do it again." Accordingly, when the session closed, I was minded to return to Baltimore and plead for permission to join the Southern Army. I even contemplated — in the event of being unable to get through the lines — to go up to the home of my aunt, Mrs. Garrett, some eighteen miles from the University, and settle down "quietly," "trying to make myself useful teaching the children French and arithmetic."

But in cherishing such an idea I reckoned without the *Zeitgeist*. Day after day the spirit of the epoch wrought in me more and more mightily till I felt that I could no longer resist the call to follow the example of my kindred, my friends, and my fellow students, and enlist in the Southern Army.

But there were two obstacles in the way: first, my rash promise just mentioned, that I would not enlist without my father's consent, and secondly this: my young cousin, Robert Breckinridge McKim, was, to

23

some extent, under my charge, and he stoutly insisted that if I joined the army he would do the same. In vain I reasoned with him that he was under age — not yet eighteen — while I had just passed my nineteenth birthday — consequently *my* duty was to my country, his was to his mother.

Unable to move him from his purpose, I said: "Very well, Robert, I will go with you to Baltimore and deliver you to your mother, then my responsibility will end."

But on our way to Winchester, intending to make our way into Maryland, I heard of the declaring of martial law in Baltimore and the planting of artillery in the public squares of our city. This intelligence swept away all further hesitation as to the course I ought to pursue. I saw that, if I did go back I should to a certainty be arrested as having been at Harper's Ferry in arms against the government. And I strongly hoped that my father could no longer stand with Mr. Lincoln's administration when he found that he "meant to establish a despotism and call it by the sacred name of Union." Many other Union men had been swung over to the Southern side by this, — surely my father would be also. I remembered, too, how he had taught me that, next to God, my allegiance was due to my country before all other obligations. The fact is that by this time the cause of the South had become identified with liberty itself, and, being of military age, I felt myself bound by every high and holy consideration to take up arms to deliver Maryland from the invaders who were polluting her soil.

At Bristoe Station, en route to Winchester, I had visited the troops at the front. There I saw several first cousins who were in the army, Wirt Harrison, and Major Carter Harrison, and Major Julien Harrison. I heard that thirty-six of my Harrison cousins were in the service. I saw many friends and fellow students in the uniform. And I confess I felt humiliated when I saw these men, already bronzed, by camp life, while my face was as white as a piece of writing paper, and I was wearing citizen's clothes.

This experience intensified the conviction which had already taken possession of my mind, and I felt that now all hesitation was at an end.

The following letter tells my mind at this period:

WINCHESTER, July 11, 1861.

MY DEAR MOTHER:

I left the University last week expecting to be in Baltimore before now, but on my way I heard of the declaring of martial law and of the unlimbering of artillery in the public squares of our city. This was more than my endurance could stand and I determined to come up here and join Willie Murray's company and aid in driving those insolent oppressors out of our city. I feel this to be my duty and I earnestly hope it will not be displeasing to either you or papa. I cannot but hope and trust that papa has before this awakened to a sense of the despotism which Lincoln is building up for himself, and that he is as desirous as I am to drive every Northerner from the State of Maryland. I would go home if I could and try and get his and your consent to my present course, but they are so strict now that I fear they would arrest me for having been to Harper's Ferry, as there are so many informers nowadays. I am very sorry not to see you once more before joining, but it is impossible. I hope I may be among those who before long shall march into Baltimore and deliver her from her oppressors. Poor Baltimore! my heart bleeds for her. Bob McKim has come up here and joined a Virginia artillery company. Duncan is in the same company I am in. He is a splendid soldier and very enthusiastic. You need not be alarmed about me, my dear mother; there is *some* danger in case of battle, but very little; the Yankees cannot shoot.

But, dear mamma, if anything should happen to me, remember that your son is not afraid to die for the liberties of his country, that he scorns being a *Tory* and that he can look up to Heaven and ask a blessing upon the cause he is engaged in, and commit his soul to God on the battle field, and then fear not the sting of death or the victory of the grave.

When we entered the train which was to take us to Strasburg en route to Winchester, whence we meant to make our way into Maryland, I called Robert to me and told him I could no longer delay responding to the call of my country, and was resolved to join the army as soon as we reached Winchester, but he must continue on his way and do his duty by returning to his mother. I shall never forget the dear boy's joy when he heard of my resolve. He sprang to his feet, clapped his hands, and said, "I shall follow your example," nor could I dissuade him from his resolve.

Arrived at Winchester, we made our way next morning, eighteen miles, to Darksville on the Martinsburg pike, where the army of Gen. Joseph E. Johnston was encamped. I enlisted July 11th, ten days before the battle of Manassas. We found the troops forming in line of battle to meet the reported advance of General Patterson, which was hourly expected. Naturally we sought the regiment of Maryland infantry, in whose ranks I soon found a place in the company of my dear friend Capt. Wm. H. Murray. But Bob McKim, unable to find a musket, went over to the Rockbridge (Va.) Artillery, and decided to enlist in its ranks, as he had several friends in the company. The brave boy met his death at the battle of Winchester, May 25th, 1862, only ten months later, gallantly serving his piece.

General Patterson did not advance, however, so we had no battle that day, but I had two little foretastes of army life which I will mention. Our captain having given instructions to the men as they stood in line of battle that, when any member of the company should be wounded, but one man should leave the field to care or him, my cousin Duncan McKim, who was immediately in front of me, turned to me and said with a twinkle in his eye and a smile on his lips, "Randolph, when you fall, I'll carry you off the field." I thanked him, with rather a sickly smile, and thought that soldiering was getting to be a serious business.

After waiting several hours for General Patterson's call, to no purpose, about four P.M. we stacked arms, broke ranks, and charged upon the camp-fires, eager for dinner, which had been interrupted by the call to arms. Having had nothing to eat since early morning, and having ridden eighteen miles, and stood in the ranks several hours, my appetite was keen, and I gladly accepted Giraud Wright's invitation to "dine" with him. My host provided the "dinner" by dipping a tin cup into a black camp kettle and procuring one iron spoon. He then invited me to a seat on a rock beside him and we took turns at the soup with the spoon, each also having a piece of hard-tack for his separate use. Alas! my dinner, so eagerly expected, was soon ended, for one or two spoonfuls of the greasy stuff that came out of the camp kettle completely turned my stomach, and I told my friend and host I was not hungry and would not take any more. Inwardly, I said, "Well, I *may* get used to standing up and being shot at, but this kind of food will kill me in a week!"

I had expected a baptism of fire, and looked forward to it with some nervousness, but instead I had had a baptism of soup which threatened an untimely end to my military career!

The real experience of a soldier's life now began in earnest. Drill and discipline were applied to the new recruit, by dint of which the raw material of young manhood was to be converted into a soldier. The man at the head of this military factory was Col. George H. Steuart, and he thoroughly understood his business. A "West Pointer," and an officer in the old army, he was imbued with a very strong sense of the value of strict discipline. The First Maryland Infantry was under his command and he very soon "licked it into shape," and it began to have a reputation for precision of drill and excellence in marching.

These qualities were to be subjected to a practical test very soon, for not many days after the experience narrated in the last chapter, Gen. Joseph E. Johnston quietly broke camp near Winchester and took up his march for Manassas, there to effect a junction with General Beauregard and help him win the first great battle of the war. We marched late in the afternoon of July 18th, and by midnight were ten or twelve miles on our way. As we approached the village of Millwood, Clarke County, I observed the home of my aunt, Mrs. Wm. Fitzhugh Randolph, brightly illuminated, and when I entered, the dear old lady met me with perplexity on her face and said, "Randolph, what am I to do? The soldiers have been coming in ever since five o'clock, and they have eaten up everything I have in the house, and still they keep coming." "No wonder," I replied, "your house is right at the cross-roads, and you have it brightly illuminated, as if you expected them. Put out the lights and shut the doors and you will soon be at peace."

Well, the door that shut out the rest shut me in, and I had a few hours sleep on a bed, after a refreshing "bite" in the dining-room. By four o'clock I was on the road again with one or two of my company, approaching the river which the army was obliged to ford. As we trudged along, with knapsack and musket, in a lonely part of the road, we were overtaken by a mounted officer, muffled up in a cloak, who gruffly demanded what we were doing ahead of our regiment, to which I hotly replied, "*What business is that of yours?*" One of my companions pulled me by the sleeve and said, "Man, that is General Elzey; you'd better shut up, or you'll be arrested and put in the guard-house, or shot for insubordination." I suppose I must have known he was an officer, and that my reply was a gross breach of discipline. But obedience and submission to military authority was a lesson I had not yet learned in my seven days of soldiering. The general, however, paid no attention to what I said, and my only punishment was the amusement of my fellow soldiers at my greenness. It was a lonely spot and it was still rather dark. Perhaps that accounts for the general's making as if he did not hear my insubordinate reply.

After wading the Shenandoah we took our way up through Ashby gap and were soon descending the eastern slope of the Blue Ridge. Near the great tree whose branches stretch into four counties we went into camp, and our mess was presently delighted by the approach of a well-furnished wagon from the farm of Mr. Robert Bolling, in charge of the old gentleman himself. He was the father of John Bolling, one of the privates in Murray's company. Both John and his father were very popular men that day in Company H, and long lingered the delicious memory of those Virginia hams and well-fed poultry and goodies too numerous to mention.

It was here I received a letter from my mother which showed that she had no idea I had enlisted in the army, or would do so. I immediately sat down and wrote her the following letter, wholly devoted to explaining my course of action and deprecating her displeasure and my father's. It must have been indited just before taking the cars which were to convey us to the battle of Manassas, fought the next day. It contained no allusion to our forced march, or to the approaching battle.

PIEDMONT STATION,
Saturday, July 20, 1861.

MY MOST PRECIOUS MOTHER:

Mr. Hall has just made his appearance and handed me your letter and dear Margie's. It grieved me to the quick to find that you are still in ignorance of my real position in Virginia now, and I confess I almost felt self-reproached when you said that you were perfectly satisfied with my promise not to join the Southern Army "without my father's consent." I recollect full well writing the letter, and that was the thing which has kept me back so long from following what I have felt my duty to my country. This made me change my mind about joining when I had almost made up my mind to it some time ago, and this made me resolve to use every effort to get home and try and get consent to do so. I would not now be in the army, and would be at home, I expect, if the condition of things in Baltimore had not rendered it pretty certain that I would be arrested because I went in arms to Harper's Ferry.

I say then in justification of my course that I could not get home safely to get advice, and I felt very hopeful that papa, as most other Union men in Baltimore, had changed his sentiments when he found that the government means to establish a despotism and call it by the sacred name of Union. I do not now believe, after learning that I am disappointed to a great extent in this expected change so far, that papa will not finally cease to support what he has believed a free and righteous government, when he finds beyond contradiction that Lincoln has overthrown the government of our forefathers and abolished every principle of the Declaration of Independence.

My dear, dear mother, I could hardly restrain tears in the midst of all the confusion and bustle of the camp this morning when I read your letter with those renewed expressions of your tender love for me. Oh, I hope you will not think me unworthy of such a love. If I have erred, do be lenient to me, you and papa both, and do not disown your son for doing what he felt to be a holy duty to his country. Papa, if you place yourself in my position, with the profound conviction I have of the holiness and righteousness of this Cause, ask yourself whether you would not have unhesitatingly done what I have done. You have yourself, in my hearing, placed the duty of country first in this world's duties and second only to the duty I owe my God. How then am I reprehensible for obeying what my very heart of hearts told me was my country's call, when I had some hope that your will would not be at variance with it, and I was unable to find out whether it was or not?

I have suffered much in mind and still do suffer. At all events I am not actuated by selfish or cowardly motives. How easy it would have been to sit down at quiet Belvidere, preserving an inactivity which all my friends would have regarded as honorable, than at the possible loss of your parental love and care, and at the sacrifice of my comforts and the risk of my life, to do what I have done — enlist as a common soldier (i.e., a volunteer private) in the cause of liberty and right! Camp life is a hard life — I know by experience. Forced marches, scanty provisions sometimes, menial offices to perform, perfect discipline to submit to, are not attractive features to anyone. Then military life has little charm for me. I have no taste for it, and no ambition for military glory. But I am ready and willing to suffer all these hardships, and, when necessary, to lay my life upon the altar of my country's freedom.

I hope I do not seem to boast or to glorify myself in speaking thus, but if I know my own heart this is the truth, and God give me grace to be consistent with this profession. Do not, my precious mother, be too much alarmed and too anxious about me. I trust and hope that God will protect me from "the terror by night" and "the destruction that wasteth at noon-day." I feel as if my life was to be spared. I hope yet to preach the Gospel of the Lord Jesus Christ; but, my dear mother, we are in God's hands, and He doth not willingly afflict or grieve the children of men. "He that dwelleth in the secret place of the most High shall abide under the shadow of the Almighty." He does all things well, and He will give you grace to bear this trial too. Farewell, dear mother and father, Telfair, Mary, and Margie. I am, in this life and the next,

Your fond and affectionate

RANDOLPH.

The following letter from my mother reflects the sentiment prevalent in Baltimore at that time:

BALTIMORE, July 1, 1860.

MY BELOVED CHILD:

.   .   .   .

The plot thickens around us here, the usurpation becoming more and more dictatorial. Thankful I feel that we are not personally endangered, but I do not feel the less indignant at the outrageous arrest of our citizens, or the less sympathy for my neighbors who are subjected to the tyranny of the arbitrary power in Washington. We are such a loyal people, that it takes only 30,000 men to keep us quiet; and our police and marshal of police arrested! There will be no stop to this until you send them flying from Virginia, then we may have a chance to show our loyalty.

CHAPTER IV

A S we disembarked from the cars on that Sunday morning, July 21st, 1861, the distant booming of cannon fell upon our ears, and we realized that now we were indeed on the fiery edge of battle. We had orders to cast off our knapsacks that we might march unimpeded to the field. Leaving them in a pile by the roadside under a small guard, we were soon marching at the double quick for Manassas. Our pulses beat more quickly than our feet, as we passed on, the sounds of battle waxing nearer and nearer every moment. It was a severe test of endurance, for the field was six miles away, and the heat of that July day was very exhausting. The weather had been very dry, and the dust rose in clouds around us, as we double-quicked on — so thick was it that I distinctly remember I could not see my file-leader.

We were by and by near enough to hear the rattle of the musketry, and soon we began to meet the wounded coming off the field in streams, some limping along, some on stretchers borne by their comrades. Stern work was evidently right ahead of us, and it did not steady our nerves for our first battle to be told, as the wounded told us, especially those whose wounds were slight, that it was going very badly with our men at the front. At length the dreadful six-mile double-quick march was over, and the firing line was right in front of us. Some few — very few — had dropped out exhausted. All of us were nearly spent with the heat and the dust and the killing pace; and a brief halt was made to get breath, moisten our lips from the canteens, and prepare for the charge. I remember how poor "Sell" Brogden, panting and exhausted, turned to me and asked for a drink of water from my canteen. I had scarcely a swallow left, but he was so much worse off than I, and his appeal was so piteous, that I gave him the last drop.

We had arrived on the field in the nick of time, at the very crisis, when victory or defeat was trembling in the balance. The Federal general, McDowell, had turned General Beauregard's flank, and only Gen. Joe Johnston's timely arrival on that flank of the Confederate position had saved him from disaster. Jackson at the head of his Virginia troops was "standing like a Stonewall" — those were the words of General Bee as he sought to rally his retreating South Carolinians. But the Confederate line was wavering, and the result of the day hung in grave doubt, when Elzey's brigade arrived on the field and deployed for attack. Of this brigade, the leading regiment (the one first on the field) was the First Maryland under Colonel Steuart, and it was the blow struck by this fine body of men, 600 strong, that turned the balance of battle in favor of the Southern Army. Looking back now, I think the moral effect of the great cloud of dust which rose as we double-quicked to the field, and which was easily seen by the Federals, was worth quite as much as our 600 muskets in action. For it gave the enemy the impression that it was at least a brigade instead of a regiment that was being launched against them at the moment of our charge. This was intensified by the shout, "*Go in, Baltimore*," which rose above the din of battle as we swept forward. It so happened that the same Massachusetts regiment which was so roughly handled by the people in the streets of Baltimore on the 19th of April was in our front on the 21st of July, and prisoners afterwards told us that when we charged the Massachusetts men said, "Here come those d—d Baltimore men! It's time for us to git up and git!" Then, after the day was won, and General Elzey, our brigade commander, was saluted as the Blücher of the day, we men of the First Maryland were proud to say that our regiment was the head of the spear that Elzey drove into the vitals of the enemy that eventful day.

I remember that after the first rush, when a brief pause came, some of us dashed down to a tiny little brook for a mouthful of water — only to find the water tinged with blood. Nevertheless not a few stooped and lapped it up where it was clearest.

The first man I saw fall in the battle was Gen. Kirby Smith, who was riding by the side of our column before we deployed for the charge. He fell in the most spectacular way — the reins falling from his grasp, he reeled in the saddle, threw out his arms and fell to the ground, seriously but not fatally wounded.

The New York Zouaves, in their red breeches, were deployed as skirmishers in our front, and did us some damage before we formed our line. One of the amusing incidents that occurred (and the Confederate soldier was always eager to see some fun in the serious work of war) was when Geo. Lemmon in his excitement fired his musket too close to Nick Watkins' head and shot a hole in his cap — fortunately not in his head — and Nick turned and said in the coolest way, "George Lemmon, I wish you'd look where you're shooting — I'm not a Yankee."

How well I remember our eager expectancy that night. We had seen the rout, and had followed the fleeing Federals some distance along the road back towards Washington. It was full of the evidences of the panic into which the Union Army had been thrown. I need not describe a scene so often described before. But with all the evidences of the demoralization of our enemy, we were confident they could be pursued and Washington taken, if the Confederate Army pressed on. This we confidently expected, and were bitterly disappointed when the next day, and the next, came and went without any serious advance.

As I lay down to sleep on the battle field that night, I had much to think of. The weariness of the day and the peril of the battle were lost sight of in the awful scenes of death and suffering to which we had been introduced that day for the first time. I had seen the reality of the battle field, its carnage, its desolation, its awful pictures of the wounded, the dying, and the dead.

Somehow I was especially moved by the sight of the battery horses on the Henry Hill, so frightfully torn by shot and shell. The sufferings of the poor brutes, not in their own battle or by their own fault, but for man's sake, appealed to me in a peculiar way.

Mingled with my devout thankfulness for my own safety was my sorrow as news came in of friend after friend, and some relatives too, who had fallen.

It was reported all over Virginia that I had been among the killed. One of my cousins, Col. Randolph Harrison, when he saw me, exclaimed, "Why, I thought you were dead." These unfounded reports were often the occasion of much needless distress to the relatives of the men in the field.

The following letter referred to the battle:

FAIRFAX, Co. H, July 30, 1861.

MY DEAR MOTHER:

I have written twice since the battle to tell you I was safe; still I will embrace this opportunity, as I know you will be glad to hear from me whenever you can. We have been here some time, ever since the fight in fact. How grateful I feel that none of our close friends in the Maryland regiment were killed, or even wounded in the fight. Yet we have to mourn the loss of two very near to us in ties of blood, and others dear by friendship. Cousin Peyton Harrison — dear sweet fellow — I saw him only a week before his death, — and Cousin Carter Harrison who fell in the battle of Thursday while bravely bringing up his men to battle.

My dear mother, I am so grateful to God for sparing me in safety through the dangers of the day for your sake and the sake of the dear girls and Telly and papa as well. I thought of you all on the field of battle, and prayed God to spare me, or, if not, to comfort you, for I know that it would be a severe blow to you to lose me in this way so soon. Still, confident in the justice of our cause, and looking to the great God of truth and justice to be our salvation, I was ready to yield up myself, if necessary, on the altar of my country. Our regiment behaved beautifully on the field; they *would* pick blackberries, though, notwithstanding the indignation of the officers. We were in that brigade which came up so opportunely just as the fortune of the day seemed to be going against us. We fired several times on the Yankees and drove them before us, though our numbers were far inferior to theirs. It was truly the hand of Providence which gave us the victory on that day, and our Congress very appropriately gave thanks to Him and appointed last Sunday as a day of thanksgiving. The panic which spread among the Northern Army was almost unaccountable; they were beaten back with half their numbers, but there was no need of such a flight as they made to Alexandria, leaving behind them all their baggage trains, ammunition, etc. We only had fifteen to twenty thousand men engaged, because we had so many points to defend, and did not know where they were going to attack us. In the same way, I suppose, they had only about 35,000. The people in this neighborhood said that when they saw the army pass here they thought we would never return again, but that the Southern army would be certainly crushed. How different the result! When they passed here on the way up, they destroyed all the private property, broke into the houses and pillaged everything; but when they returned they *hadn't time* for anything of that sort. They were perfectly demoralized; thousands had no arms at all. I have a splendid overcoat gotten from a number they left behind. Cousin Wirt Harrison was wounded in the foot. Holmes and Tucker Conrad were killed side by side.

· · · · · · · ·

CHAPTER V

A FTER the battle of Manassas, we settled down to camp life, varied by occasional picket duty at one of the advanced outposts, such as Mason's and Munsen's Hill, whence the Maryland hills could be seen and which for that reason was a favorite post with our boys. Our colonel, George H. Steuart, had no superior as a camp officer in the Army of Northern Virginia. He kept his camp in good order by careful policing. He paid particular attention to the quartermaster and commissary departments, and looked well after the interests of his men, holding every officer, including the surgeon, to the strict performance of his duty. But he drilled us hard — generally six hours a day; company drill two hours before breakfast, regimental drill two hours after breakfast; and, when he rose to be brigadier brigade drill two hours in the afternoon. Moreover, he was a strict disciplinarian, and it was not easy for any breach of his orders to escape his lynx-eyed observation. He had some tough elements to deal with in some of his companies, and when these became unruly, the colonel was severe in his punishments. It was not uncommon in his camp to see two or three men tied up by the thumbs to a cross-pole — and in those July and August days this punishment was peculiarly painful. One sometimes heard men muttering curses and threatening to "shoot old Steuart" in the first battle they got into. But after Manassas, when the good result of his strict drill and discipline was seen, he became popular with the men. The regiment soon had the reputation of being the best drilled and the best marching regiment in Gen. Joe Johnston's army; and the men, proud of this, well knew that they owed it to Colonel Steuart.

We had a large drum corps, and its quick-step march was unique in that army of 30,000 men around Manassas that summer. It was a fine sight to see the First Maryland marching with that quick Zouave step by which they were distinguished. It was a sturdy body of men, not so tall as the Virginia regiments usually were, but well set up, active and alert, and capable of much endurance. Best of all, they stood to their work and showed the same fine soldierly qualities that characterized the Maryland line in the first Revolutionary War.

Colonel Steuart was in the habit of testing his men when on guard in some lonely spot by suddenly rushing upon them on foot or on horseback, taking them by surprise if possible. One night a sentinel had been posted near the colonel's tent, and part of his duty was to protect a lot of tent-flies piled up close by. In the small hours of the night, Colonel Steuart crept out of the rear of his tent, and stealthily approaching, while the sentinel was leaning on his musket, gazing at the stars and probably thinking of his sweetheart or his mother, took up one of the tent-flies, shouldered it, and was walking off with it when the sentinel, turning, rushed upon him, and pretending not to recognize him, seized him by the shoulders and gave him such a shaking that the colonel could hardly get breath to cry, "I'm your colonel — I'm your colonel!" Then when the sentry let go his hold and apologized, the colonel slapped him on the back and said, "Good soldier! Good soldier! I'll remember this."

The regiment was divided into messes containing each about fifteen men, and two of these were detailed for the duty of cooking and chopping wood and bringing water. In many of the Southern regiments there were negro cooks, but we, of Maryland, had to do our own cooking, and first we had to learn how — a slow and painful process. Bacon and flour and salt constituted our bill of fare, with some kind of substitute for coffee, which was a mighty poor make-believe. At first we could only make "slap-jacks," — composed of flour and water mixed, and floated in bacon-grease. When sufficiently fried on one side, it was then "up" to the cook to toss the frying-pan up and cause the half-cooked cake to turn a somersault in the air and come down "slap-jack" on the pan again — if it did not happen to come down in the fire instead. But by degrees we learned to make biscuits baked in the small oven, and to boil our beef (when we had any), and make soup at the same time. Horse beef was issued sometimes, and we found it a difficult dental proposition. On a famous occasion when we had invited Captain Murray to dine with us, I suggested to my co-cook, Sergeant Lyon, that we should create an apple pie. He was doubtful if the thing could be done. The apples we had in hand as the result of a forage, but how on earth were we to make the pastry? I told him I remembered (when a smaller boy) seeing our cook Josephine make pastry, rolling out the dough thin and sticking little dabs of butter all over it — then folding it and rolling it again. So we made some dough as if for biscuit, then rolled it with a bottle on the top of a barrel, and planted it thick with small pats, of butter — doubled it over and rolled it — and repeated the process until the butter was exhausted. The pie that resulted from all this culinary strategy *we* considered fit to set before a *general*, to say nothing of a mere captain. In this connection I recall once on a march making a loaf of bread about three feet long and one-eighth of an inch thick by wrapping the dough round my ramrod and setting it up before the fire to bake. With the modern breech-loader this could not have been done.

About once a week it was my duty to cook for the mess of fifteen men, or else to chop the necessary wood and fetch the water. One of our number, Harry Oliver, a gentleman of wealth and position before he became a soldier, was an enthusiast, almost a monomaniac, about washing, spending much of his leisure time washing himself or his clothes, and I recall more than one occasion when it was his turn to cook break-fast, that when we returned from our first two hours drill, eager for breakfast, Harry was nowhere to be seen, nor was there any breakfast prepared — he was "off at the branch washing." So our mess No. 5, not without maledictions on Harry, were compelled to go out breakfastless to the second drill of two hours more. Well, I daresay it was a good preparation for the bad time coming when we had to march and fight so often on an empty stomach.

On picket duty sometimes we lived for three days on corn plucked in the fields and roasted in the shuck, a process highly conducive to diarrhœa.

On one of these occasions, after a long march, our captain at nightfall called for volunteers to perform a special duty, without specifying what the duty was. Some of us, fancying, as we were on an advanced picket and very near the enemy, that it was some exciting and adventurous task, stepped out of the ranks and offered ourselves as volunteers. What was our disgust when we discovered it was special *guard* duty! When my turn came it was very dark and raining heavily, and I was in a very bad humor with myself and everybody else for having thus put my head into the noose. Arrived at my post, the sentinel whom I relieved gave me the instructions he had received and whispered the countersign, which I could not understand, though I asked him twice to repeat it. Quite out of patience I turned to the corporal of the guard and said, "Corporal, I wish you'd tell me the countersign, I can't understand this man." He approached and whispered something like "Wanis." "Spell it," I said. In reply he whispered with staccato emphasis on each letter, "We-e-noos." Then at last I understood that the countersign was "*Venus*"! It was too funny! Here was an illiterate Irish sentinel pronouncing "Venus" in the most approved, modern European style! It almost put me in a good humor.

I would here point out that our Maryland men faced from the start some of the hardships and limitations that came to many Southern regiments at a later stage of the war. In some commands the private soldiers had their trunks with them. It is related of a young Richmond gentleman, private in the Howitzers, that he had as part of his outfit a dozen face towels besides bath towels, and that when orders were issued that all trunks should be sent back to Richmond, the elegant young dandy took offence and sent in to the captain his "resignation"!

Needless to say, our Maryland boys had neither trunks, nor cooks, nor woodchoppers.

The following letter refers to this period:

FAIRFAX, Co. H, August 3, 1861.

To MY MOTHER:

Though I have written I think three times since the battle to assure you of my safety, yet the news which Mr. —— brings, that I am reported among the killed in Baltimore, makes me anxious to embrace this new and certain opportunity of setting your mind at rest on this score, especially as the report is current at the University and in Richmond, and you may suppose it occurred in some way since the fight, on picket duty for instance. You have no idea how I long to see you and dear old Belvidere again. I lay in my tent the other morning while the rain poured in torrents outside, and pictured to myself the dear old place with the damasks on the porch, so fragrant, and then I entered the door in imagination and saw you all seated at a comfortable breakfast-table while I was almost drenched and obliged to fly to my crowded tent before completing my breakfast by half.

You should see me engaged in cooking, making fires, washing, etc. It is truly hard work and young men like Duncan, Wilson Carr and myself find that it is a difficult thing to make bread and coffee good enough to support life. Our mess consists of ten, some of whom I will mention; Duncan, Wilson Carr, Willie Colston, Giraud Wright, Charlie Grogan, McHenry Howard. We have no yeast, and so our bread must needs be heavy and indigestible as we have no means of rolling it out into biscuits. We make rice cakes though, and frequently get corn meal and make first-rate corn bread. We are able occasionally to get our bread cooked by the country people and we buy sometimes eggs, with a stray chicken or two. You have no idea how one gets accustomed to any sort of fare. I can now eat salt junk of the very fattest with great gusto, and drink coffee without milk, made in the company pot, and feel refreshed. The first hard washing of my clothes which I did, burned off the skin from my arms dreadfully. Sometimes we have been out all day and part of the night in a drenching rain. In that forced march from Winchester to Manassas we knew no distinction between night and day, but marched during both without rest almost, and almost entirely without food. Our regiment marches very fast and finds it very tiresome marching behind some Virginia and Tennessee regiments. We passed through Millwood, and Aunt Jane had her house lit up and was giving supper to all the soldiers who came in on their way. From five to six o'clock in the afternoon till three in the morning she was cooking for them, till she was eaten out of house and home nearly. We forded the Shenandoah up to our breasts and then marched on to Piedmont where we were delayed some time. We reached the Manassas Junction at 10.30 o'clock Sunday morning. As I told you, during the whole march we had not a single regular meal. Immediately after the victory we were marched back to Manassas (some six miles) and stayed there all Monday in a drenching rain, without tents, blankets or overcoats. Our company was out on picket duty night before last and we could hear the drums beating in the enemy's camp nearly all night long. We were within seven miles of Alexandria.

You would like to know how I spend a day here. The bugle sounds at half past four and then we go out to drill till six. Then we get breakfast, wash and get ready for drill again at nine o'clock. Then we drill an hour and a half or two hours. Then sleep, or write a letter, or clean up camp, or wash clothes, or put the tents in order. Then get dinner ready — drill again in the evening (the whole regiment together, battalion drill) at five o'clock. Dress parade at 6.30 P.M. Then supper. Soon after, at nine o'clock, the tattoo sounds and roll is called; then at 9.30 come three taps on the drum and all lights must instantly be extinguished. I have been very sick all day for the first time, but am nearly well now. Good-by, my dear mother, — God bless and keep you all. I am sad often thinking of my dear home and longing to hear from you. Wish I could see you again just for one little day or week.

Never cease to pray for your fond son.

Sometime in October I was detailed for duty during two days at General Johnston's headquarters at Centreville under Major John Haskell, a gallant member of a gallant South Carolina family of brothers, who did royal service in the Confederate Army. Wm. Haskell was one of my most valued friends at the University. I looked up to him with reverence. He fell at the battle of Gettysburg — a costly sacrifice to the Southern cause. Major John still lives, wearing an empty sleeve, witness of one of his many brave deeds.

During those ten days I had frequent opportunity of seeing that superb soldier and strategist, Gen. Joseph E. Johnston, whose removal in 1864 from the command of the southwestern army sealed, or at any rate hastened, the doom of the Confederacy.

The following letter refers to this period:

CENTREVILLE, October 20, 1861.

I sat up late reading, and after putting out the candle, stretched myself out on my pallet of straw, and commenced thinking. It was about midnight and not a sound could be heard but the dull pattering of the rain on the tent.

Everything that can distract the mind was hushed, and I seemed to hear only the voice of the Almighty in each drop of rain. I felt then that I was a spirit, an immortal spirit — consciousness of my bodily, mortal nature almost left me. The God that sends each drop of that rain on its separate mission, — can He not take care of all dear to me? Can He not restore us peace, and return me to my home? . . . And will not all he does be right and good and for the best?"

CHAPTER VI

THE autumn of 1861 was spent in camp at Centreville. Our tents were pitched on the summit of a bare hill, from which the encampment of the entire army of Gen. Joseph E. Johnston — about 30,000 men — was visible. At night, when the camp-fires glowed all round us for miles, it was a very beautiful sight. My cousin, W. Duncan McKim, and I used to lie there and fancy we were looking down on the city of Baltimore from Belvidere hill. He would say, "Randolph, there are the lights of Barnum's Hotel, and there is the Shot Tower, and there is the jail, and far away there are the lights on Federal Hill." Our thoughts turned, in every quiet hour, to home and kindred and friends. Duncan had a great aversion to serving as cook for our mess of fifteen men, and when his turn came round for this duty, he would do his best to exchange with some comrade for guard duty.

As winter approached, we suffered with the cold on that bleak hill-top, and some of the men excavated the entire space under their tents to the depth of three or four feet, and so slept snug and warm, while the less energetic of the company were exposed to the keen, cold winds. This, however, had occasionally its disadvantages. I remember, for instance, one night as I was going out to take my guard duty, looking

49

enviously into one of these tents and seeing the men grouped cosily together in their "dug-out," some reading, some playing cards, all quite secure from the sweep of the wintry winds; and I wished I could return after my four hours "on guard" to such a snug refuge. But before my watch was over there arose a tempest of wind and rain, and when I passed that tent again, it had collapsed, and there were six inches of water in the cosey place," and blankets and knapsacks, etc., were all afloat!

John Bolling, his cousin Robert, and I had a small "A" tent together in that camp. It was just wide enough to hold the three of us when we lay "spoon fashion," and by "pooling" our assets of blankets, we managed to sleep warm — at least the fortunate man in the middle was quite comfortable. But after lying an hour or so on the rough stony ground, our bones would begin to ache, and the man who waked up first, aching, would punch the others so that all might turn over together and preserve the "spoon" alignment, for only in that formation would the blankets cover all three. So, often during the night, the order would be given to our little squad by whichever man wanted to turn over, "Company A, right face," or "Company A, left face."

Later, I think early in December, we moved from Centreville to the vicinity of Fairfax Station, and there built ourselves huts for winter quarters. The spot selected was a forest of pines, in the midst of which we hewed out an open space large enough to accommodate huts for the entire regiment. This was unaccustomed work for many of us. Indeed, very few men in Murray's company could wield an axe, but, under the pressure of stern necessity, we learned the art just as we had learned the art of cooking. We hacked down the trees "somehow," and at last — long after our comrades in most of the other companies — we got our huts built, and set to work to make ourselves comfortable.

The composition of our mess was notable. It was certainly a rare group of men to be serving as *private soldiers*, on the munificent pay of eleven dollars per month, Confederate money. There was Harry Oliver, a country gentleman of large means, and Wilson Carr, a lawyer who left a good practice in Baltimore to shoulder a musket for the Confederacy, and Redmond, a highly educated Irish gentleman, and Wm. Duncan McKim, a graduate of Harvard, the president of the "Hasty Pudding Club" there and an intimate of Rufus Choate. Then there was McHenry Howard, a second-honor man of Princeton, and John Bolling, who had taken M.A. at the University of Virginia, an honor so difficult of achievement; and, most accomplished of all, Geo. Williamson, master of several modern languages, educated in a European university, widely read and widely travelled. He was a man of great personal charm and of the most exalted ideals. So nice was his sense of duty and honor that we dubbed him "Mr. Conscientious Scruples." We had also a candidate for Holy Orders in the Episcopal Church, and I, too, had devoted myself at the age of sixteen to the ministry of the Gospel. I may say that, in such a circle of accomplished men, the conversation in our log hut, as we lay in our bunks waiting for taps to sound, was of a very high order. In a fragment of a diary kept at this time (Jan. 24th, 1862), I find the following entry·

"I have felt my ignorance lately in listening to men in the mess of greater age and far greater reading and information than myself. In listening to George Williamson, describing the cities, and the manners of foreign countries, and the monuments of art and antiquity in Europe, I have felt a longing to travel, and to learn more of men and things; and I have sighed in contemplating my ignorance of the world of Nature, of literature and of art, and yearned to drink deep of knowledge."

I sent to the University of Virginia for some of my books, among them some nice editions of the classics that belonged long ago to my father, — only to lose them all when we suddenly broke camp in the spring and left all such *impedimenta* behind.

The following letter gives a picture of our life in winter quarters at Fairfax Station:

WINTER QUARTERS, January 27, 1862.

To MY MOTHER:

. . . .

Wouldn't you like to peep in on us some evening as we sit around our stove amusing ourselves until it is time to retire? We are a happy but a boisterous family, as the neighbors next door will tell you. Our amusements are various — reading, singing, quarreling, and writing. We employ the twilight in conversation, the subject of which is the "latest grape-vine" (i.e., rumor), or a joke on the Colonel, or when we are alone, our domestic concerns. We amuse ourselves with the many-tongued rumors which float about on the popular breeze, that England or France has recognized the Confederacy, or that the Confederates have gained a new victory, etc., etc. Then there are frequent domestic quarrels, free fights, passes with the bayonet, and hand to hand encounters, to vary the monotony of our peaceful life here. As soon as night sets in the candles

are lit and we draw round the stove and take down our
books, or else someone reads aloud till the newspaper arrives,
when other occupations are suspended, and we listen to
the news of the day. 'Then someone proposes a song and
"Maryland, my Maryland" is generally the first. We
hear that it is universally popular in Baltimore. We sang
it by request for General Beauregard some time since.
I will send you an account of it taken from the Richmond
Dispatch. I was one of the singers. The "enthusiastic
young lieutenant" was my captain. Sometimes we get
George Williamson to tell of his travels in Europe. He is
so entertaining, so happy in conversation, and so thoroughly
cultivated, that it is delightful to listen to him. He is
one of the finest men I know. Do the girls know him well?
We laugh at him about his restless energy. If he cannot be
at anything else, he will drive some nails to hang his coat
on, or make a shelf to put his books on, or something of
the sort. We visited Carvel Hall the other night (C.,
George, Mac., Jim G. and myself) and had a very pleasant
time. Some of the party played whist, and the rest (Carvel,
George and I) talked cozily around the fire. Colonel ———,
a Virginian, came in and sat down with us, and talked to
us in as friendly a way as if we had been his equals in rank.
Later in the evening we had oysters, raw and stewed, and
at intervals of about half an hour, those who drank indulged
in whiskey-toddy. When we returned to our hut ("Mrs."
Bolling and "Mrs." Redmond had promised to sit up for us)
we found the mess chest and a barrel and boxes piled up
before the door: this was followed by a fall, and then we
routed the rest out of bed and the fight that ensued made
such a noise that the colonel sent some men to arrest us.
They did not do it though. We have a cook now and live
very comfortably. It is a great satisfaction to feel that all
this is the work of our own hands. We appoint an "officer
of the day" whose duty it is to make the fire and spread
the ashes on the floor and sweep up. We have a kitchen,

outside the shanty. This morning we had inspection, and afterwards each shanty was inspected by the colonel and staff. "Ah!" said he, "this looks like a soldier's house." Our roof is of shingles, out of trees felled by our own hands. Our beds are made of light poles laid close together; they have a pleasant spring to them and I think as agreeable a bed as I ever slept in. Yesterday I put up a rack for the guns, and everything is now in first-rate order. Who knows how long we will be here to enjoy the fruit of our labors?

Our disaster in Kentucky is much to be deplored. Yet our men fought well till they were overpowered.

.   .   .   .

I have been promoted to the rank of corporal of the Color Guard, (about two months ago.) Intend trying to improve the months of inactivity by reading and studying German. I received from you the other day some gloves and sugar plums. The last article was particularly acceptable. Don't try to send me anything, for it is so uncertain, and I have everything I want. Love to all.

Among the other literature that occupied me during these few brief weeks in winter quarters, I find note of the following: some of the works of Spenser, the poet, and his Life; Macaulay's Essay on Madame D'Arblay, and the latter's famous novel, "Evelina"; also Carlyle's "Heroes and Hero-worship." And among the subjects discussed in our mess, I find the following: Vattel and Philmore on International Law; Humboldt's works and travels; the African explorations of Harth, the great German traveller, from the Atlantic almost to the Red Sea, in a line a few degrees above the equator; the influence of climate on the human features; the culture of cotton; the laws relating to property, etc. In further illustration of the high character of the rank and file of the Confederate Army,

I may mention that in the Rockbridge Artillery (Va.) (one company) there were, in 1861, seven Masters of Arts of the University of Virginia (a degree very difficult of attainment there), twenty-eight college graduates, and twenty-five theological students, — all these serving as private soldiers.

I may also mention that the present eminent professor of oriental languages in Harvard University, Dr. Crawford H. Toy, was a private in a Virginia regiment. He was found by a friend in an interval of the battle of Cold Harbor in June, 1864, lying on his oil-cloth, immersed in the study of Arabic.   Major Robert Stiles, in his fascinating book, "Four Years under Marse Robert," writes:

"I had lived for years at the North, had graduated recently from Yale, and had but just entered upon the study of law in the City of New York when the war began.   Thus torn away by the inexorable demands of conscience and of loyalty to the South, from a focal point of intense intellectual life and purpose, one of my keenest regrets was that I was bidding a long good-by to congenial surroundings and companionships.   To my surprise and delight, around the camp-fires of the First Company, Richmond Howitzers, I found throbbing an intellectual life as high and brilliant and intense as any I had ever known."

He adds that no law school in the land ever had more brilliant or powerful moot court discussions than graced the mock trials of the Howitzer Law Club.

"I have known," he says, "the burial of a tame crow . . . to be dignified not only by salvos of artillery, but also by an English speech, a Latin oration, and a Greek ode, which would have done honor to any literary or memorial occasion at old Yale."

Nor was this high type of men confined to the troops of Maryland and Virginia. By no means. In the Louisiana regiments, for instance, in Dick Taylor's brigade, besides his "gentle Tigers," who were indeed chiefly of a decidedly tough element, the Seventh and Ninth Louisiana were largely made up of planters and the sons of planters, and the majority were said to be men of fortune. And so it was in many regiments from the other Southern States.

The following from my diary shows the feeling of a youth of nineteen about the deteriorating influence of army life.

"Friday, Jan. 24th, 1862. Nearly seven months have flown by in my soldier's life, and they have been months of external activity, but activity of the body only. It has been a period of mental slumber — nay, sloth — for the mind has not even *dreamed*, it has stagnated, — the outward life, the daily duties of a soldier, have been all-absorbing, and reflection — the turning of the mind back upon itself — has been almost entirely obscured. This has been the tendency, but need not have been the *result*, except to a degree, of circumstances. The gaze of men has been upon me by day, and by night wearied nature has claimed repose.

"I wish to begin anew a reflective life, now that a breathing spell is afforded after the labors of the campaign. In this humble hut, when my companions are wrapt in slumber, I will say to my mind 'Be free!' I desire also to improve the time, and to discipline and drill my mind. To this end, daily reading, a greedy ear, and a summing up at the end of each day of what I have learned by reading, by listening, and by observation, will be conducive."

What a boy of nineteen thought of "Evelina" is thus set down under date of Feb. 1, 1862:

"I read the story before knowing anything of the established reputation and great merit of Miss Burney. The admiration then which the purity and simplicity of her style, and the vivacity of her wit awakened in me, was totally unprejudiced. I received her book as she threw it on the world, with no recommendation save its own intrinsic merits. The simple truth of her delineation of character, and the exalted morality which pervades the whole book, struck me with great force, even while ignorant of the literary period in which she wrote, when novels were generally vicious, and always indelicate. The character of Evelina approaches as near as may be my ideal of female delicacy and refinement. Yet she seems to me to have lacked firmness and decision on several occasions, and to have shown too facile and yielding a disposition. Macaulay's critique is extremely interesting. He places the author in the rank of eminent English novelists, yet denies her the first rank."

One day word came to our quarters that two ladies desired to see my cousin, W. Duncan McKim, and myself at Fairfax Station. This was exciting news, but I found Duncan very reluctant to obey the summons. In civilized life he had been rather exquisite in dress and manners, and he shrank from appearing in the presence of ladies, surrounded as they would be by well-dressed and well-mounted staff officers, in his rough private's garb. He seemed particularly sensitive about wearing a roundabout jacket instead of a coat before them. However, he yielded to my persuasions, and we prepared to go to the station, brushing and polishing up to the best of our ability. I think we succeeded in finding or borrowing, each, a white collar for the occasion!

The ladies who had summoned us were Miss Hetty

Cary, of Baltimore, and Miss Connie Cary, of Virginia.
They had ridden to Fairfax Station on the cow-catcher
of an engine to visit the army, and when we approached
they were on horseback in the midst of a bevy of
mounted officers, for they were both famous beauties,
and, besides, enthusiastic friends of the cause. When
the young lieutenant who had ridden to our camp to
deliver the message saw us coming he pointed us out
to the ladies, saying, "There come your friends."
We heard afterwards (fortunately not then) that they
told him he must be mistaken — those men could not
be the gentlemen they were expecting. Doubtless we
were much changed and looked very rough. It was
embarrassing for us; but when we were near enough
to be recognized, they were most gracious and soon
put us at our ease.

Life in winter quarters was varied by a very occasional excursion. Thus, under date of February 6, I
find the following entry:

"On Tuesday I rode to Centreville and passed a delightful
day, principally in the genial company of my dear friend
Galliard. He is a man of sweetness of disposition and such
warmth of feeling as is rarely met with; and he is withal
so intelligent in his conversation, and so spirited and resolute in his actions that no one that knows him could
withhold their admiration. I borrowed of him Carlyle's
"Heroes and Hero-worship." On my return I found a letter
from Tom Mackall. He is in his cousin Colonel Mackall's
office, and *he* is Gen. Albert Sidney Johnston's adjutant-
general at Bowling Green, Ky. His letter is full of interest,
and I have learned more from it of the Bowling Green army
and the situation of affairs in that quarter than by all that
has been in the papers since the place was occupied. The
army (he thinks) is a very fine one, equal in many respects

to our army here, — deficient in the manual of arms and in 'the cadenced step,' but familiar with the evolutions not only of the battalion and the brigade, but also of the division. He is much struck with the remarkable superiority of the horses and mules to those in this army. The army too is much better provisioned. He tells me he is confident if I get a certificate from Colonel Steuart and go out there, his cousin, Colonel Mackall, will appoint me drill master with rank and pay of first or second lieutenant."

How thankful I feel that I did not take this bait and leave the army of Lee and Jackson, but contented myself with my place as a private soldier in the Army of Northern Virginia, and so had part in the great campaigns of 1862, 1863, and 1864.

I have mentioned above the name of Gen. Albert Sidney Johnston, the commander of the western Confederate Army. He fell, as will be remembered, at the battle of Shiloh, April 6th, 1862, in the moment of a great victory achieved by his masterly strategy and his indomitable resolution. Nothing is clearer than that, had he lived to follow up his success and carry out his plans, General Grant's army would have been destroyed before General Buell with his fresh troops, 25,000 strong, could have reached him. I embrace this opportunity of paying the tribute of my reverent admiration to this great soldier and knightly Christian gentleman, and I would recall to the reader the fact that he lost his life as a result of his chivalrous act in imperatively requiring his surgeon, who should have been by his side, to go to the help of the Federal wounded on the field of battle from which their army had been driven. "These men," he said, "have been

our enemies; they are now our prisoners.   Do all you
can to relieve their sufferings."

Had the surgeon been with General Johnston when
he received his wound, he could easily have saved
his life.   He bled to death from a wound in the lower
part of the leg.   This unselfish act of his at Shiloh sur-
passes the deed of Sir Philip Sidney at Zütphen, which
has made him an immortal example of generous
chivalry.

This brief sketch of life in winter quarters would be
incomplete without some reference to the religious
services which some of us conducted in our company.
Our chaplain was a man without much force, and with
still less zeal for his sacred functions, so that we felt
the need of supplementing his efforts.   Under date
of Jan. 30th, 1862, I find the following:

"For the third or fourth time in these singular months
since July last, I endeavored to give an impetus to my
cherished idea of social prayer-meetings, and this time (the
beginning of Dec., 1861) with marked success.   They were
held nightly, instead of weekly, or occasionally, as before.
At first we met in private tents, but finally we procured a
tent for the purpose, and fitted it up with rude benches
so as to accommodate twenty-five or thirty men.   Gradually
our numbers had increased, and this would hardly give
seats to as many as would come.   Among the attendants
were some from the other companies of the regiment.
Captain Murray was a regular and devout attendant.   I
began to feel grateful for the success of the effort in its
outward manifestations, and hopeful of its inward benefit
to the soldiers of the regiment.   Giraud Wright, George
Williamson, Valiant, and myself regularly conducted the
meetings.   Giraud and I used extempore prayer; the others

the forms of the Prayer-book.   This continued till we broke up our camp at Centreville and removed to our present position.   In the hurry of departure, I forgot the tent and it was left behind.   This loss, together with the all-absorbing employment of building our winter quarters has broken up this hopeful work.   I cannot acquit myself of much blame on this account.   Thus, after five or six weeks this effort, like its predecessors, was discontinued."

But another effort was made, for on Tuesday, Feb. 4th, I wrote in my diary:

"On Saturday evening I again commenced the prayer-meetings.   Only a few came, but I felt sure the numbers would increase.   The next day I was sent over to Major Snowden's headquarters as corporal of the guard and was obliged to stay all night.   I read the xxviith chapter of St. Matthew aloud to the men on guard."

Later in the war a wave of religious interest and revival swept over the entire Army of Northern Virginia, — but it has often been described and I need not dwell upon it here.

CHAPTER VII

A S the spring of 1862 approached, the Confederate authorities were confronted by the prospect of seeing their armies melt away in face of the enemy, by reason of the fact that most of the regiments had been enlisted for but one year. So, to encourage reënlistment, a furlough of thirty days and a bounty of fifty dollars were offered to all volunteers who should reënlist "for two years" [so my diary reads, but my memory says "for the war" — and this I think is correct], "provided not more than one-fifth of a regiment shall be absent at one time." Hearing this news, I told Watkins and Inloes of it, "and proposed to them to embrace the offer." "Next day we went round and talked to those of the regiment who were in camp (the bulk of it being on picket), and finally seven agreed to reënlist." "In a few days we will get our furlough and the bounty of fifty dollars and leave this delectable place!"

Words cannot express the delight a soldier felt at the prospect of a return to "civilization" for the space of thirty days. To have the opportunity of a daily bath, or at least a daily "wash up"; to change one's clothes; to sleep in a bed; to hear no "reveille" at four in the morning; not to be disturbed in the evening by the inevitable "taps"; to sit down at a table covered with a white cloth; not to be met at every meal by the unvarying "menu" of "slap-jacks and bacon," or "bacon and soda biscuit," — yes, to feast on the "fat of the land" before the land had grown lean and hungry, as it did in another twelvemonth; to bask in the smiles of the noble women of the Confederacy; to enjoy once more their delightful society; to be welcomed and fêted like a hero wherever you went by the men as well as the women, — all this was an experience the deliciousness of which no man who has not been a Confederate soldier can have any idea of, — and the *private* soldier enjoyed it in a higher degree than the commissioned officer, for *he* generally had a few more comforts, or at least a few less hardships, than the soldiers in the ranks. True, we Maryland boys had no home waiting to open its doors to us during our furlough, but the Virginians always gave us a peculiarly warm welcome, and, because we were exiles, did their best to make us feel that their homes were ours. The soldiers of the Union were well clothed and well fed, but they could never have such a welcome as we had, or be such heroes as we were when they went on furlough, because there was no such solidarity of feeling in the North as there was in the South. The condition of the two peoples was entirely different. The Southern soldier was fighting to repel invasion. He was regarded as the defender of the homes and firesides of the people. The common perils, the common hardships, the common sacrifices, of the war, welded the Southern people together as if they were all of the same blood, all of one family. In fact, there was, independently of the war, a homogeneity in the South that the North knew nothing of. But when the war came all this was greatly intensified. We were all one family then. Every Confederate soldier was welcomed, wherever he went, to the best the people had. When he approached a house to seek for food or shelter, he never had the least misgiving as to how he would be received. The warmest welcome and the most generous hospitality awaited him — that he knew beforehand.

Such an experience, even though it lasted but thirty or forty days, was a compensation for much that he endured. The memory of it lingers delightfully after eight and forty years. We could truly say, "*Olim meminisse juvabit.*" And to have passed four years in such an atmosphere, to have felt one's self a unit in such a society, where all hearts beat as one, where all toiled together, and suffered together, and hoped and gloried together, or else bent before the same blast of adversity, — that was something to have lived for — something to die for, too — something the fragrant memory of which can never pass away.

In my case, however, there was more even than this. Allied, through my noble mother, with many of the old families of Virginia, — the Randolphs, the Harrisons, the Carters, the Pages, the Nelsons, the Lees (to name no more), — I found myself among kinsfolk wherever I went in the old State. During my thirty days furlough, which somehow was lengthened out to forty days, I visited Clarke County, and then Richmond and the James River, and Lynchburg, and Fredericksburg and Charlottesville and Staunton, and in all those places I was welcomed by people of my own blood, who knew all about me, and who received me, not only with cordiality because I was a Confederate soldier, but with affection because I was a relative.

So on my travels, those six weeks, I had "the best time going" and was as happy as the days were long.

Millwood, Clarke County, was my first objective. Taking the train at Manassas, February 7th, I got out at Piedmont, where fortunately I found a conveyance which took me as far as Upperville. To quote from my diary:

"For the second time I travelled over that road, but this time in a different direction, under different circumstances and for a different purpose. All the scenes and occurrences of the 19th, 20th, and 21st of July came vividly back. How weary and worn had I trudged with musket and knapsack over that same road, little conscious of the eventful scene I was soon to play a part in. It was a moonlight night and I recognized each turn in the road and each spring by the wayside."

It was late when I reached Bollingbrooke. The family had retired to bed, and it was with difficulty I waked them up. John Bolling was one of my mess, and news of him was welcome, even at the midnight hour. Next day, Willie, a younger son, drove me to Millwood.

"At the highest point in the gap (through the Blue Ridge), just beside the road stands a tree whose branches overshadow parts of four counties: Fauquier, Loudon, Warren and Clarke. We reached the Shenandoah before we expected to, so pleasing was the road, and so busy was my mind recalling each spot associated with the march of the 19th of July. The river was swollen many feet above the watermark of last summer. It swept on rapidly as if defying any attempt to ford it a second time. Indeed, independent of its depth, it would have been impossible for man or horse to stem such a tide. . . . Willie Bolling told me that when he and his father drove to our camp at Winchester last summer a little boy at the ford directed them purposely to drive into a deep hole, and when they were almost drowned, rolled over on his back on the river bank, convulsed with laughter. They were obliged to take the horses out and hire some men to drag the wagon out with ropes. It appears it was this boy's habit to hang about the ford and watch for strangers and make them drive into this hole for his amusement. He could not have been more than eight or nine years of age."

I was again the guest at Millwood of one of my mother's sisters, Mrs. Wm. Fitzhugh Randolph, to whom I have already referred.

"Aunt Randolph makes a baby of me. I am not allowed to wait on myself — not even to *pick up a pin!* At my age I do not particularly enjoy swaddling bands!"

Here I lingered for twelve days of my precious thirty, visiting many of the delightful country homes, dining out, spending the night in some cases, singing with the girls, sleigh-riding, attending a wedding, and other festivities.

At "The Moorings" lived the family of my quondam navy cousin, now Major Beverly Randolph. At "Saratoga" I was welcomed by my charming cousins, Mary Frances and Lucy Page. We sang together "Maryland, my Maryland," and I sang for them "The Leaf and the Fountain," "The Pirate's Glee," and "Silence," which they seemed pleased with. I dined also at stately "Carter Hall," and my diary mentions that "seven, eight, and nine o'clock struck while we were at the dinner table." They "compelled me to stay all night," — to my sorrow, for breakfast was not served next day till eleven o'clock, and this to a soldier disciplined for months to answer roll-call at four A.M. was no small trial! "Bored to death," was my memorandum of this. Another day I dined at "New Market" with my cousin Dr. Robert Randolph, and was warmly received and as usual "compelled to stay all night." Cousin Lucy (Dr. R.'s wife) "was very affectionate and kissed me." "Next morning, after prayers, seeing an old lady with a cap on come into the room," I supposed she was Mrs. Randolph, "though looking much older than on the previous evening." Accordingly "I saluted her with a kiss before the old lady had time to show her surprise," and before I discovered that it was Mrs. Burwell, Mrs. Randolph's mother. We had never met before, but nobody seemed surprised at what I had done.

I may here set down a remark in my diary to this effect: "I have never heard anyone here address anyone else by a more formal title than 'cousin.' Whatever the company, it is always the same."

This reminds me of Michelet's description of Burgundy, which is applicable in several respects to Virginia. However, the only part of it I can now recall is this, "It is a land of joyous Christmases, where everyone calls everyone else 'cousin.'" My diary mentions also the wedding of Mr. Warren Smith and Miss Betty Randolph, which took place at "New Market" at five P.M., "with eight bridesmaids." The entertainment which followed was prolonged till one o'clock next morning.

Such was the happy gayety and the prodigal hospitality in old Clarke County the first winter of our

cruel war. It had not yet felt the iron heel of the
invader. The winters that followed till 1865 would
tell a different tale. It is still a beautiful country,
and some of the fine old homesteads still survive,
though few of them are owned by the same old
families.

I next turned my steps, February 20th, to Richmond, the capital of the Confederacy, where I
found another nest of relatives and many friends.
At Piedmont, where I struck the railroad and spent
the night, "I wrote some blank verse rather to vent
my feelings than to while away the time," — the
subject whereof has not been preserved in my record!
Met many old acquaintances on the way, and made
some new ones, among them a very clever and charming young lady, with whom I had "a long conversation on the subject of matrimony," — altogether
impersonal, however!

I was just in time for the inauguration of Mr. Jefferson Davis as President of the Confederate States of
America. It took place February 22d, in the Capitol
Square, amid a downpour of rain. In the evening
the President held a levee which I attended in company with Mrs. James Lyons and Miss Mary Lyons,
enjoying myself hugely, and finding Mr. Davis very
gracious and affable. He was a man of fine presence
and of distinguished abilities, as was well recognized
in *ante bellum* days when he was Secretary of War,
and later when he represented Mississippi in the
United States Senate. It was he who first projected
a transcontinental railway. His State papers were
models of vigorous English. He was a graduate of
West Point, and had shed his blood gallantly in the

Mexican War. Had he been quite ignorant of military matters, he would have been a more successful President. In that case it is likely Robert E. Lee would have been made commander-in-chief in 1862, instead of in 1865, when it was too late.

The Southern people forgave all his mistakes and set him on high as their martyred President, when Gen. Nelson Miles put him in irons at Fortress Monroe after the war was over. He was a man of exalted character, and had a knightly soul.

In Richmond I met "acquaintances innumerable," and many relations, among the former "Tom Dudley" (destined to be a famous bishop), with whom I dined. He was, I think, in one of the departments of the government in Richmond.

The very next day, February 23d, Fort Donelson fell, and my Uncle Peyton's son, Dabney Harrison, was killed, gallantly leading his company. He was a Presbyterian minister, but felt the call to defend his State from the invader, and, doffing his ministerial office, raised a company in his own congregation and was elected its captain. His course and his fate were similar to those of Bishop Polk, who laid aside his episcopal robes and became lieutenant-general in the Southwestern Army — with this difference, that *he* had had a military education at West Point. General Pendleton, Lee's chief of artillery, was another example of a clergyman entering the army as a combatant.

The same day my uncle lost his daughter Nannie by scarlet fever at Brandon on the James River. The previous July, at the battle of Manassas, the dear old gentleman had lost another son, Capt. Peyton

Harrison, and still another, Wm. Wirt Harrison, had been severely wounded. Not long afterwards, his married daughter Mary, Mrs. Robt. Hunter, died in childbed, her illness brought on prematurely by a raid of the Federal soldiers. Still later his son, Dr. Randolph Harrison, was wounded and died, and his youngest son Harry was taken prisoner.

He bore it all like a noble Roman — or rather like a brave Christian, which he was. The story of this family is that of many another in the South.

I may here mention that I had twenty-four first cousins in the Confederate Army on my mother's side, most of them bearing the name of Harrison.

After some halcyon days in Richmond among my many friends, college mates, and kinsfolk, I took the steamboat, February 26th, down the river to upper Brandon, the home of my mother's sister, Mrs. Wm. B. Harrison and her husband. There I indulged in the sport of wild duck shooting several times with varying luck. George Harrison, a year younger than I, was at home, and we had long talks over the fire till the "wee sma' hours," much of it about the Christian ministry, to which we both aspired, and we usually ended with united prayer.

The following Sunday was the Fast Day appointed by President Jefferson Davis, and we rode horseback to Cabin Point to the Episcopal Church, and received the holy communion together.

The following Sunday was stormy, so we had the church service at home, and I read a sermon aloud. I also examined Dr. A. T. Bledsoe's "Theodicy," — a very able book, by the way.

The next day, March 3d, George and I set out for

Jamestown Island, but the boat was caught in a fog and obliged to return. On the 4th we started again and reached the island, which we found fortified with thirteen guns, Columbiads, thirty-two pounders, and Dahlgrens. How strange a spectacle — the island where the first English settlers landed in 1607 and planted the seeds of English civilization, English liberty, and the English Church, fortifying itself against the invasion of the descendants of the Puritans who landed in 1620!

George's brother and my dear friend, Capt. Shirley Harrison, was there in command of a company of heavy artillery. He was "well, and living like a lord"! Twice more we went ducking.

It is sad to reflect on the fate of my uncle's princely home of Brandon, where in the old days as many as forty guests would sometimes be entertained. It was shelled later in the war by the Federal gunboats and rendered untenantable. After the war financial disaster overtook him and his sons, and the place was sold for debt.

Lower Brandon and Berkeley were two other Harrison seats, much older than my uncle's. The family's history in America began in 1634 with Benjamin Harrison, the emigrant. It was one of the most distinguished in the old colonial days.

March 6th I returned to Brandon, and next day drove with my uncle William to Petersburg, thirty miles — roads very bad, and the journey took seven hours. We found Richmond under martial law. March 8th I proceeded to Fredericksburg, where I was the guest, at Kenmore, of another aunt, Mrs. Randolph Harrison. Visited also "Santee," the home of Mr.

Sam Gordon. Saw more Harrison soldiers, my cousins. The following extract from a letter to my mother, written just before returning from furlough, may illustrate the spirit of the Southern people at this time:

KENMORE, March 10, 1862.

. . . .

Our affairs look dark, but not hopeless. The war may be a long one, but it *can* have but one termination — our independence. We are stimulated to new exertion, our people are roused to action, and there exists a deep-seated resolve in the heart of the nation, to choose extermination before subjugation. "God and the Right" is our motto. For my part, I have cast my lot irrevocably with this sacred cause. I have reënlisted, and shall continue to do so until the end is accomplished. If I fall, do not grieve for me. Your son would prefer such a death to any but a martyr's, and you will not be ashamed to think that I have died in my country's cause. But I have *no presentiment* whatever, — I only speak of *possibilities*.

Good-by, father, mother, brother, sisters. God bless you all is my prayer.

On March 11th I set out again for Millwood — why, I do not know, for my thirty days furlough was at an end, and I have no record of its extension — though I conclude it must have been, for I would not have been insubordinate, I am sure. I travelled by stage as far as Mt. Jackson, but did not reach Millwood, for Manassas had been evacuated, Winchester also, and Clarke County was now in possession of the enemy. I passed through Staunton, where I found more Harrison relations, and then stopped at Greenwood Depot with another sister of my mother, Mrs. Dr. Garrett. Then to Charlottesville, where of course I met many friends, and also another daughter of my Uncle Peyton, Mrs. Hoge, and the widow of my cousin Dabney Harrison.

March 17th I set out again for camp, but was "stopped" at Gordonsville and obliged to return to "Edge Hill," where I had a nest of Randolph cousins — among them Cousin Sarah, who later wrote that charming book, "Domestic Life of Thomas Jefferson." We had a most interesting horseback ride together to Monticello, Jefferson's seat.

March 22d set out once more for camp, and on the 23d, by walking ten miles from Culpeper Court House, reached the regiment encamped on the Rappahannock, having been absent six weeks.

I have given some account of my visits to different parts of Virginia during my furlough because they reflect the spirit and the life of the people at that period of the war, February and March, 1862. There was still much comfort, even luxury, in the manner of living, and a spirit of joyousness and gayety among the young. The war had not yet begun to press heavily on the resources of the South. There had been in Virginia but one great battle, and that had resulted in so great a victory that there was an absolute confidence among all classes of the ultimate success of the cause. This feeling was damped by the reverses in the west at Fort Donelson, the last week in February; and the surrender of so large a force, in face of the indignant protest of Gen. N. B. Forrest, was galling to the pride of the South. I found everywhere I went a deep religious feeling. At the great houses in Clarke County I was generally asked to conduct family worship. The churches in Richmond and elsewhere were largely attended. Among the young men, I found it easy to introduce the subject of religion. The following entry in my diary illustrates this:

"While at Brandon, George and I had some very sweet interviews. One of them is peculiarly pleasant to recall. He was speaking of his future prospects in life, and I turned the conversation to the ministry, and was delighted to find that he had himself frequently thought of it. I endeavored to strengthen and encourage his inclinations to enter the sacred calling. He told me it had been his sainted mother's wish that he should devote himself to God, and that his father echoes the same desire. Then I invited him to join me in prayer, and with tears of penitence and humility we sought God's blessing. . . . Never did we embrace with as much tenderness and emotion as when we rose from that prayer at the still midnight hour."

I brought back with me to camp thirty-four copies of the New Testament for distribution and made this entry:

"The campaign now opening is likely to be a very active and also a very bloody one. How necessary to enter upon it with a soul at peace with God, and a mind prepared for any event!"

CHAPTER VIII

EARLY in March the war entered upon a new phase. General McClellan had withdrawn from Johnston's front at Manassas, and transported his army by water to Fortress Monroe, and was now advancing on Richmond by way of the peninsula, making the York River and the James his bases. Undoubtedly this was good strategy on his part, for it enabled him to advance under protection of the Federal gunboats nearly as far as Williamsburg. In fact, McClellan established his lines on the Chickahominy, within a day's march of Richmond, with very small loss, fighting only one battle, the unimportant battle of Williamsburg, in securing a position so near the capital of the Confederacy. It cost General Grant, two years later, a long and hard-fought campaign, with many bloody battles, involving the loss of nearly one hundred thousand men, to get as close to Richmond as his predecessor had done with only trifling loss. So far, surely, the strategic honors were with McClellan, and had he been given in 1862 the supreme authority which Grant wielded in 1864, enabling him to summon to his aid, as he earnestly wished to do, General McDowell with his forty thousand men from Fredericksburg, it is doubtful whether the army of

Lee could have achieved the victory it did in those seven days battles before Richmond.

Before my return to camp, Gen. Joseph E. Johnston had transferred the bulk of his army to the peninsula to contest the advance of McClellan; Gen. T. J. Jackson had been sent to the valley, and the division of General Ewell was left on the old line. Our regiment was attached to his command. Manassas had been evacuated. Our log huts at Fairfax Station had been left, and all our little accumulations of comfort lost. Our tents had been burned at Manassas, for what reason I do not know, and I found the regiment bivouacking under their blankets stretched over poles on a little rocky hill back of the Rappahannock. My precious store of books had of course been left behind and lost. We now had two months of marching and countermarching, without any object that we could divine, under conditions of more acute discomfort than we had ever known before, enlivened by an occasional skirmish or artillery duel. The following sketch, under date of March 28th, may serve as a sample:

"On the banks of the Rappahannock. The bridge is on fire at both ends — the flames of a house on the opposite side of the river darting fiercely up to the sky. Our regiment in line of battle. A shell has just passed hissing over our heads. The bridge blows up as I write with a double explosion. The Yankees are shelling the woods as they advance. Our artillery on our left has just opened. I suppose we intend protecting General Steuart's retreat. It is not desired to fight unless the Federals press us hard. — Another shell. — Another — An officer rides up and asks for five rounds of cartridges from each man of our regiment. He has but fifteen rounds to a man. We have forty. —

The Baltimore Light Artillery fires its first shell. This is their maiden engagement. The Federal infantry advances toward the river; they are saluted by the Baltimore Light Artillery from an eminence on our right. The enemy's artillery changes position. As yet they have not found our range. The bridge falls in with a rattle like the discharge of musketry, or the rattling of wagons. The Baltimore Light Artillery are firing round shot, and not shell, as I supposed. — Infantry firing in rapid succession. One of our companies (Goldsborough's) is engaged, deployed as skirmishers. Now they are moving double quick (still as skirmishers) by the left flank. The Artillery at the other side has slackened its fire. — Chesney (Elzey's adjutant-general) dashes past at full speed between us and our skirmishers. — Musketry again from skirmishers. — Another rattling crash, from the bridge, I suppose. — The Federals discover the Baltimore Light Artillery and begin to open on them. They reply, and it seems probable we shall have a brisk artillery duel. They seem to have gotten the range of our battery. . . . Wagons are seen on the other side of the river. It may be an armed reconnoissance in force after forage. The battery on our right has limbered up, and is moving off. A shell bursts between — [Here we were called to attention and moved off a mile or so from the river. It was nearly dusk. The enemy shelled us as we retreated up the railroad, but without doing us any damage. General Elzey and Captain Brockenbrough had a very narrow escape: a shell burst just between them, throwing light on their faces. The Baltimore Light Artillery did good practice, driving the enemy's artillery twice from their position. Our cavalry next day crossed the river and found two (artillery) horses dead, and that several cannon balls had passed through the house behind which the enemy took refuge.]"

On Good Friday, April 18th, we had another artillery duel.

The weather was very severe through March and far into April — "much rain and sometimes sleet or snow. As late as April 10th the ground is covered with snow frozen and the air is very keen. The mountains look beautiful in their white garments." Marching and bivouacking without tents (which were not supplied us again till April 6th), we had many rough experiences, often drenched to the skin, and as the wood was wet and soggy, sometimes it was next to impossible to light a fire. A favorite device was to get three fence rails and rest them at one end on the ground, placing the other end on the third rail of the fence, the middle rail depressed below those on either side. This made a bed which kept us out of the mud, while we covered with our blankets and made out to be fairly comfortable — only the knots or other protuberances of the rails made themselves objectionable.

In one of those "driving sleets"

"John Post and I constructed a bunk together with blankets stretched over and straw to lie on. We were obliged to retreat into it about one o'clock. We talked as long as we could about old times and Monument street girls. He read me an extract from a letter from R. N., and showed me the daguerreotype of a mutual friend. Then we went to sleep and would not have waked up till morning but for the cold and rain on our feet and the water which gradually crept under us. We went off about eleven o'clock from a camp where the mud was ankle deep to a warm country house (Mr. Wise's) just above Brandy Station, where we stayed till next day."

Another entry, March 30th, is as follows:

"We awoke to the most disagreeable consciousness that the rain of the day preceding was unabated, that our feet were wet and cold, that the straw on which we were lying was almost saturated, and our bodies of course chilled with the wet and cold."

The Mr. Wise mentioned above, who treated us so hospitably (refusing compensation), used to keep the Warm Springs, Va., and knew my father and grandfather. It was Sunday, and Post and I sang hymns together. Then we read the New Testament and wrote letters to our people in Baltimore.

During the weeks of March when we had no tents and when the weather was so inclement and our exposure so unusually severe, we would slip off to some private house whenever opportunity offered and leave could be obtained, and sometimes without leave. Only in this way, I think, could we have endured the ordeal. Often our only meal in camp was a piece of hardtack and a piece of bacon toasted on a forked stick. And when at length the tents were furnished, orders were issued that they should be pitched every night and struck every morning early — evidently to prevent the enemy discovering our whereabouts.

I give here part of a letter written to my mother on my twentieth birthday:

TUESDAY, April 15, 1862.

.   .   .   .

After dinner. — The regiment has gone out to drill, but I am excused as cook. I have not told you of the receipt of three letters from you all a few days ago. One dated February 28th, from you (in which I am glad to find you so cheerful, my precious mother); a second containing one from Telly (Feb. 28), one from Sister Mary (Nov. 8th!!!), and a third from Marge written on the 4th and 5th. How exultantly I seated myself on my bunk and, strewing my

letters around, devoured them one by one, over and over
again. I gave George Williamson your message, for which
he thanks you warmly; he sends kindest regards to you all.
So does Jim Howard. Telly's letter amused and entertained me greatly: he has "broken out" in so many new
places, I shall not know him when I see him. Tell him,
however, to stay where he is. He is so full of Shakespeare
and the classics that he will despise such a rough soldier
as his brother has gotten to be. But the funniest meta-
morphosis in the boy is his conversion to the creed of Byron
and Cupid. He need not flatter himself that he can cut
me out in Annapolis. When I come home "from the wars,"
I will throw him in the shade completely by my "honorable
wounds," "deeds of valor," etc.! I can't thank you all
enough for your frequent letters; every one attests the spirit
of a love which I have not deserved and can never repay.
There was one for Duncan from sister Mary too, enclosed
in mine. He is, you know, on General Trimble's staff, his
aide-de-camp. You never saw such a change in a man in
your life. When he returned from Richmond with his
sunburnt hair cut off, his beard shaven, except mustache
and imperial "staff" boots replacing his old "regulations,"
and his dirty uniform exchanged for a nice new suit, it was
hard to recognize him. You may imagine how he was
changed by camp life, when I tell you that Mr. Hollingsworth was introduced to him as Captain Jones, talked with
him some time, and finally left him to go in search of *his
friend Duncan McKim*, who *he learned* was in the hotel.
How fortunate he is to be with Carvel, Jim L., Wm. C.
(Carvel's brother-in-law), and on General Trimble's staff.
We were so amused at an incident over there some time since
before Jim and Duncan had their appointments. Geo. W.,
Duncan, and one other of our mess took dinner at the
General's. A Colonel Kirkland from Mississippi (or N. C.)
came in; after our boys left he remarked to Carvel: "Those
men are very well educated and have remarkably good

manners for *privates*." I have been enjoying myself lately in visiting about in the neighborhood (generally in quest of meals). One day I got lost in an immense forest twelve miles long; it was a sleety, misty day, and the water was an inch deep all the way. I walked from eleven to three before I came to a house; then I went in to dry myself, and was invited out to dinner; returning I slept at another house where were two very pretty ladylike girls; we talked together some time, then I sang "Maryland" to a new audience, and took my departure, though the old white-haired father asked me to stay all night. I have been there once since, and borrowed a volume of Mrs. Hemans' poems. There is a beautiful stanza at the commencement of the "Forest Sanctuary," which I will transcribe:

"The voices of my home! I hear them still!
    They have been with me through the dreamy night —
    The blessed household voices, wont to fill
    My heart's clear depths with unalloyed delight!
    I hear them still, unchanged: — though some from earth
    Are now departed, and the tones of mirth —
    Wild, silvery tones — that sang through days more bright,
    Have died in others, — yet to me they come,
    Singing of boyhood back — the voices of my home."

The poetry was certainly not of a very high order of merit, but the sentiment waked a warm response in the heart of the exile soldier boy.

On the evening of April 18th, Good Friday, orders were received to leave our camp on the Rappahannock and take up the line of march for Culpeper.

This is my entry on that occasion:

"We started at dusk after standing drawn up in line of battle for an hour and a half in a furious storm of rain. We could only turn our backs upon it and take it. At last, thoroughly drenched, we set out (along the railroad track), and what with the darkness and the mud and the culverts and cow-catchers we had a most miserable march. We would move three or four steps and halt, then three or four more and halt again — this, from dusk till two o'clock in the night when we reached Culpeper, — six miles in seven hours! Then laid us down in the rain and slept till morning. No rations served out! Charlie Grogan and I were most hospitably entertained by a Mrs. Patterson near Culpeper. She gave us also ground coffee and green coffee, and offered us sugar and salt." — "Marched four miles on the road to Madison Court House. Halted a couple of hours. Then marched back in a drenching rain over muddy roads at almost a double quick. Still no rations. Men almost broken down with the weather and with fasting. Halted a mile above Culpeper for the night; still raining hard. Ground wet, wood soggy, air cold, men starved. In the morning [it was Easter Sunday] set out again up the railroad in a cold, driving rain. Redmond and I walked a mile ahead and got a plain breakfast and tried to dry ourselves. Rejoined the regiment and marched twelve miles to Rapidan. Still no rations furnished. Stopped at Colonel Taliaferro's to see Miss Molly. Had an elegant dinner — enjoyed 'civilization.'" "Rode up from Rapidan to Orange on the cars—five miles; got in ahead of the regiment; stayed at a private house on the outskirts of the village, at Mrs. Bull's. She and her pretty daughters pleased me much. She invited me to stay all night, which I did. After I got into bed, the door opened and two gentlemen came in with a candle. I started up and asked if I had made a mistake. They said 'No,' and soon General Trimble and I recognized each other." "Monday, April 21st, 1862. Rained pitilessly all day. The regiment rode up to Gordonsville ten or twelve miles on open cars. This is one of the severest experiences we have ever had. Friday evening, Saturday, Sunday, and Monday exposed constantly to cold, drenching rain, with no shelter, and during two whole days without anything to eat. Our blankets and clothing were soaked with water: we marched wet, slept wet, and got up in the morning wet. On the evening of Monday we got tents . . . orders to march in the morning with two days cooked provisions."

These quotations (rather tedious, I fear, to the reader) show several things very clearly. First, the wretchedness of our commissariat; second, the hardships of the Confederate infantrymen; and third, the never-failing hospitality of the people of the country, rich and poor alike.

What a debt of gratitude we poor weary, starved men owed them, and especially the women, for their goodness. They heartened us for our severe work, and inspired us with fresh resolve to defend the country from the invaders. How one would like to express to them now (to such as may be still living) our heartfelt thanks for what they did for us eight and forty years ago!

In the light of a narrative like this, the fortitude and steadfast devotion of the Confederate soldier stands out in strong light. How patiently he trudged along those muddy roads, carrying musket and knapsack, cold and wet and hungry day after day — without murmuring, without ever a thought of giving the thing up, without regretting his act in leaving home and exiling himself for the Confederate cause, though his State had not seceded. I do not remember that any of our men deserted then, or at any time during the war. Not many of that regiment were as I was; for Virginia was a second home to me, and everywhere I went I found my mother's kin. This made it more natural and easier for me to stand up to the work and stick to the Cause.

The frequent absences from the regiment, even over night, which I have mentioned, seem to show a lack of the strict discipline of which I have spoken on a previous page as the characteristic of Colonel Steuart. But I think that about this time he was promoted to be brigadier-general, and given another command; and besides two things are to be considered: first, that under such circumstances, discipline was necessarily and wisely relaxed, and, second, that our commanding officer knew he could trust us to report for duty in any emergency that might arise. Yet failure to perform camp duty, or absence from roll-call would bring its punishment. Several times I mention having been put under arrest for the latter omission, and once that I was made sergeant of the guard for the night because of my absence at Orange Court House.

The inclement weather of that unfriendly spring continued nearly to the end of April. As late as the 25th we had snow, and about the same time my record is, "In camp we have no shelter and it is almost impossible to cook. This morning it is again raining hard." And again, "Poor Giraud Wright sat up all night in the rain over the fire, and is now sleeping with his head resting on a chair."

Notwithstanding the cold, whenever the sun *did* come out, Redmond and I would plunge into the chill waters of the swift Rapidan and have a swim. Bathing was a rare privilege, and so much valued that it was my habit during the winter at one of our camps to break the ice and take a plunge in a pool of water by the side of the railroad.   Under the genial sun we would soon forget our miseries and enjoy the beautiful scenery sometimes spread out before us in our marches.   Here is a note of April 25th:

"This is a beautiful country, and highly cultivated. Tobacco is successfully grown.   Farms are large.   Dwellings, all the way from Culpeper to Gordonsville and from Gordonsville to this point on the Rapidan, are large and handsome. . . . The spring has arrived very suddenly. Vegetation has sprung as it were from death to vigorous life without the usual intermediate stages.   Fruit trees are all in bloom except the later varieties.   Even pear trees are beginning to blossom.   The wheat is luxuriant and wears a constant and fresh verdure.   The banks of the river just above our camp are enchanting.   The river flows narrow, but deep, and very rapid.   The banks, from which the water has receded, are covered with the wildest and rankest growth of weeds and flowers, the usual denizens of marshy ground.   Running along parallel to the right bank is a rocky cliff, about forty or fifty feet high.   It is covered with trees, some of them growing out of the clefts in the rocks, and many of them (wild cherry, dogwood, etc.) covered with bloom.   Ferns hang gracefully over the rocks, while the level at the foot is completely carpeted with moss; from wild flowers of every variety and hue spring up."

About this time Giraud Wright was made second lieutenant in Doctor Thom's company.   He was the eighth member of our mess (No. 5) who had received a commission.

I have alluded to the fact that some of our companies were enlisted for only twelve months.   Well, on April 29th, an order came from General Elzey to these companies to elect their officers in accordance with the terms of the Conscript Act.   Col. Bradley Johnson harangued the men and tried to induce them to conform to the order, but they refused to elect any officers, holding that the Conscript Act did not apply to Marylanders. The number of the men who had reënlisted in February and taken the furlough was not large. This was not because their interest in the cause, or their loyalty, had cooled, but because almost every man wanted to enter some other branch of the service, — the cavalry, for instance, or the artillery. Col. Bradley Johnson was much chagrined by the action of the men just mentioned, and when, on May 17th, Company "C" was mustered out of the service before the rest of the regiment, and marched off to the rear, he called out dramatically, as he pointed in the opposite direction, "Men of the First Maryland Regiment, *there* is the way to the enemy."

In a letter written about this time, I said, "It seems probable we will miss all the great struggles likely to occur before this month is out." How little we knew what was before us!

The first week of May — I believe it was May 2d — we left Standardsville and marched across the mountain, fifteen miles, and camped in "Swift Run Gap," which we reached about nine P.M. Here we came in touch with Stonewall Jackson's division. That astute and able commander, in order to deceive the enemy's scouts, gave orders that Ewell's division should occupy the camp of his division, which marched out in the dark, leaving its camp-fires burning, so that it should appear that Jackson was still there. Then making a forced night march, he was many miles away before the morning light, marching to attack Milroy, west of Staunton, and leaving Ewell to await his return.

Now began that campaign of Jackson in the valley which has been so famous ever since and which established his reputation forever as a great soldier and a brilliant strategist. But of this more later on.

While Stonewall was marching to West Virginia, beating Milroy, and marching back again — which occupied about three weeks — we remained in camp at Swift Run Gap perhaps two weeks, where the monotony was varied for some of us by visits to the refined and hospitable home of Doctor Jennings, whose charming daughters greatly attracted us. There we had music and song and bright and merry converse, which speedily banished the memory of the hardships of the past two months. There came to our camp here three Frenchmen whose errand and whose identity much mystified us. One of them, de Beaumont, claimed to be an officer in the Chasseurs d'Afrique. They were suspected of being spies, but we had no proof.

May 16th we marched seventeen miles (in the rain, of course) over a bad road and camped near Columbia Bridge. May 17th marched to the top of the mountain as if Gordonsville were our objective, — "beautiful scenery, delightful atmosphere, and water bursting, sparkling and cold, from the rocks." Under this inspiration and without any emergency that I can recall, we made the three and one-half miles in forty-five minutes, though the mountain road was steep. We were in the habit of making seven miles in two hours, but that day we beat our record.

After spending Sunday the 18th on top of the mountain in sight of Culpeper and Luray, we marched next day down the mountain and back to Columbia

Bridge, a distance of thirteen miles. The weather was very warm. As soon as we had stacked arms there was a break for the Shenandoah, where hundreds of men were soon to be seen all along the banks standing on the water's edge or in the water, washing themselves or their clothes. The river was in flood, and no one dared to attempt to swim across, till Redmond, the athlete of our mess, a well-developed, well-seasoned man of about thirty years of age, plunged in and struck out for the opposite shore. He was watched with breathless interest by almost the entire regiment, and when at length he accomplished the feat, and stood safe on the other bank, a great shout went up from hundreds of throats. Not willing to be outdone, even by Redmond, I also made the plunge and tempted the flood. I crossed successfully, losing less distance than he, and stepped out on the shore in triumph, receiving, as he had received, the acclaim of the crowd. But unfortunately I was seized with a chill the moment after, and when I tried to swim back, my strength left me after a few strokes, and I was at the mercy of the current. I made up my mind that my end had come and said my prayers accordingly, but, the river making a sharp curve just there, I was carried by the current near to shore, and by a desperate effort succeeded in making a landing.

Two other misfortunes awaited me before that day was done. I found myself afflicted as the Egyptians were on a famous occasion (see Exodus viii. 16). The plague which baffled the magicians, and of which they confessed to Pharaoh, "This is the finger of God," had long since visited the Confederate camps, but till that unlucky day I had been exempt. But now my turn had come.

The same evening I yielded to temptation and "supped at the hospitable board of Mr. Long, where we had music and conversation." The result is thus tersely stated in my diary: "Put under arrest in consequence."

The first of these occurrences marks an experience which was the very acme of our trials borne for the cause. No hardship, or enforced self-denial of food, or rest, or comfort, was as hard to bear. It brought a sense of humiliation that is difficult to describe, although it was just the inevitable consequence of the conditions under which we lived. I set down the unpleasant fact because my object in these pages is to give a true picture of the life we led as private soldiers.

CHAPTER IX

ON the 22d of May, 1862, General Jackson returned from his successful expedition against Milroy and united his division with that of Ewell. From that day the First Maryland Regiment was under "Stonewall's" immediate command and marched and fought under his eye. It will always be our pride and boast that we had an active part in that marvellous campaign of his in the valley of Virginia, from May 22d to June 10th, and that we so conducted ourselves as to win his confidence and to be assigned such duty as could only have been given a command which he thoroughly trusted.

Of this great soldier a few words may here be said. From the hour when, at the battle of Manassas, General Bee pointed to him and cried to his wavering South Carolinians, "There stands Jackson, like a stone wall!" the rank and file of the army gave him their complete confidence, and were ready to follow wherever he led, and to attempt whatever he commanded. Not so the authorities at Richmond. Not so all the officers of high rank in the field. Generals who had known him at West Point and remembered that his scholastic rank was low, and that only by patient plodding could he keep up with his class, found it difficult to believe that Jackson could be a

90

LIEUT. GEN. THOS. J. ("STONEWALL") JACKSON

brilliant soldier. Those also who had known him as the quiet and by no means inspiring professor at the Virginia Military Institute felt the same scepticism. They acknowledged his steadfast courage and his unflinching resolution. Those qualities had been displayed by him in the Mexican War at Vera Cruz, Contreras, and Chapultepec,[1] and now again at Manassas and at Kernstown, but his critics said, first, that he was indeed the man to lead a forlorn hope into the jaws of death, but had not capacity to command a brigade; and when he had disproved this in battle, they said that he could fight a brigade under the eye of a capable superior officer, but could never fill an independent command, which required strategy and judgment. It will be remembered that, owing to the representations of General Loring, in the winter of 1861, the Richmond authorities so hampered and interfered with Jackson that he wrote his resignation, resolving to enter the ranks as a private soldier, and that it was only with great difficulty he was induced to withdraw it. The prejudice he encountered in high quarters was such that at each step forward that he made toward military greatness his detractors had fresh objections to make to his further advancement. "He might do to command a brigade, but not a division." Next, "Well, he had done pretty well as a division commander, but could never handle an army independently." It was not till after the brilliant series of victories which he won in the valley in 1862

---

[1] When asked after the close of the Mexican War if he felt no trepidation when so many were falling around him at Chapultepec, he replied, "No, the only anxiety of which I was conscious during the engagement was a fear lest I should not meet danger enough to make my conduct conspicuous."

that the voice of detraction was silenced. And even
after that at Malvern Hill, when Jackson ordered a
charge, General Whiting was heard to exclaim, "Great
God! Won't some ranking officer come, and save us
from this fool!" He came!

All the while the soldiers of the army adored
him. His appearance at any part of the line always and instantly roused the greatest enthusiasm,
and wild shouts rent the air as long as he was in
sight. On these occasions he would put spurs to
his horse and gallop out of sight as soon as possible.
This popularity was the more remarkable when it is
remembered that he was very stern, very silent, very
reserved, and by no means an ideal leader in appearance. His figure was bad, his riding was ungraceful
(he rode, as I remember him, with short stirrups and
with one shoulder higher than the other), and his uniform usually rusty, with scarce anything to mark him
out as a general. He never made a speech to his soldiers, he was a stern disciplinarian, exacting implicit
obedience not only from the rank and file, but from the
brigadiers and major-generals. Let one of these fail
to march with his brigade or division at the hour
prescribed in Jackson's orders, and he might expect
to be put under arrest with no more ceremony than if
he had been a second lieutenant or a sergeant of the
guard. And then the men knew that Stonewall would
march them hard, and fight them hard, and require
the greatest sacrifices of them. At the battle of Kernstown General Garnett held his position until his brigade
had been decimated and then, overwhelmed with numbers, retreated without Jackson's order. For this
Jackson rebuked him and put him under arrest.

In nearly all these respects he was a contrast to Gen. Robert E. Lee, who was elegant in person and handsome in features, a superb rider, the very beau ideal of a soldier, urbane, also, and gracious in manner, with a native dignity which stamped him as a king of men. He had also the rare gift of a rich and melodious voice, which alone would have marked him out in any company. While no man, not even Jackson, could have been a more lion-hearted and aggressive fighter than Lee, yet he lacked the other's strictness and severity as a disciplinarian. It has been said of him that he was too epicene, too gentle, and indeed, if he had a fault as a commander, it lay in that direction. There were occasions when more of Jackson's sternness and inflexibility in dealing with his generals would have been conducive to success on the field of battle.

These two great soldiers were types respectively of the Puritan and the Cavalier. Jackson was a Presbyterian, with many of the Puritan's characteristics. He was Oliver Cromwell, without his selfish ambition. Robert E. Lee, on the other hand, was a devout and loyal son of the Episcopal Church, a Cavalier in bearing as he was in blood, but with a simplicity and purity of character that was certainly not characteristic of King Charles's gallant and dashing leaders. But though they were thus men of very different types, they completely trusted and understood one another, and formed a combination that was well nigh irresistible. Lee regarded Jackson as his right arm, while it is on record that Jackson said of Lee that he was the only man he would be always willing to follow blindfolded.

I need say nothing of the great place this modest

and reticent soldier, Thomas J. Jackson, made for himself among the great captains of history. Distinguished military critics like Lt. Col. G. F. R. Henderson (whose two volumes on the life and career of Stonewall Jackson are the classic on the subject) have said all that need be said on that subject — and said it with authority. I remember hearing General Miles (at that time commander-in-chief of the United States Army) speak of him with the most enthusiastic admiration. In his estimation Jackson was beyond question the greatest soldier developed in our Civil War. His name was equivalent in value to a *corps d'armée*. He said that in the Federal Army he inspired at all times the greatest apprehension. "We never knew whether he would descend upon us on the right flank, or the left, or out of the clouds. He was the very embodiment of the genius of war, and, had he lived, in my opinion the South must certainly have succeeded. I have gone carefully over the history of the campaigns that followed his death, and there were at least half a dozen critical occasions when, in my opinion, his presence would have certainly insured victory to the Confederate Army."

I give this utterance of General Miles, not as expressing my own opinion (which of course is of no consequence on a subject demanding the knowledge of an expert military critic), but only as a sample of the exalted estimate in which General Jackson is held among military men. What I think most extraordinary is, that this plain soldier wrote his name so high on the roll of the great soldiers of the world's history in so short a time. It was less than two years between his first battle, that of Manassas, July 21st,

1861, and his last immortal victory at Chancellorsville on the 3d of May, 1863. Indeed it might be said that he carved his great fame in one short twelvemonth, — for the battles that have made his name immortal were all fought between May 25th, 1862, and May 3d, 1863.

I will only add that unquestionably one of the features of Jackson's character which commanded the confidence of the soldiers was his sincere piety and his strong faith. The men of that army believed in God, and they liked to feel that the leader whom they followed was a man of God and a man of prayer.

There are many anecdotes that might be told in illustration of "Stonewall's" devout religiousness, but they are probably familiar to most of those who will read these pages.

He was a man of prayer, and often while his soldiers slept, this devout soldier was pouring out his soul in supplication,

> "Appealing for his native sod,
> *In forma pauperis* to God;
> 'Lay bare thine arm — stretch forth thy rod,
> Amen.' That's Stonewall's way."

After his death one of his grim veterans said the Lord sent his angels to escort "Stonewall" to heaven, but they could not find him anywhere in the precincts of the camp. So they returned to the heavenly courts to make report to that effect, when to their astonishment there he was. "Old Jack" had outflanked the angels and got to heaven before them!

It was on the 22d of May that Jackson united his two divisions near Luray and began his movement against Banks.   The following is the entry in my diary:

"Marched through to Luray in fine spirits to the music of our 'sullen drums,' and in the light of 'brightest eyes were ever seen.'   Made about seventeen miles on the road to Front Royal.   General Jackson with his army joined us and created great enthusiasm.   Next morning (23d) army commenced moving at daybreak.   Ewell's and Johnson's divisions passed us, while we halted.   Orders came for the Maryland regiment (our own) to take the advance.   We passed the two divisions without making a halt, marching twelve miles on a stretch, seven of which we made in two hours.   Great enthusiasm as we passed through the army at our rapid, swinging Zouave step, singing 'Baltimore, ain't you happy?'   Bradley Johnson made a stirring appeal to some of Smith's men who had refused to do duty [because their term of enlistment had expired]: they took up their arms again.   Halted some four or five miles outside of Front Royal to rest.   Then we advanced rapidly, capturing the enemy's picket as we went.   The Maryland regiment (ours) was formed in line of battle and burst suddenly into the town, driving the whole Federal force out at the other end.   Women and children, wild with delight and gratitude, some with tears in their eyes, welcomed us as their deliverers.   I never felt the bliss of aiding my fellow men so much as then.   Fought several hours outside the town with the First Maryland (Union) Regiment.   Repulsed them.   Captured immense stores and 1400 prisoners.   Saved the bridge and several railway trains.   That night the First Maryland 'Rebels' stood guard over the First Maryland 'Loyals.'   Next morning we carried them in triumph into Front Royal, the scene of their former domination."

While the bullets were whistling through the streets of the little town, a lovely girl of about fifteen years ran out of one of the houses and, waving a Confederate flag, cried, "Go it, boys!   Maryland whip Maryland!" She was much excited and seemed unconscious of her danger.

General Jackson's order that our regiment should take the front and make the assault on the town was due to the discovery that it was occupied by the First Maryland Federal Regiment.   He thus put us on our mettle to show which were the best men and the truest representatives of Maryland.   It must be acknowledged that the "loyal" Marylanders were made of good stuff.   They put up a gallant fight and when, on their defeat, they were pursued by our cavalry, they would form in small squares and fight to the death. My record says "only a score or two escaped."

Allusion is made above to our singing as we marched. That we often did, and with fine effect — upon our spirits!   I have seen our men weary with a long march, and dragging along without any semblance of order, fall into line and march with cadenced step, almost forgetting their fatigue, when some one would start one of our familiar songs and the whole column would instantly take it up.

Neither words nor tune had any merit, but there was rhythm in it, at least, which appealed to the ear and helped the step.   One of our favorites was:

> "Baltimore, ain't you happy,
>   We'll anchor by and by;
>   Baltimore, ain't you happy,
>   We'll anchor by and by.
>   We'll stand the storm, it won't be long,
>   We'll anchor by and by."

The verses were all identical, except that the apostrophe was different. "Maryland" was invited to be "happy," and "old soldiers" likewise, and "Southerners" and "Confederates," etc.

Still another prime favorite was "Gay and Happy." the chorus of which ran:

> " So let the wide world wag as it will,
>   We'll be gay and happy still;
>   Gay and happy, gay and happy,
>   We'll be gay and happy still."

This resolve to be "gay and happy" might be considered heroic under the conditions that often environed us. But sung by a ragged regiment, marching through rain and mud, with weary limbs and empty stomachs, the element of the ludicrous was often more conspicuous than the heroic.

Another favorite ran thus:

> "As I was going to Derby,
>   'Twas on a market day,
>   I saw the biggest ram, sir,
>   That ever was fed upon hay.
>   The wool upon his back, sir,
>   It grew full two yards high,
>   And the horns upon his head, sir,
>   They reached up to the sky."
>   *Chorus:* "Oh, what a lie! Oh, what a lie!"

The verses that followed were of the same high order of poetical merit! They were always sung by a little fellow who had a high tenor voice and the chorus was then sung by the rest of the regiment. The effect of several hundred voices roaring out, "Oh, what a lie! Oh, what a lie!" was very grotesque and amusing.

The fact is we were soldier boys, and sometimes the "boy" was more in evidence than the "soldier." In camp we had a more varied repertoire of songs, such as "Maryland, my Maryland," "The Bonnie Blue Flag," "There's Life in the Old Land Yet," — and of course, "Dixie." We had also some of our college songs on occasion. A Richmond gentleman added the following verses to Mr. Randall's "Maryland":

> "Cheer up, brave sons of noble sires,
>   Of Maryland, my Maryland!
> Strike for your altars and your fires,
>   Maryland, brave Maryland!
> The tyrant's power must soon grow less,
> Virginia feels for thy distress,
> Thy wrongs she surely will redress,
>   Maryland, brave Maryland!
>
> "When the despot's power is flown,
>   From Maryland, dear Maryland;
> And liberty's regained her throne,
>   In Maryland, old Maryland;
> Then shall her sons once more be free,
> Her daughters sing of Liberty,
> And close united ever be
>   Virginia and Maryland.

I may here transcribe some verses that appeared in the *Baltimore South:*

> "What will they say down South,
>   When the story there is told,
> Of deeds of might, for Southern right,
>   Done by the brave and bold?
> Of Lincoln, proud in springtime,

Humbled ere summer's sun?
They'll say, ' 'Twas like our noble South,
They'll say, ''Twas bravely done.'

"What will they say down South,
    When hushed in awe and dread,
Fond hearts, through all our happy homes,
    Think of the mighty dead?
And muse in speechless agony
    O'er father, brother, son?
They'll say in our dear gallant South,
    'God's holy will be done!'

"What will they say down South,
    The matron and the maid,
When withered, widow'd hearts have found
    The price that each has paid,
The gladness that their homes have lost
    For all the glory won?
They'll say in our dear, noble South,
    'God's holy will be done!'

'What will they say down South?
    Our names both night and day
Are in their hearts, and on their lips,
    When they laugh, or weep, or pray.
They watch on earth, they plead with Heaven,
    Then foremost to the fight!
Who droops or fears when Davis cheers,
    And God defends the right!"

After the fight at Front Royal referred to above, the army moved on Winchester in two columns, Jackson by Strasburg, Ewell by the straight road from Front Royal. Our regiment made twenty-two miles that day, with only dry crackers (nothing else) for rations. We seem to have left our blankets behind, that we might march the faster, so that when night came we "couldn't sleep," — it was so cold without them. This was on Saturday, May 24th. Of the next day, Sunday, the 25th, I shall always have a vivid remembrance. It was my first battle at Winchester. By three A.M. we were in line of march, five miles from Winchester:

"As the sun rose, the Sabbath stillness was broken by General Jackson's artillery on our left. Then the battle commenced along the whole line. We pressed on through the smoke and mist till we were nearly in the town."

For some time we could not see friend or foe, but through the fog we could hear the orders of the Federal officers to their men. Well, after three or four hours heavy fighting the enemy yielded before the charge of the Louisiana Brigade, and the whole line dashed forward, entering the town by 8.30 A.M. "For the first time in the valley, 'the Rebel yell,' that strange fierce cry which heralded the Southern charge, rang high above the storm of battle."

I would like to pay a passing tribute to that fine soldier and gallant gentleman, Gen. Dick Taylor, who commanded the Louisiana Brigade. Enough to say that he speedily won the confidence of Jackson as a resolute and skilful commander, — though when he heard him utter an oath he said, "I'm afraid you are a wicked fellow." His conduct and that of his splendid brigade on this occasion elicited universal admiration. Ewell cheered himself hoarse as he witnessed their charge. It was in truth a gallant feat of arms.

Strange sights were seen in those two days of fighting before Winchester, — Federal cavalrymen strapped

to their saddles, so that when made prisoners and
ordered to dismount they couldn't obey till time was
given them to unstrap themselves, — and soldiers
equipped with breastplates to protect them from the
musket balls!

In the rush into Winchester that morning of May
25th I suffered a serious loss — serious in my eyes, at
least, at the time.

At Front Royal I had filled my haversack with "good
things" from the captured stores; and during our
rush at double quick into the town, the strap broke,
and away went all the rich stores it contained! I
groaned in spirit that I could not stop to recover that
precious haversack.

My diary proceeds:

"We were received with the most enthusiastic demon-
strations of joy by the inhabitants, who thronged the streets
regardless of the death-shots flying around them. Our
timely arrival saved the city from being blown up. The
storehouse was on fire at one end. The retreating miscreants
took delight in telling the women and children they would be
blown up. We saved the medical stores too. Colonel Dorsey
behaved with gallantry and was wounded. I found him
at Mrs. Hugh Lee's. I was detailed to take care of him and
stayed till the Wednesday afternoon following, revelling in
the enjoyment of ladies' society in particular and civilized
life in general."

That was a joyous breakfast table that Sunday
morning at Mrs. Lee's. The battle was over. We
were all "heroes" and "deliverers" in the eyes of the
charming women of the family, and all was proceeding
gayly till the entrance of my friend Berkeley Minor
brought me the sad news of the death of Robert Breck-

inridge McKim, my young cousin, who had joined the
Rockbridge Artillery near this very town less than
eleven months before. He fell gallantly serving his
piece in the battle. It was a painful shock to me, for
I was warmly attached to the noble boy. Procuring
a horse, I rode out to the field and found him laid out
in a barn, with a label attached, on which was his
name. The minie-ball had pierced his head just above
the forehead, leaving the face undisfigured. His
features wore a peaceful expression, and I believe his
soul was at peace with God in the better world. How
joyous he used to be and how well he sang our college
songs, "Lauriger Horatius," "The Irishman's Shanty,"
etc.

I remember once, at a Sunday afternoon students'
prayer meeting, Bob was called on to pray, and promptly
answered in the phrase we used in the lecture room
when the lesson had not been studied — "unprepared!"
To this call to meet his Maker in the storm of battle,
dear Bob had no need to make that answer. He was gay
and joyous, but true and good, and he had given himself to Christ. This is a fair sample of the checkered
life we led. Joy and sorrow were strangely mixed.
Whenever possible, we were "gay and happy," as
one of our favorite marching songs had it. The dear
women of the South, young and old, always met us
with smiles, and did everything to cheer our hearts,
even when their own were sore and sad for some loved
one who had fallen. As the war went on and became
more and more bloody, there were few families which
did not mourn a father, or a husband, or a brother
who had fallen in battle. The valley of Virginia was
for four years a constant battle ground. Up and down,

all the way from Staunton to Shepherdstown, the two armies swept, till at the end it was reduced to a scene of desolation. I myself participated in five battles at or near Winchester, and it is said the town changed hands more than eighty times during the war. To Winchester I had come with the University companies en route to Harper's Ferry, in April, 1861. To Winchester again Robert and I had come in July, 1861, to join Johnston's army. At Winchester now Robert had yielded up his life. At Winchester and at Stevenson's Depot I was to see severe fighting in June, 1863. Near Winchester again I was to be in the fatal battle of September, 1864, and at Cedar Creek the following October I was to see Gordon's victory turned into defeat by General Early's mistakes, — at least, that is my opinion.

Its people were devotedly loyal to the Confederacy, and my heart warms to-day to the dear old town, as I think what a warm welcome it always gave us.

In this battle General Jackson, by his brilliant strategy, ably seconded by the blindness and the blunders of the Federal commander, General Banks, had succeeded in attacking the army at Winchester with a force double its numbers. He led a force of 17,000 men, infantry, artillery, and cavalry. Three or four weeks before this disaster, General Banks had written to Mr. Stanton expressing regret that he was "not to be included in active operations during the summer." On that 25th of May, the Confederate commander relieved him of that regret in very rude but effective fashion.

This unexpected blow delivered at Winchester by

Jackson reverberated with telling effect through the whole North. Mr. Lincoln and his cabinet were alarmed for the safety of the Capital. Stanton wrote the governor of Massachusetts: "There is no doubt that the enemy in great force are marching on Washington." General McDowell, who was just starting to reinforce McClellan, was stopped, and his 40,000 men cancelled from the advance on Richmond. Frémont was ordered to support Banks. Even McClellan was ordered either to attack Richmond at once, or come to the defence of Washington. Such was the alarm that in one day nearly 500,000 men volunteered to save the Union.

Thus this great soldier had in a single engagement transformed the whole military situation in Virginia, — and the cause of the South, till then shrouded in gloom, had suddenly been irradiated with hope. By an unfortunate and almost inexcusable refusal to obey an order of Jackson because it did not come through Ewell, the pursuit of Banks's defeated army by our cavalry was delayed until the splendid opportunity was lost. Three days later part of the army advanced as far as Halltown, and the Stonewall Brigade, with our regiment and a battery of artillery, was pushed forward to Bolivar Heights, which was within range of Harper's Ferry. There we had some fighting — chiefly a duel of artillery—but the only man I remember seeing injured was an artilleryman who was shot in the thigh by a rifle ball at a distance of approximately 900 yards. That was looked upon as a remarkable achievement at that period in the history of war. How different it is to-day! I also recall that the wound was a horrible one — the flesh was dreadfully torn and lacerated.

The enemy had resorted to the reprehensible practice of using explosive bullets.

While this was going on the Federal generals were laying their plans to cut off the retreat of General Jackson, and "bag" him and his whole army. Four armies were set in motion from different directions against him — that of General Shields, detached from McDowell's army at Fredericksburg, 10,000 men; another force of 10,000 under General Ord; Frémont coming from the west with 15,000 men; besides 15,000 more under Banks and Saxton, moving south from the Potomac, — in all 50,000 men against Jackson's 15,000. I recall, while at Bolivar Heights, seeing a courier ride up in haste and hand General Jackson a despatch, and I noted his face and manner when he read it. He gave quick orders to a member of his staff and then, putting spurs to his horse, dashed off in the direction of Winchester. The information he had received was that Shields and Frémont were marching upon his rear to cut his communications and intercept his retreat. The bulk of Jackson's army was not far east of Winchester, which is about thirty miles west of Bolivar Heights. As soon as orders could reach them, these troops were put in motion up the valley towards Strasburg, which lies at the foot of the Massanutten Mountain.

Thus there was a gap of thirty miles between us and the rest of the army, and when we began our retreat at daybreak next morning, our officers realized that we were in grave danger of being cut off and captured. All day long, through the rain and mud, we trudged on, till at dark we reached Winchester; but we did not tarry here, but pushed on with weary limbs till we passed Newtown, having marched, with musket and knapsack, forty miles between dawn and nine or ten o'clock at night. We lay down to rest by the road-side just as we were, making no camp, lighting no fires, too much exhausted to care for anything except rest. I may here remark that the constant marching in this campaign, day after day and week after week, so hard-ened our muscles that when fatigue came there was no soreness or stiffness of the muscles, but just a gen-eral exhaustion — a "caving in" of the energies.

By early dawn we were again on the march, with rather depleted ranks, for not a few of the men had dropped by the way, unable to keep up the pace. It was Sunday morning — one week after our victory at Winchester — and now it looked as if our turn for defeat had arrived — or rather for defeat and capture — for what could our one brigade do against the Fed-eral army that might be already interposing itself between General Jackson and us? It was a silent and a gloomy column that trudged along the turnpike that morning. Officers and men were silent as the grave, — occupied all with the same gloomy appre-hensions. I fancied that even the gallant and intrepid General Winder (who commanded the Stonewall Bri-gade, to which we were temporarily attached) looked chagrined and gloomy. Not a few of us, I imagine, offi-cers as well as men, were secretly indulging in criticism of General Jackson for allowing us to be isolated as we had been, thirty miles in advance of the army. These anxieties came to a climax when, about eight o'clock, we heard the booming of artillery ahead of us. The men exchanged glances, but no one spoke a word, though the same thought was in every mind, "We are cut off now — it is all up with us." But not so! The guns we heard were Jackson's guns. He did not wait for Frémont to reach the valley pike, but advanced a part of his army several miles to meet him, threw out skirmishers, placed artillery in position, and opened upon the advancing Federals. In this way he held Frémont several hours till Winder and his brigade had time to make a junction with the rest of the army at Strasburg. How different our feelings then! Our spirits rose; we forgot our fatigue and were ready to sing

"Baltimore, ain't you happy?"

What the men said to each other then was of a different complexion, — "Old Jack knows what he's about! He'll take care of us, you bet!" From that hour we never doubted him.

And now began the retreat of our army up the valley, vigorously pursued by the Federal army under General Frémont. On our left ran the Massanutten mountain, and on the other side of that great barrier was General Shields with his army of 10,000 men. Could these two armies unite, they would overwhelm us by superior numbers; but General Jackson did not intend that they should unite. It was his purpose to fight them separately, and having beaten one, then to throw himself upon the other. Meanwhile, our Maryland regiment was given by Jackson the post of rearguard, — an honor which we highly appreciated and were determined to show that we deserved. For a week this retreat continued, and we were under fire every day and nearly all day. We would be deployed as skirmishers to hold the enemy in check while the

wagons and the ammunition train pursued its slow
and tortuous course. A battery of our artillery co-
operated with us in protecting the retreat of the army,
saluting the Federals with shot and shell as they
advanced — then limbering up and galloping off to
a new position, while our skirmish line slowly withdrew, taking advantage of every little hillock, or clump
of trees, or outcropping of rocks, to stop and fire upon
the pursuing cavalry. This operation was constantly
repeated during the day, and day after day. It was
exciting and perilous and fatiguing work, but I think
we did the business to "old Jack's" satisfaction. Now
and then a cavalry dash would be made and the enemy
would win some small advantage, but the trains were
protected, and the army moved with due deliberation
up from Strasburg to Harrisburg.

Three miles beyond that place a severe engagement
took place, in which the First Maryland took part,
encountering and beating the gallant Pennsylvania
"Buck-tail" rifle regiment. Among those who fell
on our side was Turner Ashby — a great loss, for he
was one of the most daring and skilful cavalry leaders.
Jackson mourned his loss as irreparable. His daring
feats of arms on his famous white charger had become
the theme of song and story. In his report, Stonewall
said of him: "His daring was proverbial, his powers
of endurance almost incredible, his character heroic,
and his sagacity almost intuitive in divining the purposes and movements of the enemy." This, I think,
was on Friday, June 6th. Next day all was quiet.
Our guns were silent the first time in fifteen days.
Sunday morning, June 8th, I was sent for betimes by
Brig.-General Geo. H. Steuart, who, after a brief ser-

vice with the cavalry, had been assigned to an infantry brigade. I went at once to his headquarters, expecting a reprimand, or to be ordered under arrest, because I had, with John Gill, slipped out of the column in the dark and spent a night (or rather part of the night) in a house in Harrisburg, where we were refreshed with food and a wash. "Has the general found this out?" I said to myself. What was my relief when he informed me that he had decided to make me his *aide-de-camp*, as he had observed "that I had been a good soldier and had been the first man in the regiment to set the example of reënlisting for the war." I thanked him, and returning to my mess began packing my knapsack preparatory to moving up to headquarters. Observing this, the men asked me what I was doing, and in reply I told them I was tired doing the duty of an infantryman and was going up to headquarters to be on the general's staff. I have mentioned that most of my immediate friends had preferred not to reënlist, and as the day approached (it was now only two weeks off) when our company was to be mustered out, I had been made the butt of many a gibe as to what would be my fate after that. I would, said they, be drafted into E.'s company — which was made up of roughs — and what would I do then? Well, now it was my turn to laugh, as I told them that the general said one reason he had selected me was that I had been the first to reënlist.

My cousin, Wm. Duncan McKim, had, previous to this, been appointed *aide* to General Trimble, and McHenry Howard had been given a place on General Winder's staff.

I entered at once on my duties, but was embarrassed

LIEUT. RANDOLPH H. McKIM, 1862

by the fact that I had neither horse, nor sword, nor spurs — and of course no uniform but my gray jacket with the chevrons of a sergeant on the left arm, having been made color sergeant not long before. I had hardly reached headquarters when the enemy was reported advancing, and in a very short time the bloody battle of Cross Keys, Sunday, June 8th, had begun. General Steuart bade me mount a beautiful black horse belonging to Major Kyle, the quartermaster, who was absent. I felt happy and proud when I found myself astride of that fine animal.

I need not describe the battle that ensued. That has been done with admirable accuracy by Lieut.-Col. Henderson in his "Life of Stonewall Jackson," and by various other writers. Ewell, with 6,000 infantry, 5 batteries, and a small cavalry force, defeated Frémont, with over 10,000 infantry, 12 batteries, and 2,000 cavalry. It is amusing now to read Frémont's despatch to Shields, who was just across the mountain. "The enemy need only a movement on the flank to panic-strike them. No man has had such a chance since the war commenced. You are within thirty miles of a broken, retreating army." In two days that "broken army" was to smash up the two armies of Shields and Frémont, numbering 25,000 men!

As the battle progressed, I was sent by General Steuart with a despatch to Major-General Ewell, who was in active command. I found him surrounded by his staff of young officers, well mounted and handsomely equipped. He gave me an order to take back to General Steuart, but when I turned to go, Major Kyle's horse positively refused to face the very heavy artillery fire directly in front. In vain I dug my heels

into his side.   Whereupon General Ewell laughed aloud
and said, *"Ha! Ha! a courier without any spurs!"* [1]
This, in the presence of his staff, was too much to bear
patiently.   I was very angry and felt the blood suffuse
my face.   To call me a "courier" when I was a "First
Lieut. and A. D. C.," with pay of 135 Confederate
dollars per month and allowances, — almost enough
by 1864 to purchase a pair of cavalry boots!   And to
do this before his whole staff on the field of battle!
However, I could only swallow the affront and obey
the general's suggestion, "Young man, you will have to
go back another way."

So I started back "another way," but before
long struck a Virginia regiment lying down in the
long grass in support of our batteries which were
hotly engaged just in front.   I reined up and asked
if there was any officer who would lend me a spur,
as I was bearing an important despatch and my
horse would not "face the music" of the Parrots.
Then up rose an officer, who, I afterwards learned, was
Major John Ross.   He kept rising till his stalwart figure was six feet three inches in the air, then he stooped
and unbuckled one of his spurs and handed it to me.
I dismounted, buckled it on, remounted, and thanking
the major, rode off, not by the "other way round,"

[1] General Ewell is thus described by Gen. Dick Taylor in that
racy volume of his "Destruction and Reconstruction":

"Bright, prominent eyes, a bomb-shaped, bald head, and a nose
like that of Francis of Valois, gave him a striking resemblance to a
woodcock; and this was increased by a bird-like habit of putting
his head on one side to utter his quaint speeches."

He was a bold horseman, a fine fighter, and a fine commander.
He had a supreme admiration for Jackson, and used to say "he
never saw one of Jackson's couriers approach without expecting an
order to assault the North Pole!"

but the direct way, across the bare horseshoe knoll, right in front, where, I think, all of our artillery was concentrated, and upon which the enemy's cannon were directed from several different points, like the spokes of the section of a wheel converging on the hub. It was a very hot place indeed, and the hottest spot was a little in rear of our batteries, where the lines of artillery fire met and crossed. I noted it in my diary as "a perfect hail of shell, cannon-balls, and bullets." My beautiful black was not to be blamed for not wishing to spoil his beauty in such a terrible place! But now, with the sharp spur plunged into his side, he had no option but to obey his rider; so away we went full speed across the infernal spot. Well, just in the middle of it, a round shot tore up the ground underneath us and passed harmlessly to us on its deadly path, and at that moment my little infantry cap flew off my head. Then ensued in my mind a brief but fierce battle (it lasted just about one second) between Pride and Fear. Fear said, "If you get off this horse to pick up that cap, you are a dead man!" But Pride promptly replied, "You won't ride up to the general's staff with no cap on your head!" Well, Pride conquered, and I was fool enough to rein up, dismount, and pick up my worthless cap, — but I enjoyed that immunity which the proverb says is given to children and fools, for neither my noble horse nor I was touched just then by any of the flying missiles of death.

In that battle I saw two men absolutely overcome by "panic fear" — and I do not recall any other examples through the whole war. One of these was an artillery man who had taken refuge under the caisson, where he crouched trembling like a leaf. I saw a sergeant ride up and point a pistol at his head, saying, "Come out from under there and do your duty, and you'll have some chance of your life, but if you stay there, by the Eternal, I'll blow your brains out." I didn't stay to see what the result was. Then, shortly after, I saw another soldier crouching in terror behind a tree. The next moment came a round shot, which went through the tree and absolutely decapitated the man! Major Stiles tells a story of a little army dog named "Bob Lee," who became demoralized at the battle of Chancellorsville and took shelter behind a tree, "crouching and squatting as a demoralized man might have done." He, however, escaped with his life!

I suppose these two men might, under other circumstances and on other occasions, have stood up to their duty as good soldiers. He who, on one particular day and under certain mental or physical conditions, may play the coward, may be steady and true on another day in face of danger. It is certainly a familiar fact that the bravest troops are sometimes for some unaccountable reason seized with panic. I may here say that I never felt inclined to dodge when a shell came shrieking through the air — simply because I always said to myself, "Why, you are just as liable to dodge your head into the shell as away from it — for you don't know at what point it will pass."

Another thing I saw that day, which is, I think, unusual, was this: a Parrott shell leaped into the midst of a group of men and exploded, killing and wounding several. It was close to me, and I saw the shell as it dropped. That was the unusual circumstance, — to see the shell come. Later in the battle my beautiful black was shot under me.   The ball went right through his head.   I heard the "thud" as it struck, and then the noble animal tumbled and fell, but I quickly withdrew my feet from the stirrups and as he fell over on one side, I sprang off on the other.   My first thought as he lay there before me was, "How shall I ever pay Major Kyle for that horse?"

I left the field instantly to procure another horse, but before I returned, my chief, Gen. Geo. H. Steuart, had been shot by a canister ball, which pierced the upper part of the chest and lodged in the back.

It was then my duty, as of his personal staff, to procure an ambulance and carry him off the field, and after that to find quarters for him in some safe place within the lines.

The battle ended, as all know, in victory for Ewell. Jackson was on the field, but did not interfere with his subordinate.   No officer contributed more to the success than our gallant Marylander, General Trimble. During the beginning of the battle of Cross Keys a sharp encounter took place on the other side of the mountain at Port Republic between some of Jackson's force and the advance brigade and cavalry of General Shields.   The latter were driven back in confusion and with serious loss.

I find the following entry in my little diary on June 15th at the University of Virginia:

"Here I have been since Wednesday morning with General Steuart, who was wounded on Sunday in that terrible battle with Frémont's forces.   This campaign with Jackson from May 23d to June 9th has been a most eventful one, fraught with danger and hardship beyond anything I have ever experienced.   Yet God has brought me safely through it all. I have been in three pitched battles and numerous skirmishes. Last Sunday I had a horse shot under me, but my life has been graciously spared, and to-day I am a monument of God's merciful protection. . . . Last Sabbath, while riding backwards and forwards in a perfect hail of shell, cannon-balls, and bullets, I was deeply impressed with my entire dependence on God's care, and in gratitude for my preservation, I inwardly resolved to devote myself more perfectly to his service, and especially to urge my fellow men to repent and turn to God."

The battle of Port Republic was fought the next day, and Shields' army was hurled back down the Luray valley in confusion, with heavy loss in killed, wounded, and prisoners.

By these operations of Stonewall Jackson, McDowell's army of 40,000 men and 100 guns, which should have gone to McClellan's aid in his advance against Richmond, were held back, and thus Richmond was saved.

CHAPTER X

A S a member of the personal staff of Gen. Geo. H. Steuart it was now my duty to be in attendance on him in the hospital until he should have recovered from his wound, or until he assigned me to some other duty. Accordingly I was a good deal with him at the University of Virginia, where he remained for some time during his convalescence. I also spent some time in Staunton, where I went to purchase a horse and other equipment — uniform, sword, pistol, spurs, etc.—suitable to my rank as a staff officer. While there I made the acquaintance of Miss Agnes Gray Phillips, who became my wife on the 26th of February, 1863.

I would here make mention of the generous hospitality extended to all Confederate soldiers by Rev. R. H. Phillips and his wife. There my cousin, Major Wm. Duncan McKim, was nursed for months after his serious wound received at the battle of Sharpsburg, Sept. 22, 1862. There another cousin of mine, Joseph Irving, was nursed at a later stage of the war till he died. There all our soldiers, and especially exiled Marylanders, found ever a welcome and a home. All that hospitality and kindness and sympathy could do to cheer and help them was freely given in that lovely Christian home.

117

The latter part of June I made a visit to Richmond to secure my commission and equipment. The following letter refers to this period:

RICHMOND, June 24, 1862.

MY DEAREST MOTHER:

Still in Richmond, you see, though the 1st of June has come and gone, and still the "Young (very young) Napoleon" tarries outside the Capitol. It is almost impossible to realize, as I sit quietly at the table in Mrs. Nicholas' dining room, that there are two immense armies lying opposite each other scarcely five miles from the limits of the city. A battle may occur at any moment: when it comes it will be fearful in carnage and most momentous in its result; it will decide, it seems to me, whether our independence will be at once established or whether this war shall drag its weary and blighting length over years yet to come. But, mother, I have confidence in God's help and guidance and in the valor and fortitude of our Southern troops. You are wondering what I am doing here. Well, I will tell you. If you have received a letter I wrote you from Charlottesville last week, you know that I am now General Steuart's aide-de-camp, that he was wounded severely in the shoulder, that I came off the field with him and brought him to Charlottesville where he now is. I have just arrived here. My business is to get my commission and equipment. On my way I stopped in Lynchburg at Mrs. Blackford's. Saw Vinnie and her husband, and received from Mr. Tom Taylor the loan of a beautiful sword captured at Manassas; it has "U. S." on the hilt, but that means (for me) "United South."

They were all very affectionate and kind. We are all brothers and sisters now in the South. I always feel sure wherever I am that I will be a welcome guest on account of the proud title I bear, "a soldier of the South." We are suffering many privations now; everyone is obliged to deny themselves the luxuries of life; you would be astonished at the universal scarcity of what were once considered the necessities of life. Tea is $10 a pound, for instance; fine uniform cloth $13.75 per yard; beef $1.00 per lb.; chickens $1.00 apiece, etc. But still you hear no complaint; the people seem willing to bear this, and much more, if necessary. It is astonishing to see how cheerfully people give up those nearest and dearest to them as sacrifices to the great cause. Nothing could surpass the devotion with which the ladies have nursed and watched the sick and wounded. They cook regularly for them themselves; all the delicacies are given up to them; the little white sugar left in the Confederacy is always laid aside for them. It is beautiful on the other hand to observe the fortitude and patience which the wounded soldiers show in the hospitals. While at Charlottesville I several times went through one of the hospitals, and talked to some of the wounded, and read the Testament to them. One poor Georgian, dangerously wounded, interested me deeply. You know I have been through all that campaign with Jackson in the valley, and would not have missed it for my commission. If any American general is like Napoleon, he is. Our gallant First has been in the advance, and then covered the retreat all the way. It was badly cut up, but covered itself with glory. Phil Coakley slightly wounded — Willie Colston dangerously. These are the only two you know, except poor Nick Snowden who was killed.

. . . .

When the general was somewhat recovered, he ordered me to Richmond to open headquarters for the organization of the Maryland Line. This was early in August, 1862, but I cannot remember that much was accomplished there in that enterprise.

During the summer the First Maryland Regiment was disbanded, its term of enlistment having expired. This was done at Charlottesville. Very soon — almost immediately afterward — the Maryland Battalion of infantry was organized. It was afterward known as the Second Maryland Regiment.

Early in September, 1862, General Steuart, though still unfit for active duty in the field, was ordered to Winchester, and given command of the Maryland Line, then being organized there. It consisted of infantry, artillery, and cavalry. We, who were members of his staff, including Capt. Geo. Williamson, Lieut. McHenry Howard, Major Kyle, and myself, were much occupied in the duties connected with this organization and its equipment with arms, uniforms, and supplies. Our general had command also of the post and of the region of country in that part of the valley. The roads to Romney, to Martinsburg, and to Berryville were carefully picketed. Prisoners were sometimes brought in from the front, once or twice in sufficient numbers to require a detail of a considerable number of men to escort them up the valley to Staunton.

We had a busy but an uneventful autumn and winter. Owing to these post duties with my still disabled chief, I took no part in the stirring campaign which embraced the two great battles of Second Manassas and Sharpsburg, or in the winter campaign marked by the battle of Fredericksburg. And it was not until the following spring that General Steuart was able to resume active duty in the field.

Of this whole period I have no diary to refer to, and therefore I pass it over, unwilling to rely on my memory for the narrative of events. This is of little moment, however, for I am not attempting in these pages to tell the history of the war, or to give a full record of my experience in it, but only to present such sketches of the life I led as may assist in a better understanding of the everyday experiences of the Confederate soldier in that great struggle.

During a considerable part of this post duty at Winchester, I performed the duties of adjutant-general, Captain Williamson having been invalided to Staunton, where Major W. Duncan McKim was enjoying himself while he slowly recovered from his wound. The Second Maryland Infantry was with us there. Lieut.-Gen. Jackson was often in Winchester the early part of the winter. During this period I continued to write to my brother Telfair, urging that it was his duty to stay at home and care for his father and mother, who were growing old — and not come South to enter the army. It was hard for the gallant boy to take my advice, but he did, though I know it took more courage than to shoulder a musket and follow Jackson.

I insert here a letter referring to the life at Winchester at this time:

HEADQUARTERS, WINCHESTER,
November 20, 1862.

TO MY MOTHER:

Again I write a letter which I expect to leave behind me in Winchester when we evacuate the town. This time I think we shall certainly leave here, as some of the troops already have marching orders. Flying reports, which I don't believe, come to us of General Hill being defeated and General Longstreet attacked. *Jackson*, with a large army, is here, though, and we may be overwhelmed, but *never* defeated. General Steuart has been commandant of this post for more than two months, as you know, perhaps. He is charged with the rear-guard in the movement with the Maryland Line. This is the second time Marylanders have been the last to leave Winchester. I am sorry to leave it. I like some of the people very much, particularly the Conrads, whom I know very well. They would correspond exactly with sister Mary's idea of refinement and culture. They have been very kind to me. I hope you may meet them. I will give this to them and possibly some lines, which mamma will recollect, "Wife, Children, Friends." Grandpa used to sing them. I have added three verses to the song and I want you to see them.

George Williamson is in Staunton on sick furlough: I am acting adjutant-general. I have a great deal of work to do, and sometimes it gives me quite a bad headache. Of course George is staying at Mr. Phillips' and enjoying himself hugely. Duncan has left Staunton and is staying at Edge Hill. He has entirely recovered, I believe. All other friends are well, I believe. Yesterday I saw Mr. Hill of La., who stayed with Mr. Sam Smith on Park Street, and knew you all. I was in the office attending to business when he came in and enquired for Lieut. Randolph McKim. I have not yet received the letter sent by him. Have heard frequently from you lately, my last was Oct. 30th.

.   .   .   .

Give my warmest love to all my friends in dear old Baltimore. I love them and my native town more the longer I am separated from them. I cherish no hopes that do not include Baltimore and Maryland in the bounds of our Confederacy. I love every stone and every tree in both of them, however much I may love the South and my Southern friends. They are all kind and good to me, but cannot take the place of those I have bid such a long farewell to.

.   .   .   .

After serving as commander of the Post at Winchester for about three months, General Steuart found that his wound was growing worse and that he was unfit for the duties of the office. He therefore requested a furlough of three months, and took his departure for Savannah, Ga. This threw me out of active service, and some time in December, 1862, I went to Staunton and arranged to remain there until such time as General Steuart should be able to take the field.

Here I spent the Christmas of 1862, referred to in the following letter. The picture it gives represents a rare oasis in our Confederate experience.

STAUNTON, December 27, 1862.

.   .   .   .

We are just through the *"festivities"* of Christmas and Duncan and I have been wondering how you all enjoyed yourselves on that day. I said "the festivities" of Christmas; they consisted only of a very nicely prepared and beautifully set out family dinner. We had *everything* that you could think of, except ice-cream and iced fruit, etc. Our plum-pudding too did not have any raisins in it, but cherries made a very good substitute. Shall I give you our bill of fare? — Oyster Soup — Roast Turkey, Ham, Round of Beef, Fresh Beef, Fried Oysters, Lobster Salad — Hominy, Potatoes, Beans, Salsafy, Rice, Dried Fruit — Plum-pudding, Charlotte Russe, Jelly, Pound Cake, and Jelly Cake, Puffs, etc., and Java Coffee! That will *do* for the Southern Confederacy, where everybody is starving! You must not suppose people generally, however, are so fortunate. Mrs. Phillips is a capital housekeeper, and had large supplies of everything on hand when the war broke out. I only make this enumeration to show you how well Duncan and I fared on Christmas Day. The day was a very happy one to me. We had breakfast about nine, and then family prayers. We attended at the Episcopal Church and heard a beautiful discourse from Dr. Sparrow. I am much delighted with *"the dear old Doctor"* as he is called. So much learning and piety are seldom found combined with so much simplicity of character and such childlike meekness and love. His prayers and his exhortations are peculiarly delightful.

I utilized the time in Staunton (besides teaching a small class in Latin, French, and English) in general reading and in particular in the investigation of the question of primitive Church government. It was during this winter of 1862–63 that I finally decided to enter the Episcopal Church.

My mother was an Episcopalian, having been confirmed by Bishop Moore, and all but two of her eleven brothers and sisters were of the same faith. The Harrison family, which had been identified with Virginian history since 1634, had always been of the Church of England. The same was true of the Randolphs and the Carters and the Carys — from all of which families my mother was descended. In Baltimore my mother and father had attended Christ Church when it stood east of the Falls, and also the second Christ Church on Gay Street, of which the two brothers Johns had successively been rectors. My first recollection of any church service was of this latter church and of Dr. Henry Johns vested in his black gown. Later my father decided to attend Dr. Plummer's Presbyterian Church, in which faith he had been brought up, and of that church I became a member when I was fifteen years of age. But at the University of Virginia I had become much interested in the Episcopal service, so that now, when I was considering my preparation for the ministry, I decided to investigate the question of Church government for myself. The result of this decided me to become a candidate for orders in the Episcopal Church, which I did in the spring of 1863.

My Uncle Peyton Harrison was a stanch Presbyterian, and when we met after the war, he said, "Well, Randolph, you have left the Church of your Fathers." "Yes," I replied, "I have returned to the Church of my Forefathers."

When General Steuart's three months furlough expired, he found himself still unfit for duty in the field, and as a consequence I became restless and dissatisfied at my long absence from the army. I had now been out of active service for four months.

Accordingly I made application through my cousin, Major W. Duncan McKim, for an appointment on General Trimble's staff. This plan failed, as that general's staff was already excessively large. My cousin, however, wrote me that Gen. Rooney Lee (W. H. F. Lee) had expressed a desire to have me on his staff. However, before this could be consummated, General Steuart wrote that he would shortly require my services. Of this I was glad, as I fully shared the sentiment expressed by my friend McHenry Howard, that a commission as captain of ordinance had no attraction for him if it could separate him from the Maryland Line. We were proud of our State. We were fighting to set her free to choose her lot with North or with South, and we were confident what her choice would be. The army, never turned northward, but we began to hope that we should soon help to liberate our native State. That General Steuart would be in command of the Maryland Line, or some part of it, I did not doubt. And so the event proved, for at Winchester in June, 1863, the Second Maryland Infantry was attached to his brigade.

CHAPTER XI

O N Sunday, May 24th, 1863, I received orders to report to my chief, General Steuart, at Fredericksburg. The great battle of Chancellorsville, which displayed so brilliantly the military genius of both General Lee and General Jackson, had been fought on May 2d and 3d, resulting in a great victory for the Confederate Army. It has been described by an able military critic (Colonel Henderson) "as the tactical masterpiece of the nineteenth century." General Hooker's strategy appears to me worthy of all praise. It only failed because it was confronted by the superior strategy of Lee and by the indomitable valor of the army which he commanded. Sedgwick, with 22,000 men, was thrown across the Rappahannock River below Fredericksburg on April 29th. But this was not the real line of attack, but was meant to deceive Lee, while Hooker with the main body of his army was marching to the upper fords in order to turn Lee's right flank. This operation was carried out so successfully that, on the 30th of April, General Hooker issued a general order to his army, felicitating them and himself on what had been accomplished, in the following terms: "The operations of the last three days have determined that our enemy must either ingloriously fly, or come out from behind his defences and give us battle on our own ground, where certain destruction awaits him."

He would have done well to remember the scriptural admonition, "Let not him that putteth on his armor boast as he that taketh it off." Lee was not deceived by the movement of Sedgwick on his right flank. He divined that the real attack would be on his left, and accordingly leaving Early with 9,000 men to hold Sedgwick in check, moved with Jackson to meet Hooker. The Federal general, with six army corps, was intrenched at Chancellorsville in an apparently impregnable position. To meet this host of more than 90,000 men, Lee had but 48,000 of all arms, and it is not surprising that Hooker should have so confidently expected that with such a force in such a strong position on his left flank and Sedgwick with 22,000 men (perhaps as many as 30,000) moving on his right rear, the Confederate general would be compelled to retreat. His plan was admirably conceived, and thus far admirably, as well as swiftly, executed. But there was an unknown quantity in the problem which upset all Hooker's calculations. That was the audacious strategy of Lee with the incomparable Jackson at hand to put it into execution. Hooker cannot be blamed for not anticipating the audacity of the plan which his great antagonist now proceeded to develop. Lee had already divided his army, by leaving Early at Deep Run, below Fredericksburg, twelve miles away. He now decided to still further divide it by sending Jackson with his whole corps to turn Hooker's right flank and crush it by a sudden and unexpected blow, while he, with only two divisions, those of Anderson and McLaw, numbering less than 14,000 men, stood facing the great army of his antagonist, 70,000 strong at this point. In deciding upon such a plan, Lee took a tremendous risk, but a general who, with 57,000 men of all arms, is opposed to an army of more than twice his own numbers (130,000 was the strength of the Federal Army) can only hope for success by taking great risks.[1] Two circumstances justified this audacious movement, — first, that the density of the forest growth made it possible to screen the march of General Jackson around Hooker's right rear, and second, that Lee possessed in Stonewall Jackson a lieutenant who was so brilliantly qualified to execute it with celerity, with resoluteness, and with skill.

With such secrecy and swiftness did Jackson march his corps around Hooker's right flank that he was in position to deliver his assault before the enemy had any information of his approach. It is almost pathetic to read Hooker's despatch to Sedgwick, dictated at 4.10 P.M., May 2d, bidding him "capture Fredericksburg and vigorously pursue the enemy," and adding, "We know that the enemy is fleeing to save his trains" — this while Jackson was actually preparing to launch the thunderbolt which was to overwhelm his right wing, inflicting a staggering blow upon "the finest army on the planet," and rendering abortive all the well-laid plans of its commander.

Mr. Lincoln, in one of the most remarkable letters

[1] The Confederate Army was thus separated into three parts: Early ten or twelve miles away, southward, with 12,000 men facing Sedgwick with 23,000; Lee, with about 13,000, facing Hooker's entrenched force of 70,000; and Jackson with 30,000, marching twelve miles away to turn Hooker's right flank. Then there was Reynolds, with 16,000 Federal troops as a reserve corps. To all this host must be added the numerous Federal cavalry.

ever addressed to the commander of a great army, had given General Hooker, in closing, this advice, "And now, beware of rashness! Beware of rashness! but, with energy and sleepless vigilance, go forward and give us victories." I do not think he can be accused of rashness of action in this campaign, but he was certainly rash in speech when he boasted to his soldiers and to his officers of the certain defeat of the Confederate Army, — first, before he had struck a blow, and secondly, in the midst of the battle, at the very hour when Jackson's crushing blow was about to descend upon him. In his order book he displayed an audacity which is astounding—it surpassed the audacity of Lee on the field of battle — for, after his magnificent army had been driven defeated and humiliated across the Rappahannock, back into the camps from which it had marched with such triumphant expectations a week before, General Hooker issued an order congratulating his army "on its achievements in the last seven days," and adding, "The events of the last week may swell with pride the heart of every officer and soldier in this army."

It would be a work of supererogation for me to give any extended account of this famous battle, so thoroughly described by various military critics, but I may make one or two further remarks to complete the general view I have given of the plan of Lee and the manner of its execution. After Jackson had fallen by the fire of some of his own men at dusk on the 2d of May, in the full tide of victory, Gen. J. E. B. Stuart, a soldier of whom Colonel Henderson, the English critic, says that he was "no unworthy successor of Stonewall Jackson," had been placed in command of his corps, but he did not arrive until midnight, so that nothing could be done until the next morning. Then, in coöperation with Lee, he delivered blow after blow, with great effect, against the army of Hooker, and Chancellorsville fell into the hands of the Confederates. At this moment, ten A.M., when preparing an assault on Hooker's third line of intrenchments, which must have been fatal to the Federal Army, the arm of Lee is arrested by the news that Sedgwick has captured Marye's Heights at Fredericksburg, has swept Early out of his path, and is marching with his 25,000 or 30,000 men on Lee's rear.

This was disquieting news indeed. Lee had intended that Early should keep between him and Sedgwick. Instead, Early had retreated on the Plank road in the direction of Richmond. Thus he had become separated from Lee, and could render him no assistance. It was a critical moment. The battle was not yet won. On the contrary, it might easily be turned into defeat for Lee, with Hooker in his front and Sedgwick in his rear.

But the genius of Lee was equal to the emergency. He resolved on a movement "even more daring," says the Comte de Paris, "than that which, the day previous, had brought Jackson upon the flank of the enemy." Suspending his attack on Hooker, he turned with McLaws' and Anderson's divisions, advanced swiftly against Sedgwick, attacked him, and drove him back over the river. This operation, necessary for Lee's salvation, was the means of delivering Hooker from his perilous situation; for when the Confederate chieftain returned to strike Hooker the *coup de grace* which Sedgwick's advance on his rear had arrested, the

Federal general had withdrawn his army and the next day he made good his retreat by the very fords which Jackson would have seized had he not been cut down by that deplorable accident.

I will only add that the battle of Chancellorsville illustrates the consummate genius and audacity of the two great Southern commanders not more conspicuously than it displays the sublime devotion and intrepidity of the rank and file of the Confederate Army.

It had for me a painful personal interest (although I took no part in it myself) because my gallant cousin, Major Wm. Duncan McKim, was killed in the conflict of May 3d, during one of the assaults on the intrenchments of Hooker. I was told afterward that he was the only officer in the division who remained mounted in the midst of that frightful hail of bullets, there in the thick woods. An officer of the Stonewall Brigade went to him and besought him to dismount — indeed remonstrated with him seriously upon the foolhardiness and uselessness of his keeping the saddle under the circumstances; and when he could not prevail upon him to take his advice, returned to his company saying, "Well, it is only a question of minutes when he will fall." And so it was — very soon he was seen to reel in the saddle and fall to the ground. His death must have been almost instantaneous. But in fact it was not, I believe, foolhardiness that made him thus sacrifice his life. It appears that the day before he had received a severe contusion on the leg from a grapeshot, and the brigade surgeon told him he was unfit to go into the battle on the 3d. But Duncan could not be restrained. He got into the saddle somehow, and marched with his command. Then, when Capt. Wm. Randolph begged him to dismount, he refused because he knew he could not walk. He had been ever a gallant soldier, cool and fearless on the field of battle. At Sharpsburg in September, 1862, he had been shot through both thighs and was taken to the residence of Rev. R. H. Phillips, in Staunton, where he was tenderly nursed for months by Mrs. Phillips and her daughter Agnes. It was, I think, about the 1st of February, 1863, that Duncan returned to the field, though even then his wound had not entirely healed. I here pay my tribute of love and admiration to this noble man and brave soldier. Fascinating in manners, handsome in person, charming in conversation, high-spirited, a man of high ideals and warm affections, brave to a fault, and always good company,—there were few young men who laid upon the altar of the Confederate cause a more costly sacrifice than did he.

I went to the battle-field about ten days, perhaps two weeks, after he fell, found the spot where he was buried, and had him disinterred. He had been wrapped in his blanket and buried without a coffin, and mother Earth had so closely held him in her embrace that when we lifted him up and unwound the blanket, he lay before us as perfectly preserved as if he had fallen only a few hours before. We buried him in the cemetery at Staunton, whence, upon the conclusion of the war, he was removed to Greenmount Cemetery, Baltimore. There he rests in peace — "Siste viator, heroa calcas." I was now the last survivor of the three of my name who had entered the Confederate service at the outbreak of the war.

CHAPTER XII

THE OPENING OF THE GETTYSBURG CAMPAIGN

THREE weeks after the battle of Chancellorsville I received, as I have said, orders to report for duty at Fredericksburg, and on Wednesday, the 27th of May, I set out from Staunton for the army.[1] On Thursday, after a ride of twenty-seven miles, I reached General Lee's headquarters at 1.45 P.M. The general received me graciously and asked me to dine with him, which I was, of course, glad to do. The highest officer in the army would have esteemed it a great honor — what,

[1] RICHMOND, May 23, 1863.

MY DEAR MR. McKIM:

I have just time to say that I received an order this morning to report to General Lee at Fredericksburg for assignment to duty, and will leave without delay. From what Gen. A. P. Hill said this morning, I expect to be assigned to command of a brigade in Jackson's old division. Come to Fredericksburg immediately by the shortest route, if they will not take your horse on the cars. It will be better anyhow to ride from Gordonsville to the army. I hope the battalion and staff officers will be ordered to join me. I fear the Maryland Line is broken up, never to be together again, the same as it was anyhow. It will be a great disappointment if I cannot have the staff officers with me, and the battalion after all the trouble I have had for more than a year past. I had hoped to have had command in the valley. When I see you I will have much to say. Mr. —— goes up in the morning and will take this. You will find me somewhere with the army. With the battalion I would have a magnificent brigade.

Believe me,
Most sincerely yours,
GEORGE H. STEUART.

then, were the feelings of a young "first lieutenant
and A. D. C." in sitting down at the board of the great
soldier who was the idol of the armies and the people
of the South? The simple courtesy and genial hospitality of General Lee would have put me at ease, if
I had been a stranger; but he had several times been
a guest at my father's house in Baltimore, when he was
in charge of the construction of Fort Sollers in the
Patapsco River, so that I felt at home in his presence.
Our families were on very friendly and familiar terms.
Indeed the general was a cousin of my mother, both
being descended from the famous "King" Carter.

As I talked with him after dinner, he cast his eyes
across the Rappahannock to the camps of General
Hooker's army and said to me, "I wish I could get at
those people over there." That was the expression by
which he uniformly designated the Federal Army. He
was very friendly, talked of the days when he used to visit
Belvidere, and inquired after my father and mother
and my sisters. I spent that night, or the next, at
the headquarters of Gen. Edward Johnson, who was
to be such a familiar figure to me in battle in the
approaching campaign. There I saw Carvel Hall, who
gave me a full account of Duncan McKim's death,
describing his magnificent gallantry.

On Saturday, the 20th, General Ewell arrived in
camp with his wife — a new acquisition — and with
one leg less than when I saw him last. From a military point of view the addition of the wife did not
compensate for the loss of the leg. We were of the
opinion that Ewell was not the same soldier he had
been when he was a whole man — and a single one.

I dined with General Colston, and later the same

GEN. ROBERT EDWARD LEE, 1862

day General Steuart assumed command of the Third Brigade, and I the duties of assistant adjutant-general, in the absence of Captain Garrison. The brigade consisted of the following regiments:

10th Virginia, Colonel Warren.
23d Virginia, Lieutenant-Colonel Walton.
37th Virginia, Major Wood.
1st North Carolina, Colonel McDowell.
3d North Carolina, Major Parsley.

Major Stanard was our chief commissary, Capt. N. S. Byrd was acting quartermaster. The strength of the brigade was as follows:

10th Virginia.	On the roll	627,	present for duty			342
37th Virginia	"	" 740	"	"	"	347
23d Virginia	"	"	"	"	"	269
1st North Carolina	"	" 927	"	"	"	510
3d North Carolina	"	" 921	"	"	"	473
Total present for duty						1941

The Maryland regiment joined us later.

I note that the daily ration was $\frac{1}{2}$ lb. bacon and $1\frac{1}{8}$ lbs. flour per man, and for every 100 men 6 lbs. of sugar, 15 lbs. of peas, 2 lbs. soap, and 3 lbs. salt.

The men were armed with long-range guns, calibre 58. There were but 1,069 bayonets in the brigade and 1,480 muskets; 51,000 rounds of ammunition in the hands of the men, and 50,000 in the ordnance train.

Four of our five regiments had chaplains:

1st North Carolina, Rev. W. R. Gaultney (Baptist).
3d North Carolina, Rev. Geo. Patterson (Episcopalian).

23d Virginia, Rev. Mr. Morton (Presbyterian).
10th Virginia, Brother Balthus, Exhorter.

My duties as adjutant-general were soon over. I barely had a chance to make out and send in the monthly report of the brigade when Captain Garrison arrived and assumed his duties, I taking again my proper office as *aide-de-camp*.

That was my first Sunday with the brigade, and I attended service in the First North Carolina camp and, after a sermon by the chaplain, I rose and addressed the men. There was a large attendance. The influence of the revival the preceding winter was still felt.

In this connection I may mention that I had resolved when about sixteen years of age to devote myself to the Christian ministry. At the time I entered the University, at seventeen years of age, and during my course there, it was my intention to go to China as a missionary. It was not till later that I concluded I might be more needed at home than abroad. The inward call to preach Christ to my fellow men pressed strongly upon me in my camp life, and I find many entries in my little diaries showing my sense of responsibility in relation to it. Thus on June 3d:

"Read, talked, and prayed with about fifteen men at a log house near camp. Gave them tracts. They asked my name and on my return, as I was riding by, they stopped me and asked what chapter it was I had read to them. It was the 27th Psalm, 'The Lord is my light and my salvation; whom shall I fear? The Lord is the strength of my life; of whom shall I be afraid?' One of the poor fellows was under sentence of death."

I found General Steuart very willing to have me

conduct prayers in his tent in the evening; often the adjutant and he and I were the only persons present. The general read his Bible and Prayer-Book regularly. Throughout this thrilling campaign, I found many opportunities of trying to help my comrades and fellow officers in the spiritual life. Looking back now over forty-five years of ministerial life, I am prepared to say that in my whole experience I have never found men so open to the frank discussion of the subject of personal religion as the officers and men of Lee's army. The example of our great commander and of Stonewall Jackson and of "Jeb" Stuart—indeed of most of our officers of high rank—had much to do with this, in my estimation.

So wide was the door of opportunity, and so great the need of consecrated men to preach Christ in the army, that I often wished I was already ordained and commissioned as a chaplain. There were occasions when I was mistaken for a clergyman.

It was on the evening of June 3d that we received orders to break camp at Hamilton's Crossing, cook three days rations, and take up the line of march northward. That day may be said to mark the opening of the Gettysburg campaign, although it does not appear that General Lee had yet formed his plans with definiteness — certainly he did not have Gettysburg in his eye at that time.

The army had been organized into three corps, commanded respectively by General Longstreet, General Ewell, and General A. P. Hill. Longstreet had now his whole corps present, McLaws' division, which participated so effectively in the battle of Chancellorsville, and the divisions of Hood and Pickett, which, unfortunately for Lee, had been at Suffolk and did not arrive in time, as Major-General French, in his Memoir, thinks they ought to have done. These two divisions only were transported by rail direct from Richmond to the vicinity of Culpeper. McLaws' division marched June 3d. Ewell's corps followed on June 5th. A. P. Hill's was left at Fredericksburg, to make Hooker believe that Lee's whole army was still in front of him on the Rappahannock. The ruse succeeded.

Our division took up the line of march June 5th at two A.M. — this unusually early start being intended, I suppose, to prevent our movement being discovered by the gentleman who daily ascended in the balloon to spy upon us and report to General Hooker. We marched in the following order:

The 2d Brigade, General Jones;
The 4th Brigade, General Nicholls;
The 3d Brigade, General Steuart;
The 1st Brigade (Stonewall);

all under command of Gen. Edward Johnson, a vigorous man and a stalwart fighter. Marching by way of Massaponax Church and Spottsylvania Court House, we halted several hours at the latter place to let Early's division, also of Ewell's corps, pass us. In spite of our very early start we made only fifteen miles and went into camp about 2.30 P.M.

Next day reveille sounded at three A.M. and by four A.M. we were in line, but received countermarching orders and returned to camp.

About this time General Pleasanton, in command of Hooker's whole cavalry force, was making preparations for crossing the Rappahannock and attacking

"Jeb" Stuart, who, with the bulk of the Confederate cavalry, was camped near Brandy Station on the Rapidan. It is just possible some rumor of this movement may have reached our commander and this may account for our countermarching. However, by three P.M. we were again in motion, and we "marched till night . . . and were overtaken by a violent rainstorm."

June 7th we marched at 4.30 A.M. and struck the Plank road fourteen miles from Orange Court House. Verdiersville lay in our route and here "we filed right and took the road to Raccoon Ford, nine miles distant. The weather was fine, the roads excellent, the men in good spirits, but *they have had no rations.*" One of them remarked good-humoredly, "They put a fellow in the guard-house now for taking a drink of water; and as to *eating* — that's out of the question." The same day we crossed the Rapidan, not at Raccoon, but at Somerville Ford, in the usual Confederate way. No pontoons for us!

June 8th. Reveille at four, marched at six, passed through Culpeper Court House at 10.30 A.M., and camped at three P.M.

It was at this time that I began to become acquainted with Rev. Geo. Patterson, chaplain of the Third North Carolina Regiment, who had two conversations with Duncan McKim, and administered to him the holy communion the Sunday before he fell. Though I was on the staff, he asked me if I was a clergyman — some of the officers had told him so. That evening at dusk, in the tent of Major Parsley of his regiment, we solaced ourselves by singing songs. Patterson was present. I found the men all much attached to him — *malgré* his eccentricities and his very rigid churchmanship. He was a true and a brave man and did his duty faithfully as he understood it. Before the war he had been a chaplain on a plantation of North Carolina, where there were 500 negroes, of whom 180 were communicants of the Episcopal Church. The master paid him a salary of $3,000 a year for his services as chaplain. "Their chapel was too small to hold them at daily morning and evening prayer." Though they could not read, they joined earnestly in the responses, having committed them to memory. He had also taught them one or two of the Psalms, so that they repeated them responsively in the service. By the master's orders no work was done on fast days or feast days, nor of course on Sundays. Such was Patterson's influence over them that the previous winter he had "brought away 175 of them out of the Federal lines, under shell fire and without any guard, and entirely of their own accord." He told them Lincoln had made them all free, but had no right to do it, and they would be sinful to leave their masters, but could do as they chose. And I was told that not one of the 500 ran away.

Tuesday, June 9th, was an eventful day. As we marched toward Sperryville, cannonading was heard in the direction of Culpeper Court House. We halted instantly and soon orders came to march back. This was about three in the afternoon. General Pleasanton after a night march had crossed the Rappahannock at two points with the intention of destroying General Stuart's cavalry, which was massed in Culpeper County. In a very severe fight, characterized by great gallantry on both sides, our superb J. E. B. Stuart had routed both of Pleasanton's brigades and captured a good deal of his artillery and hundreds of his troopers. Again, as at Chancellorsville, General Stuart showed a very high degree of skill in handling his brigades. Owing to the thick fog on the river, the Federal cavalry were able to cross without being discovered, and the Confederates were taken by surprise; but by the valor of the officers and men, both of the cavalry and artillery, and by the brilliant leadership of their chief, the tide of battle was turned, and both Gregg and Buford driven back over the river, Stuart having beaten them in detail.

It was a hard-fought battle — this of Brandy Station. "General Gregg's battery was captured and recaptured several times." Doubtless it was to guard against the possible emergency of Stuart's defeat that our brigade was ordered back toward Culpeper.

Notwithstanding these stirring events, we had eyes for the beautiful scenery through which we were passing, as the following extract shows:

CAMP NEAR CULPEPER,
June 9, 1863.

TO MY MOTHER:

We left Fredericksburg, as you know, on Friday and have been on the march ever since until to-day. We came through Spottsylvania C. H. and struck the plank road to Orange a few miles from Verdiersville. There we turned off to the right and took the road to Somerville Ford, which is a few miles above Raccoon Ford on the Rapidan. This brought us through a beautiful country and we began to catch glimpses of the distant Blue Ridge. The view from the crest of the hills which extend along the south bank of the Rapidan was enchanting. The ground sinks almost precipitately within a hundred yards of the river. The river itself was swollen from the recent rain, and the water as red as Albemarle soil. The banks on either side were lined with willows which dipped their branches in the stream and made a beautiful feature in the landscape. Just above the ford there was a waterfall and an old mill in the last stages of decay. The north bank rises more gradually. Just upon the summit of a little knoll opposite the ford two tall chimneys mark the spot where once stood a large old-fashioned country house. From this point the ground ascends very gently and broad fertile fields lie on either side of the road, with here and there a pretty white cottage. Beyond rises the Piedmont Range and the dim blue mountains form the background. You can better imagine than I describe, how beautiful the aspect which was spread out beneath us for miles as we reached the crest of the range of hills I have described. Now cast your eye down the road that leads to the ford and see that dense column of men stretching down to the river, across its swollen current up the farther bank, and extending for miles until lost where the road enters a thick grove of trees. Many of the men took off shoes and stockings, but some regiments marched straight through without breaking ranks. The water was nearly waist deep, but the men pushed on with shouts, in fine spirits. It was one of the most picturesque scenes I have ever witnessed, and the second of the kind in which I have borne a part since the war began. It was Sunday, but the air was fresh and cool, the roads in splendid order, and I enjoyed the march very much. . . . The orders about rails have been very strict and the general ordered me to go through every regiment in the brigade and see if there was a single rail taken, and if so, to make the men carry it back to the fence. It was a very disagreeable duty, and, I felt, put me in the light of a *spy* before the men. Still, I made no complaint, but rode up and down our five regiments, among the poor weary fellows, and executed his order faithfully. When I returned, and had unsaddled and unbridled, I reported to the general, and he ordered me to saddle up again and ride through the wagon yard and search for rails. This provoked me, and the discomforts of our mess arrangements added to my vexation, and induced me to write as I did. Let me tell you now what a good dinner we had yesterday. I exchanged a pound of sugar for more than half a pound of fresh butter and a quart and a half of buttermilk. Then we had some bread toasted and some black-eyed peas boiled and some ham fried, and though we ate with our pen-knives, we enjoyed it very much.

.   .   .   .

June 10th we resumed our march, but not till four P.M., and at dark were only fourteen miles beyond Culpeper Court House, and six miles this side of Sperryville.

June 11th we again had an early reveille and marched at 4.30 A.M., passing through Sperryville and Little Washington, and making camp at 1.30 P.M., having made sixteen miles.

Friday, June 12th, we had reveille at three, and at 4.30 A.M. took up our march via Flint Hill for Front Royal, where we arrived at two P.M.

"Dined luxuriously (!) with Samuels, inspector of our brigade. At four we crossed the Shenandoah on Confederate pontoons — that is, by wading straight through in column of fours. Forded both branches, the men cheering and in fine spirits. I never saw a ford so well made. The march has been remarkable, scarcely any stragglers. Made twenty-three miles to-day and two fords. Halted fourteen miles from Winchester at dark. Supped with Mrs. ——, a very pretty and very rebellious lady! Probability of a fight to-morrow. Held prayers!"

This march of Ewell's corps was remarkable in several respects. In the first place four brigades of infantry with baggage and ordnance trains had marched from Fredericksburg to Winchester in seven days, though one day had been lost by a countermarch. (The itinerary I have given shows a succession of very early starts from two A.M. to four A.M.) In the next place, the movement was so well planned and carried out that the Federal commander-in-chief had no idea that Ewell had left his camp at Hamilton's Crossing. Stuart's cavalry screened the inception of the movement and after we got a good start the Blue Ridge masked our march. That so large a force should have been withdrawn from General Hooker's front without his having an inkling of it, in spite of his balloon, and that this force should have marched from the Rappahannock River to the lower valley without being discovered by the Federal scouts, is truly astonishing. It is not creditable to General Hooker, or to his chief of cavalry, General Pleasanton, or to his chief of scouts, whoever he was.

And now Ewell was preparing to swoop down upon General Milroy, like an eagle on his unsuspecting prey. That officer was in command of an army of 9,000 men, and was occupying Winchester, which he had strongly fortified. He did not dream that any of Lee's infantry had crossed the Blue Ridge. He had been warned of a possible raid by Stuart's cavalry, but that he did not fear. Indeed for weeks the minds of Hooker and Pleasanton seem to have been wholly preoccupied by that cavalry raid of Stuart, which they were certain he was preparing. The way in which this idea held them amounted almost to an obsession.

As to the advance of Lee's army, which had been going on for a week, this is what Milroy says in his self-exculpation for being caught napping by Ewell:

"I deemed it impossible that Lee's army with its immense artillery and baggage trains could have escaped from the Army of the Potomac and crossed the Blue Ridge through Ashby's, Chester's, and Thornton's Gap, in concentric columns. The movement must have occupied four or five days; notice of its being in progress could have been conveyed to me by General Hooker's headquarters in five minutes, for telegraphic communication still existed between Baltimore and Winchester."

But no notice or warning of Ewell's approach came to him, and when on the 12th he sent out the 12th Pennsylvania Cavalry on a reconnoissance in the direction of Front Royal, and its commanding officer reported to Milroy that at Cedarville, about twelve miles from Winchester, he encountered a large force of the enemy composed of cavalry, infantry, and artillery, — the general discredited the report.

Out of this false security the Federal general at Winchester was rudely awakened by the guns of Ewell on June 13th about 11.30 A.M. Our brigade moved at 4.30 A.M., our men much fatigued. We were to support the Stonewall Brigade.

"Early begins the attack on the Strasburg road. Occasional artillery firing all day. Heavy rain in the afternoon [which probably delayed operations]. About nine P.M. I was ordered to post three companies on picket on our right flank. It was very dark and stormy, and having with difficulty got the men together, I led them through the thick undergrowth and at last struck the road. Became thoroughly drenched and much fatigued. With ditches,

fences woods to obstruct, I did not finish my task till eleven
o'clock, when I regained camp only by the sagacity of my
horse. Slept in the rain covered by a wet blanket.

"As usual, Sunday was the day of the real battle. Though
we expected to be in the assault on Milroy's strong works,
it fell to the lot of Early's Brigade on the opposite side of
the fort to do this. It was a picturesque battle. Early's
Artillery opened vigorously on the north of the forts. We
could see the flash of his guns, sixteen discharges per minute,
while the Stars and Stripes waved defiantly amid the bursting
shells in the rolling smoke, the sun sinking red and angry
behind the western clouds, the advance and retreat of the
skirmishers with the sharp crack of the rifle, while cavalry
and artillery gallop into position and infantry file in column.
This, with the frowning line of breastworks along the range
of hills on the left of the Martinsburg road, forms a scene
I have leisure to admire and note down, as I sit on my horse
on an eminence comparatively safe from danger."

The rebel yell of Early's men, as they charged position after position, could be plainly heard above the
din of battle. Our own brigade had taken a position
east of the forts and the Martinsburg road and north-
east of Winchester, where we could protect the right
flank of our division. We were expecting every moment
to be ordered forward, but the order did not come, and
at no time during the battle were we heavily engaged.
I heard some of our men chaffing and joking about
the expected charge. One said, "When we charge
the intrenchments, boys, recollect the crackers inside."
"Yes," replied his comrade, "but they'll serve out
rations of ammunition to us first." A third "jolly
Reb" took up the conversation with the remark, "Well,
if Mr. Early's gang and Mr. Rodes' gang would charge
those works without us I wouldn't mind." Then

another, "It's a lottery business, if we go in."   "Yes," was the rejoinder, "and some of us will draw a capital prize."

I give this as a sample of the way our men would crack jokes with one another on the very edge of battle. The fighting continued after the sun had disappeared. The flashes of the guns in the succeeding darkness produced a lurid, weird effect.   The operations of the day had given us possession of the outer defences of Milroy's position.   It remained to complete on the following day the work so well begun.

But would the Federal general, thus hemmed in by superior forces, wait to be attacked next morning? There was apprehension that he would make an effort during the night to withdraw his forces.

CHAPTER XIII

IN anticipation of such an attempt as referred to at the close of the preceding chapter, the brigade of General Steuart moved, as soon as night set in on Sunday, June 14th, down the Berryville pike to its junction with the road to Jordan's Springs, where it turned head of column left so as to strike the Winchester and Martinsburg pike at a point about four and a quarter miles from the former place, at Stephenson's Depot.

Here, at 3.30 A.M., a halt was made at a wooden bridge which carried the road across the railroad cut, about 400 yards from the Martinsburg pike, which ran at right angles to the road. Gen. Edward Johnson, our division commander, rode across the bridge with some staff officers to reconnoitre. I happened to be in front and was thus the first to discern in the dim dusk of early morning the approach of a column of the enemy's cavalry. The leading files fired and wheeled, and I sent a pistol shot after them. The expectation of our officers was justified — Milroy had evacuated the forts and was retreating to Harper's Ferry. There ensued a severe and hotly contested engagement. General Milroy had his whole force behind him, while only part of one of Johnson's brigades was up, viz., our own, with a strength of less than 2,000 men, a battery of artillery and no cavalry. At first, indeed, we had less than half that number in position to contest the advance of the enemy.

Our infantry was at once formed in the railroad cut to the right and left of the bridge just mentioned. The enemy came bravely on in our front, cheering and firing. Their fire passed for the most part over the heads of our infantry posted in the railroad cut, and partially protected by the embankment, but the general and staff officers on horseback on the nearer side of the railroad cut were much exposed. The Tenth Virginia and the First and Third North Carolina regiments alone stood the brunt of the first attacks, until our battery of artillery arrived (Dement's), when two guns were unlimbered on a slope in rear of our line and to the left of the road, while the intrepid officer in command pushed one gun forward and planted it on the bridge flush with our firing line, and another to the left and rear. Both these pieces were in easy musket shot of the enemy. Our artillery fire demoralized the enemy a great deal, as they could not reply, having abandoned all their artillery in the Winchester forts in their retreat. After the failure of their first and second frontal attacks on the bridge, they sought to turn our left flank by a force of cavalry and infantry which General Johnson, "old Alleghany" as he was called, met by forming a line perpendicular to our front line with part of the Louisiana Brigade which had just come up. I can see him now, as I write, riding up and down, vehemently giving orders, and waving the big cane which he carried instead of a sword, because of the lameness which resulted from his wound at the battle of Alleghany. His bravery and regardlessness of danger was an inspiration to the men, who responded with alacrity to his example. The staff officers had a busy time in carrying out the orders of our chiefs at this stage of the battle. It was now that I had a narrow escape. In riding from our centre to the left flank I rode a little too high on the slope occupied by our artillery before mentioned, when, at one of the discharges, a solid shot from one of our guns passed so close to my head that the wind of it almost knocked me from my horse.

While this effort to turn our left flank was still in progress, Milroy made a vigorous attack upon our right, which rested in a wood, and was "refused" at a sharp angle toward our rear. Thus we were assailed in front and on both flanks, and for some time our right, was in great danger, until the old Stonewall Brigade, arriving in the nick of time, saved the position there.

The centre now engrossed our attention, for the enemy were making desperate efforts to break through at the bridge. The situation was serious, for the ammunition of the Third Brigade was all but exhausted — one round only left. That little wooden bridge witnessed one of the most superb displays of dauntless intrepidity that was seen during the whole war. The men serving the piece planted there were fearfully exposed. It was the key of our position, and the fire of the enemy was especially directed to disabling that gun, which had so long held them at bay. Lieut. C. S. Contee was in command. His men fell around him till all were killed or wounded but himself and one other, but they continued undauntedly serving their piece in its perilous position, unsupported except by a line of bayonets below in the railway cut. At every discharge the recoil carried the gun almost over the side of the bridge, but before it could roll over, these brave men were at the wheel rolling it back into its place. Two sets of cannoneers, thirteen out of sixteen, were killed and disabled.

But now Lieutenant Contee's leg was broken, and there was but one man left (he is living to-day), and he could not serve the gun alone. The enemy were pressing forward in another determined charge when Lieutenant Morgan and I came to the help of the one hero remaining on the bridge unhurt.[1] I had seen the desperate situation of the gun and had ridden up as rapidly as my tired horse could carry me to see if I could render any help. Springing from my horse and throwing the reins over the arm of a poor fellow lying wounded in the fence corner, I ran to the caisson, and taking four canister shot in my arms, ran up the bank to the bridge where Morgan met me. Together, with the assistance of the one cannoneer, we served the Federals with grape and canister just in time to smash up their charge and save the bridge. They were within less than forty yards of it. I then mounted my horse (who was wild with excitement) and set out

[1] I append an extract from the Report of Major-Gen. Edward Johnson, Rebellion Records, vol. xxvii., p. 502. "Before closing this report, I beg leave to state that I have never seen superior artillery practice to that of Andrew's battalion in this engagement and especially the section under Lieutenant (C.S.) Contee (Dement's battery), one gun of which was placed on the bridge above referred to, and the other a little to the left and rear. Both pieces were very much exposed during the whole action. Four successive attempts were made to carry the bridge. Two sets of cannoneers (13 out of 16) were killed and disabled. Lieutenant-Colonel Andrews and Lieutenant Contee, whose gallantry calls for special mention, fell wounded at this point. Lieutenant John A. Morgan, First North Carolina Regiment, and Lieutenant Randolph H. McKim took the place of the disabled cannoneers, rendering valuable assistance, deserving special mention."

in a full run for reinforcements. Meeting two regiments of Nichol's Brigade, commanded by Colonel Williams, I cried to them to hurry forward and save their comrades and the fortunes of the day at the bridge. The Louisianians readily responded, but their commanding officer, "thinking it best not to expose himself," declined to accept orders from me, which of course he had a perfect right to do. Whether he ought to have refused my appeal is another question. General Steuart was on the right and Major-General Johnson on the left. In the centre there was no general officer, so there was no one who could command the regiments to move forward. At length they responded to my appeal, however, and moved forward to support the Third Brigade, but by this time the enemy had had enough of Morgan's canister and gave over the attempt to capture the bridge.

Captain Garrison now went to the rear after the ammunition wagons, and was nearly captured by a body of the enemy which had gotten in our rear between us and our wagon train. Fortunately they were only intent on making their escape.

By this time our whole division was up, and the advantage in numbers, which for several hours had been with the Federals, was now with us. The Stonewall Brigade on our right, led by General Walker, now charged with a yell and swept the enemy before them. Beaten back at every point and unable to break our lines, the enemy in our front surrendered. The number of prisoners captured in this battle was upward of 3,000. Total here and at Winchester more than 4,000. Also a train of about 200 wagons, 22 pieces of artillery (taken at Winchester): viz., 15 three-inch rifles, 5 twenty-pound Parrott guns, and 2 eighteen-pounder howitzers.   The enemy's loss at Stephenson's Depot, in killed and wounded, was heavy, ours much less.   General Milroy with his cavalry succeeded in making his escape.   Colonel Mosby, in his recent book, says Ewell had plenty of cavalry.   If so, I never saw them, and it is a pity that General Ewell did not discover them and send them to intercept Milroy on this occasion.

Thus the battle of Stephenson's Depot terminated successfully for Ewell — disastrously to Milroy.   The operations of the 13th, 14th, and 15th were a complete surprise to the authorities in Washington.   As late as the 14th a telegram from General Halleck informed General Schenck that it was "reported that Longstreet's and Ewell's Corps had passed through Culpeper Court House in the direction of the Valley."   In fact Longstreet was still encamped in Culpeper County on the 14th of June, and it was not till the 15th, the day of the battle at Stephenson's Depot, that his three divisions — Hood's, McLaws', and Pickett's — took up the line of march northward.   But though this affair ended in disaster to Milroy, it was a close call. G. H. Steuart's Brigade arrived at the bridge in the nick of time.   One hour later, or even half an hour, would have been too late.   And it was with great difficulty Steuart was able to hold his own against Milroy's determined attacks with superior numbers during the first hour of the engagement.   But for the heroism of those Maryland cannoneers serving the gun on the bridge and the other near by, Milroy's infantry must have broken through and escaped, with disastrous results to the Third Brigade.   They stood to their guns till fifteen out of sixteen fell, and even then the one man remaining on the bridge would not give up the gun. But the question arises, Ought such a risk to have been incurred? If there was apprehension that the enemy would try to escape by that road, ought not at least two or three brigades have been there to meet him, instead of one? The others were so far back that they arrived almost too late to save that one from disaster.

All honor to the men of Steuart's Brigade for what they did that morning. I visited the battle field many years after, and thought I recognized the very fence corner where the wounded soldier lay who allowed me to hitch my horse to his arm, while I ran to Contee's help on the bridge. Some three years ago I was attending the decoration of the graves of the Confederate dead in Arlington Cemetery, and was sitting on the platform waiting for my turn to speak, when an arm was thrust up from the crowd below and my hand warmly grasped. The owner, looking up, said, "I was one of the men lying wounded on the bridge that day at Stephenson's, when you came up."

CHAPTER XIV

ON Wednesday, June 17th, at two P.M. we took up our line of march northward, halting at Smithfield, and marching again next morning at four. This I have noted as a "very oppressive march" — probably because of the heat. We crossed the Potomac near Shepherdstown on Thursday about half past two. My chief, Gen. G. H. Steuart, and I rode side by side through the river, and our horses' feet touched the sacred soil of our native State at the same moment; but before I could guess his intention the general sprang from his horse, and dropping on his hands and knees, kissed the ground. This act of his was the expression of a feeling of love and loyalty which was deep and strong in the hearts of us all. We loved Maryland. We were proud of her history, of her traditions. We felt that she was in bondage against her will, and we burned with desire to have part in liberating her. She had not seceded. There was no star in the Confederate battle flag to represent Maryland. But we believed, in spite of the division of sentiment in the State, that if she had been free to speak, her voice would have been for the South. At the very inception of the struggle, her Legislature had been invaded by the military arm, and a number of its members had been thrown into prison, but the last act of that Legislature, before it was deprived of its liberty, was to pass a resolution declaring coercion an unconstitutional act, subversive of freedom, and expressing its sympathy with the South and its desire for the recognition of the Southern Confederacy.

Marylanders who joined the Confederate Army are sometimes blamed for their act, on the ground that they had not the excuse which the men of Virginia and other Southern States had, that they were obeying the mandate of their native State in the course they pursued. But the State of Maryland, in its last free utterance, had in effect forbidden her sons to aid in the subjugation of the Southern States, on pain of partaking in the crime of subverting liberty. Had we then remained at home, we should have been liable to conscription in the armies raised for this very purpose — the subjugation of the Southern States. Were we not, then, justified by our loyalty to our State in exiling ourselves from Maryland to avoid having part in a service which she had branded as an assault on constitutional liberty? And if our State had declared by the voice of her Legislature that the Southern Confederacy ought to be recognized, did not loyalty to Maryland justify our act in giving what aid we could for the establishment of the independence of the Confederacy? In fact, as the case presented itself to our minds, we were compelled to choose between the love of the Union and the love of liberty. We could not feel ourselves blameworthy, because we preferred Liberty without Union to Union without Liberty. I speak now of what we believed — of our deep and solemn convictions. Those who differ with us may challenge, if they will, the correctness of our judgment; they cannot fairly impeach our patriotism.

Believing as we did that the war was a war of subjugation, and that it meant, if successful, the destruction of our liberties, the issue in our minds was clearly drawn as I have stated it, — *The Union without Liberty*, or *Liberty without the Union*. And if we are reminded that the success of the Federal armies did not involve, in fact, the destruction of liberty, I answer by traversing that statement, and pointing out that during all the long and bitter period of "Reconstruction," the liberties of the Southern States were completely suppressed. Representative government existed only in name. In the end, by the blessing of God, the spirit of the martyred Lincoln prevailed over the spirit of despotism as incarnated in Thaddeus Stevens and Charles Sumner, and after long eclipse the sun of liberty and self-government again shone south of Mason and Dixon's line.

There were not less than twenty thousand Marylanders who went into voluntary exile that they might fight for the Southern cause, and wherever they were, in whatever branch of the service, they made an honorable name for fortitude and valor. Many of them rose to positions of distinction. Maryland furnished three major-generals to the Confederate Army and eleven brigadiers. I may repeat here what I have written elsewhere, that "to be a Confederate soldier meant for the Marylander, in addition to hardship and danger, exile from home and kindred. It meant to be cut off from communication with father and mother, brother and sister, and wife. It meant to have an impenetrable barrier of forts and armies between him and all

he loved and cherished best in the world.   Oh, the lone-
liness of the Maryland soldier of the Confederate Army
on his solitary post, when on guard duty — or in the
silence of the night wrapped in his blanket under the
stars — or lying wounded on the battle field, or sick
in hospital! Oh, the unutterable longing then for the
faces of those whom he had left behind!"

It was natural, then, that whenever in our campaign-
ing we came in sight of the hills or the shores of Maryland, our men would be wrought up to a high degree
of excitement, and the hope would leap up in our hearts
that we might soon be marching triumphantly to our
old homes again.

The Second Maryland Battalion (successor to the first
regiment, which had been mustered out in the summer
of 1862) was about this time attached to Steuart's
Brigade; and when we reached Shepherdstown on
Thursday, June 18th, on our way to cross into Maryland, it was given the front of the column. The citizens of the town — especially the ladies — gave us
an enthusiastic reception. The general and all his
staff had bouquets presented them. It was a gala
day for the Maryland men. When we were well over
the river and had gone into camp, the Maryland battalion had songs and great rejoicings, and Lieut. Jas.
Franklin made an appropriate address. I made this
record:

"It was an hour full of hope long deferred, and now,
actually on the soil of my native State, which my feet have
not pressed since the first of May, 1861, I find it difficult
to realize that it is not all a dream."

The following Sunday, June 21st, found us camped
near the battle ground of Sharpsburg, which had been

fought Sept. 17th, 1862. With intense interest we recalled the thrilling story of that tremendous conflict, the bloodiest of the war up to that time, when Lee, with 35,000 men, held his ground successfully against McClellan with 87,000, in that fierce struggle, when American manhood on both sides displayed its highest qualities of valor and intrepidity. That the Federal general, when the disposition of Lee's several corps was revealed to him by the mysteriously intercepted despatch, should not have destroyed the Confederate Army in detail, separated as its two wings were, must forever tarnish his reputation as a commander, excellent as he was as an organizer and as a tactician! A study of this battle reveals the marvellous intrepidity and determination of General Lee. He stands out here as a daring and aggressive fighter, second in these qualities not even to his great Lieutenant Stonewall Jackson. The Council of War at the close of the battle vividly reflects this fact. Going over part of the field, the extreme left of the Confederate position, we saw trees that had been cut down as if by the teeth of a saw by the concentrated musketry fire, — silent witnesses of the destructive volleys of the opposing armies.

The same morning we had received from the ladies of Shepherdstown a battle flag for our brigade headquarters. The women in that town were always distinguished for their devotion to the Confederate cause. How many a poor fellow was their debtor for help and sympathy in time of need. In Sharpsburg, too, we were pleased to find decided evidences of the sympathy of the people.

Looking over the notes which I kept of this campaign in a little pocket note-book about four inches square —

kept in pencil, by the way, in a very fine hand and yet distinctly legible after the lapse of over forty-five years — I am impressed anew with the religious suscepti-bility of the rank and file of Lee's army. I find fre-quent mention of religious services by the chaplains, and of prayer-meetings, conducted sometimes by my-self. Thus the day after we crossed the Potomac I "attended and conducted one of the prayer-meetings of the Maryland Regiment with much pleasure."

And on Sunday, June 21st, the Rev. Mr. Patterson of the Third North Carolina "held service, preached, and administered the communion." Again, on June 22d, Monday:

"This morning, after reading and praying in the woods, I saw a group of our men looking at some soldiers' graves, and, with their permission, read (the Bible) and prayed with them."

These brave men who followed Lee with such sub-lime devotion felt no incompatibility in their calling as soldiers with the profession of a Christian. They were not soldiers of fortune; they were not mercenaries; they were soldiers of duty. And they were not waging a war of aggression, or of conquest, but of self-defence. They were in arms to protect their homes and their firesides from the invader. This invasion of Pennsyl-vania on which they were entering was a defensive operation. It was to draw the Federal armies out of Virginia. And I may here say that Lee's army strictly observed the order of their noble chief, in which he charged his soldiers not to molest private property. "The duties exacted of us," said he, "by civilization and Christianity are not less obligatory in the country of the enemy than in our own." Compare with this the statement of General Sherman as to his famous march to the sea:

"I estimate the damage done to the State of Georgia at one hundred million dollars, at least twenty millions of which inured to our benefit, and the remainder was simply waste and destruction."

Again and again in this Pennsylvania campaign the citizens told us that we treated them far better than their own soldiers did. I can truly say I didn't see a fence rail burned between Hagerstown and Gettysburg.

Supplies of cattle and other necessaries were taken and paid for in Confederate money, the only money we had. Major Harry Gilmor, in his account of this business says, "My orders were, in all cases where the horses had not been run off and hidden, to leave a pair of plough horses to each family, and to take no milch cows at all."

Colonel Fremantle of the British army bears testimony to the good conduct of our men. He says: "I went into Chambersburg and witnessed the singularly good behavior of the troops toward the citizens. . . . To one who has seen, as I have, the ravages of the Northern troops in Southern towns, this forbearance seems most commendable and surprising."

I append General Lee's order on this subject.

HEADQUARTERS ARMY OF NORTHERN VIRGINIA,
Chambersburg, Pa., June 27, 1863.

GENERAL ORDER No. 73.

"The commanding general has observed with marked satisfaction the conduct of the troops on the march, and confidently anticipates results commensurate with the high spirit they have manifested. No troops could have displayed greater fortitude or better performed the arduous marches of the past ten days. Their conduct in other respects has, with few exceptions, been in keeping with their character as soldiers and entitles them to approbation and praise.

"There have, however, been instances of forgetfulness on the part of some, that they have in keeping the yet unsullied reputation of the army, and that the duties exacted of us by civilization and Christianity are not less obligatory in the country of the enemy than in our own. The commanding general considers that no greater disgrace could befall the army, and through it our whole people, than the perpetration of the barbarous outrages upon the innocent and defenseless and the wanton destruction of private property that have marked the course of the enemy in our own country. Such proceedings not only disgrace the perpetrators and all connected with them, but are subversive of the discipline and efficiency of the army, and destructive of the ends of our present movements. It must be remembered that we make war only on armed men, and that we cannot take vengeance for the wrongs our people have suffered, without lowering ourselves in the eyes of all whose abhorrence has been excited by the atrocities of our enemy, and offending against Him to whom vengeance belongeth, without whose favor and support our efforts will prove in vain.

"The commanding general, therefore, earnestly exhorts the troops to abstain, with most scrupulous care, from unnecessary or wanton injury to private property, and he enjoins upon all officers to arrest and bring to summary punishment all who shall in any way offend against the orders on this subject.

"R. E. LEE,
"General."

I have now to make brief mention of an expedition under Gen. G. H. Steuart to McConnellsburg, Fulton County, Pennsylvania, which lies beyond the Tuscarora Mountains, which constitute the western boundary of the great Cumberland Valley that runs from Hagerstown to Harrisburg. A glance at the map will show that McConnellsburg is as far west of Hagerstown as Gettysburg is east of it; that its latitude is considerably north of that of Gettysburg; and that in order to reach it, General Steuart's force had to cross three subsidiary ranges of mountains.

The force under Steuart's command consisted of the Third Brigade (which included now the Second Maryland infantry in addition to the three Virginia regi-

ments and the two North Carolina regiments), a
battery of artillery, and Major Gilmor's cavalry.   The
column moved from Sharpsburg at five A.M., Tuesday,
June 23d, and passed through Hagerstown about noon,
receiving there an enthusiastic reception from the ladies
of the town.   "It was a proud day for the Maryland
men, and they stepped out beautifully to the tap of the
drum."   Camp was made five miles north of Hagerstown near the Pennsylvania line at three P.M., after
a march of seventeen miles.   The march thence to
McConnellsburg, a distance of upward of twenty miles,
was made on Wednesday, by way of Greencastle,
Upton, and Mercersburg, passing through two gaps
in the mountains.   When we were already eleven
miles on our march, the general sent me back to Hagerstown after the Maryland cavalry, which had not yet
reported to him as ordered.   We were marching
through the mountains in the enemy's country, far
from any support, without any cavalry to feel the way
before us.   I had a lonely ride back, also through a
hostile country, and did not find Major Harry Gilmor till after I had reached Hagerstown.   He and I
then rode ahead, the cavalry following some distance
behind.   Gilmor was one of the most daring and reckless of the cavalry leaders in the army, — a man of
great stature, powerful build, and great physical endurance.   His "Four Years in the Saddle" is full of exciting and daring episodes, illustrating the character of
the man.   Stopping at a farmhouse for refreshment
for man and beast, Gilmor entered into conversation
with the farmer, and I was much amused to hear him
tell the farmer that we were certain of success, because
our army, from General Lee down, was wholly com-

posed of Christian men — his own conversation being punctuated meanwhile with many an oath. He explained that he was a rare exception. Indeed, he looked more like one of Claverhouse's dragoons than a leader in an army of saints. My horse and I had covered fifty miles before night. General Steuart was an exacting chief, and what with the reveilles before daylight, the forced marches, and the many orders to be executed, I had not had for a long time more than three or four hours sleep a day. I find a note in my diary in this campaign, that in five days I had had but twelve hours sleep all told.

The behavior of the men since we entered Pennsylvania had been most exemplary. At McConnellsburg there had been one breach of General Lee's orders, but that was the solitary exception. I find this note, "Our division has not burned a fence rail since we have been in Pennsylvania," and also this, "The people were frightened to death, and only asked us to spare their lives and not burn their houses. But finding us so quiet and orderly, they became calm and said we treated them much better than their own men."

What a contrast was all this to the behavior of the Federal armies in Virginia and throughout the South from the beginning to the end of the war, with some honorable exceptions. In their very first march, from Alexandria to Manassas, the Union soldiers pillaged the houses of the people and committed many depredations. When, after that battle, we passed through Fairfax Court House, the people had much to tell of what they had suffered during the forward march of McDowell's army. General Sherman's famous dictum that "War is hell" is undoubtedly true of war as conducted by him in Georgia and the Carolinas, and as conducted by Sheridan in Virginia. It has no application to war as conducted by General Lee in Pennsylvania — always excepting the horrors of the battle field. When General Sheridan visited the head-quarters of the Prussian Army before Sedan, he told Bismarck that the correct principle on which to conduct an invasion was to "leave the people nothing but eyes to weep with."[1] Those words well embody the ruthless spirit in which he ravaged the valley of Virginia in 1864.

From McConnellsburg we marched on Friday, June 26th, eastward again, passing through the gap to Loudonton in Franklin County, and thence through St. Thomas almost to Chambersburg in the Cumberland Valley, a distance of over twenty miles. Major Gilmor captured near St. Thomas "sixty head of cattle, forty horses, some mules, and a few militia." We had now marched about fifty miles in Pennsylvania and had encountered no opposition of any kind till the appearance of the "few militia" now mentioned. Nevertheless, we had marched with due precaution, a squadron of cavalry in front, then one regiment of infantry, then a section of artillery, then the rest of our infantry, then another section of artillery, then ambulance and wagon trains, and lastly a rear guard of cavalry.

Saturday, the 27th, we passed through Chambers-

---

[1] General Sheridan thus expressed himself: "The proper strategy consists, in the first place, in inflicting as telling blows as possible upon the enemy's army, and then in causing the inhabitants so much suffering that they must long for peace, and force their government to demand it. The people must be left nothing but their eyes to weep with over the war." Secret pages of Bismarck's history by Moritz Busch, vol. I., p. 128.

burg and Green Village and on to Shippensburg, through which we pressed to Stoughstown, seven miles farther, and camped at Big Spring near Springfield. "At Springfield I bought seven copies of the New Testament" for distribution among the men. The surprise of the storekeeper when an officer of the terrible Rebel Army desired to purchase copies of the New Testament may be imagined. Perhaps he thought if the rebels would read the Good Book, they might repent of their wicked Rebellion. This recalls a familiar story of General Lee. Some time after the war, he received a letter informing him that the writer had learned that the Arlington family Bible was in the possession of a lady in a certain Western city and suggesting that if the general would write to her and claim it, it might be restored to his possession. But General Lee said in reply that he would not disturb the lady on the subject, adding, with that quiet humor which distinguished him, that if she would read the Good Book and reflect upon its precepts, perhaps she would restore it of her own accord.

On Sunday, the 28th, we were still marching northward toward Harrisburg, and were now within less than a day's march of Carlisle. My notes mention that the men were much broken down, many of them having marched barefooted.

The object of this expedition of ours into the mountains west of the Cumberland Valley was, I suppose, the capture of cattle for the supply of the commissariat. If I recollect aright, it had not been very successful in this respect, though the sixty head were a welcome auxiliary to the needs of the army.

But now evidently we were marching to effect a

junction with the other divisions of our corps. Ewell had been instructed by Lee to move towards the Susquehanna, and threaten Harrisburg. At this time part of his corps was at Carlisle, about eighteen miles southwest of Harrisburg, and part, under Early, was at York, about twenty-five miles southeast of Harrisburg, and within, say, eight miles of the Susquehanna.

Ewell had sent forward his engineer, Captain Richardson, with Jenkins' Cavalry to reconnoitre the defences of Harrisburg, and "was starting on [Monday] the 29th for that place, when ordered by the general commanding to join the main body of the army at Cashtown, near Gettysburg." No doubt, therefore, our brigade was pressing on to join General Ewell in front of Harrisburg, but on that same day, Monday the 29th, at nine A.M. we received orders to "march back toward Chambersburg." This countermarch was continued that day and Tuesday, the 30th, till we reached Green Village, when we moved, head of column left, and marched east toward Fayetteville. Then Wednesday, July 1st, we passed through Fayetteville and through the gap to Cashtown. "On top of the mountain we heard rapid cannonading." The battle of Gettysburg — so big with fate — had begun.

CHAPTER XV

BEFORE proceeding to record my personal experiences and observations on this eventful field, I shall endeavor to explain, as best I can, the significance of the operations of the Confederate Army up to this point, and the plan of campaign which the commander-in-chief apparently had in mind.

Well, it is clear in the first place that the object of General Lee in the invasion of Pennsylvania was to draw the Federal armies out of Virginia, and to relieve that State of the war at least for a brief period. This Pennsylvania campaign, although offensive in form, was defensive in purpose. This is made clear by General Lee's letter of June 8th to Mr. Seddon, Secretary of War at Richmond, and his letter to Mr. Jefferson Davis from Williamsport on June 25th.

Secondly, when entered upon, it was not Lee's intention to fight an offensive, but a defensive battle. He says in his Report of July 31st, 1863, "It had not been intended to fight a general battle at such a distance from our base, unless attacked by the enemy."

Thirdly, up to the night of June 28th, at which time Lee was at Chambersburg with the corps of Longstreet and Hill close at hand, it was Lee's intention to continue the advance northward, and apparently to concentrate his entire army at Harrisburg. This is affirmed in both his Reports, that of July 31st, 1863, and that of January, 1864. We cannot suppose so crucial a point would have been twice affirmed by the commander-in-chief if it had not been true. He says in the former Report, "Preparations were now made to advance upon Harrisburg." In the latter, "Orders were therefore issued to move upon Harrisburg."[1]

Fourth, that plan was abandoned for a reason which is thus stated in Lee's second Report, "The advance against Harrisburg was arrested by intelligence received from a scout on the night of the 28th to the effect that the army of General Hooker had crossed the Potomac

---

[1] Colonel Mosby says in his book, "Stuart's Cavalry in the Gettysburg Campaign" (p. 115), "If General Lee had intended to take his army to Harrisburg, as Marshall says, he would not have turned to the east at Chambersburg, and would not have sent Heth on to Cashtown."

To prove these facts he quotes Colonel Fremantle, the English visitor who states that he found Generals Lee and Longstreet camped on the Gettysburg road, three quarters of a mile east of Chambersburg — this on June 27 or 28 — and he also quotes Jacob Hoke's "Great Invasion" which states that on Friday, 26th, Rodes division and Johnson's also moved down the Harrisburg road, and that about 8 A.M. Heth's division of Hill's corps entered Chambersburg, but instead of following Johnson's and Rodes' divisions, turned east in the direction of Gettysburg and encamped near Fayetteville. Hoke concluded from this that Baltimore and Washington were Lee's destination — Now do these facts certainly prove that Lee had not at that time any intention of concentrating his army at Harrisburg? I do not think so. It does not seem to have occurred to Colonel Mosby that the movements which Mr. Hoke witnessed might have been intended to produce on the minds of the Federal authorities at Washington (to whom they would certainly be reported) the same impression which they produced on the mind of Mr. Hoke — in other words to deceive the enemy as to his real design.

But there is another explanation. General Hill in his Report states that he was ordered to move through York, cross the Susquehanna, and then move against Harrisburg.

and was approaching the South Mountain. In the absence of the cavalry it was impossible to ascertain his intentions; but to deter him from advancing further west, and intercepting our communications with Virginia, it was determined to concentrate the army east of the mountains."

Fifth, this eastward movement, and concentration east of the South Mountain, does not explain the battle of Gettysburg. It did not necessarily result in a battle at that place. The orders given, and the reports of Ewell and Early, make it plain that the purpose of the Confederate commander was to concentrate the army in the vicinity of Cashtown, where it would have held a very strong defensive position — impregnable indeed — and where Lee if attacked could have fought a defensive battle, as he purposed to do.

This, then, was the situation when the sun rose on July 1st. A. P. Hill's corps had marched from Chambersburg east to Cashtown, and all his divisions except Anderson's were already east of the mountains. Ewell's divisions were on the march for the same point; Edward Johnson, having marched southwest from Carlisle by way of Shippensburg and Fayetteville, on the west of the great South Mountain; Rodes' division having marched from Carlisle directly south across the South Mountain, and on the east side of the same, by way of Heidlersburg and Middletown; and Early's division southwest from York by way of Hunterstown and Mummasberg. Longstreet's corps was marching from Chambersburg east to Cashtown.

What the purpose of the Confederate commander-in-chief was in this concentration at Cashtown can

perhaps only be inferred. Longstreet had advised
Lee to concentrate east of South Mountain and "bear
down to meet the enemy." But Lee himself had,
before leaving Virginia, expressed his determination
not to fight a great battle unless attacked. Colonel
Mosby's ingenious suggestion has, therefore, much
in its favor. Arguing from the fact that Lee left all
the gaps south of Cashtown open, he thinks Lee meant
by so doing to entice Hooker to cross into the Cumberland Valley, "seize Lee's communications and strike
him in his rear." "That was Lee's own favorite ma-
nœuvre, and no doubt he calculated that Hooker would
follow his example; if so, he would flank Hooker and
go on to Washington." Colonel Mosby adds that
Hooker took the bait, and intended to do what Lee
hoped he would do, but Halleck interposed his veto,
and Hooker indignantly asked to be relieved. On
June 28th, in the afternoon, at Frederick city, Hooker
was relieved of the command of the Army of the Potomac. This fact, according to the testimony of General
Longstreet, became known to General Lee that same
night before midnight.

Sixth. The battle of Gettysburg was precipitated
by the advance of Lieutenant-General Hill the early
morning of July 1st. Lee had certainly given his
lieutenants to understand that he did not wish a
general engagement brought on. Ewell says in his
Report that on the 1st of July he was moving with
Rodes' division *towards Cashtown*, and had ordered
Early to follow, but before he reached Middletown,
which is about nine miles east of Cashtown and nearly
the same distance north of Gettysburg, he "received
notice from General Hill that he was advancing upon

Gettysburg," and that he therefore "turned the head of Rodes' column towards that place by the Middletown road, sending word to Early to advance directly on the Heidlersburg road." General Ewell also says that he "notified the general commanding of his movements, and was informed by him that, in case we found the enemy's force very large, he did not want a general engagement brought on until the rest of the army came up." Now as General Lee's headquarters that morning were at Greenwood, nine miles west of Cashtown, it must have taken several hours for Ewell to send him this message and receive his reply. In fact, before General Lee's answer arrived Ewell says Hill was heavily engaged, Carter's artillery of his own corps was in action, and heavy masses of the enemy were moving into position in his front. There is no evidence that General Lee expected a battle that day. In fact, he was fifteen miles away when Hill began his forward movement. He wrote General Imboden from Greenwood, July 1st, 7.30 A.M. that his headquarters for the present would be near Cashtown, — eight miles west of Gettysburg — this while Hill and Heth were already marching into battle northwest of Gettysburg. No one claims, I believe, that the commander-in-chief ordered this advance of Lieutenant-General Hill.[1] So that we appear justified in the conclusion that General Lee was dragged into this great battle by the unauthorized action of one of his lieutenants in advancing without orders and fighting a battle. In his report General Hill says he advanced for the purpose

[1] Gen. E. P. Alexander says, "Hill's movement to Gettysburg was made of his own motion, and with the knowledge that he would find the enemy's cavalry in possession." Memoirs, p. 381.

of making a reconnoissance — to ascertain if the enemy were in force near Gettysburg.

There were nearly 50,000 men engaged in the battle that day, Rodes and Early having come to Hill's assistance in his extremity. They turned the tide in favor of the Confederates, who till their arrival had had the worst of it. The charge of Gordon's Georgia brigade of Early's division at three P.M. gave the *coup de grace* to the Federal line. It has been thus described:

"Without waiting for artillery to prepare their way, or for skirmishers to feel for the enemy, the array of Georgian troops descended on both wings of the 11th Corps, and, with the precision acquired on many battle fields, swiftly and silently moved forward to the assault without firing a shot. The sight of Jackson's veterans once more threatening to close with them in hand to hand conflict struck a chill to the hearts of men they had so recently defeated, and who now had to face that long brown line hardly distinguishable from the corn over which it trampled, save for the fringe of steel glittering above it in the July sun, and for a dozen crimson standards which flaunted defiantly the starry cross of the Confederacy. Like the sickles of a great line of reapers the sharp bayonets came nearer through the ruddy gold of the ripening wheat; then the line disappeared, only to emerge a minute later unbroken and unhesitating from the willows which lined the little stream. The sight was too much for the nerves of Barlow's men. Some there were who gallantly stood to be bayoneted when their comrades fled. Barlow himself and many superior officers fell in the fire which preluded the Southern charge, but the first line was borne back half a mile before it rallied on its reserves at the Almshouse."—CAPT. CECIL BATTINE, "Crisis of the Confederacy," pp. 196, 197.

The battle, which lasted six hours, resulted disas-

trously to the Federals. General Reynolds was killed,
the 11th Corps was almost annihilated, 5,000 prisoners
were taken, including two general officers, and three
pieces of artillery, and the enemy driven two miles
into and beyond Gettysburg.

But it was a costly victory, for it compelled Lee
to accept the alternative of retreating or fighting
—fighting on a field where the Federal Army had every
advantage of position, where it must be assailed at
great disadvantage to the assailants, whether on the
right or the left flank or in the centre. Whoever has
visited the field will recognize the great difficulty of
a concerted attack by the forces of Lee, and also that
when Meade was attacked in one part of his line, he
could hurry troops easily and quickly from another
part to its succor, because his line was like a horseshoe,
or rather like a fish-hook.

And yet General Lee's decision to attack the Federal Army the next day was justified by the situation
at nightfall of July 1st. The enemy to the number of
about 25,000 had been defeated with great loss and
driven from the field in disorder. One of his corps
was almost annihilated. The finest officer in the Union
army had been killed. Lee's army was well concentrated, Longstreet's corps (the last) having bivouacked
within four miles of Gettysburg, while a large part
of the Federal Army was still far from the field. And
the key of the position, Little Round Top, was within
his grasp, — if he might count on his orders being
obeyed. General Lee could not foresee that the first
corps, then four miles from the field, would not be
launched against Little Round Top till four P.M. instead of nine A.M. the next day.

But to proceed with my observations. I have intimated that General Stuart was not the only one of Lee's lieutenants who failed to accomplish what might have been expected of him in the Gettysburg campaign.[1] The serious error of Gen. A. P. Hill has already been referred to. That was followed by the grave mistake of Lieutenant-General Ewell in not pressing the pursuit of the enemy and seizing Cemetery Hill. General Lee did not arrive in sight of the field until 2.30 P.M., and could not therefore grasp the situation in all its features, but he promptly sent a staff officer to General Ewell, saying that he could see the enemy in retreat over the hill and suggesting, but not commanding, that he should be pursued and Cemetery Hill seized. General Early, General Gordon, and General Trimble were all urgent with General Ewell to advance. Col. E. V. White, about dark, "saw the enemy leaving Cemetery Hill," and reported to General Ewell what he had seen. No advance was made, and the enemy proceeded leisurely, during the night and next morning, to fortify their position and make it impregnable. Had it been attacked on the evening of July 1st, it would have been easily taken, as we now know, and the great battle would have been fought on another field, or else would have terminated disastrously for the Federal Army.

The next failure was on the part of General Longstreet. The Confederate commander, upon his arrival on the field after the battle of July 1st was over, had immediately seen the great importance of Little Round Top. I saw him sweep the horizon with his glass, and noted that he scanned that elevation with great atten-

[1] See Appendix, B.

tion. Accordingly General Longstreet was ordered to move the next morning "*as early as practicable with the portion of his command that was up*, around to gain the Emmitsburg road on the enemy's left" (Longstreet's statement). This order he took the responsibility of disobeying (by his own confession), preferring to wait till the last of his brigades was up; and so the movement which should have been made early in the day (his troops bivouacked within four miles of the battle field the night before) did not take place till four P.M. Thus the golden opportunity was lost which would have given Lee the key of the battle field. Even then, at that late hour, it was discovered during the attack that Little Round Top was unoccupied, and Longstreet was asked by one of his generals for permission to make a flank movement and seize it, — which could easily have been done; but he refused, saying his orders were to attack in front.

This looks like a sullen refusal of a great opportunity by one whose advice the evening before had been dissented from by the commanding general. Major F. G. R. Henderson, the distinguished English military critic, comments as follows:

"His summary message to the divisional commander to carry out the original plan, at least, lays him open to the suspicion that although he was prepared to obey orders, it was like a machine and not like an intelligent being."

If he hesitated to act on his own initiative, the commander-in-chief could easily have been consulted.

By this fatal and inexcusable delay the advantage of superior numbers which was with the Confederates on the morning of the 2d of July was thrown away.

Before Longstreet attacked, the advantage of numbers had shifted to the other side by the arrival of large bodies of Federal troops.

Had this been seized by the Confederates, Meade could not have held his position. It dominated the whole Federal line. But there was great and unaccountable delay; so that the Federals got possession of it, arriving about twenty minutes before the column of Longstreet. It would appear that Hancock marched twenty miles while Longstreet was marching six.

Now there can be no doubt that that eminence of Little Round Top was the key of the battle field, and Lee's recognition of this, with the knowledge that his troops were near enough to seize it, completely justifies his decision to fight on that field. He could not anticipate the unnecessary delay in the execution of his order. No wonder he showed impatience the next day as hour after hour passed, and still Longstreet's column did not appear. Colonel Taylor says it was the only occasion during the war when he ever saw General Lee impatient.

Captain Battine, the English military critic, in discussing the question whether Lee should have attacked the Gettysburg position, says:

"The point on which the question really depended was what chance the Confederates had of inflicting a decisive defeat, and there can be no doubt that the opportunity was the brightest they had made for themselves since they let McClellan escape from the banks of the Chickahominy. One third of the Federal Army had been severely defeated, the remainder were concentrating with difficulty by forced marching; a prompt deployment of all his available forces would have placed victory within Lee's grasp. The resolution to attack was therefore sound and wise, — the failure lay in faults of execution which were caused to some extent at any rate by the want of sympathetic co-operation of the corps commander."—"Crisis of the Confederacy," p. 207.

Into the question whether the charge of Pickett's division on the third day ought to have been ordered — whether Lee had a right to expect that it would succeed — I do not propose to enter. I will only say, he did not have the cordial coöperation of his second in command, and the charge was not made, and was not supported, as he directed. Major Henderson, the English military critic and author of the "Life of Stonewall Jackson," has left a valuable discussion of the battle of Gettysburg in which he says that it was the purpose of General Lee that the charge should have been made by 30,000 men. Instead, 15,000 made the charge, while the rest of the army looked idly on!

Thus it appears that in this great crisis of the war, the Confederate commander-in-chief was not properly supported by his subordinate commanders. All three of his lieutenant-generals failed him at need, as well as his chief of cavalry. Never had Lee commanded so fine an army as when he crossed the Potomac to enter upon this Pennsylvania campaign. It was better equipped than ever before. Its discipline was excellent, its morale superb. It had the prestige of victory. It was full of confidence and enthusiasm. It had unbounded trust in the genius of its commander. Never was it so confident of victory.

That victory did not crown its efforts does not appear to have been due to the failure of its chief or to any lack of heroic courage on the part of the rank and file of the army, but to the strange and unaccountable shortcomings of four splendid soldiers upon whom Lee was accustomed to rely with confidence, and who had ever been loyal to him. It must also be admitted that Lee's tactics in this battle were not at all up to the standard of his strategy. There was a strange failure to coördinate the attacks of the several corps of the army. Splendid assaults were made at different points of the line; but in no instance were these supported. There seemed to be a paralysis of the coördinating faculty all along the line. If we seek the ultimate solution of the mystery of this failure when all the omens pointed to success, we can only say, "It was not the will of God." Like Hector at Troy, Lee was fighting against the supernal powers. And yet it can hardly be said that Gettysburg, though a Confederate failure, was a Federal victory. It was rather a drawn battle. The first day was marked by a splendid success for the Confederates, with large spoils of war, in prisoners (5,000) and in artillery (20 pieces). The second day Sickles was almost annihilated by Longstreet. The third day Pickett's magnificent charge was repulsed, and the charge of Johnson's division on Culp's Hill likewise.

But Lee was foiled, not beaten. The morale of his army was not shaken. He offered battle on Seminary Ridge all day of July 4th, but Meade did not accept the gage. It was not considered by him or his corps commanders prudent to do so. The Federal Army was more seriously shaken than its opponent. Its losses were considerably larger.

When Lee decided to retire into Virginia, after Meade had declined his offer of battle on July 4th, his retreat was so deliberate that in twenty-four hours he only marched seven or eight miles.

Here is the record in my diary:

"On Saturday night (July 4) we left camp at Gettysburg, marching very slowly in consequence of the length of the ordnance and artillery train, and the ruggedness and mountainous nature of the road. The enemy pursued us with great caution, not daring to attack. By Sunday night we had made about seven or eight miles. Monday we marched as far as Waynesboro just beyond the mountain."

Then on Tuesday we continued our march and made eight miles, going into camp on the Leitersburg road, three miles east of Hagerstown. Wednesday we were still in camp at the same place. Thursday we "lay in camp." Friday we moved camp to a point three miles beyond Hagerstown. The Federal cavalry was twice defeated in attacks on his trains, once July 6th, at Williamsport, by Imboden, and again at Hagerstown, July 7th, by General Stuart.

Near Hagerstown Lee again offered battle on July 11th, a week after the conflict ended at Gettysburg, — his only defences being the light breastworks thrown up by the men with their bayonets. Sunday, the 12th, his army was still in line awaiting attack, but no attack was made. Meade had called a council of war to consider whether he should attack or no. Mr. Lincoln was telegraphing him that he had only to close his hand and crush Lee; but Meade's generals counselled him against it — they realized that if he did, he would find he was closing it on a hornet's nest.

It is a great mistake to suppose that the army of

Lee was at all shaken or demoralized by the battle. It was on the contrary as full of fight as ever — as ready to obey the commands of its idolized chief. Very few brigades had had so hard fighting or suffered such heavy losses as that of Gen. Geo. H. Steuart (the third brigade of Johnson's division), but our men were eager for the Federals to attack us at Hagerstown, and confident we could repulse them.

This spirit and this confidence is reflected in my diary and in my correspondence. In a letter to my mother I wrote:

HAGERSTOWN, July 7, 1863.

"The army is in fine spirits and *confident of success* when they again meet the enemy. This you may rely upon and so you may comfort yourselves with it. A *military blunder* was committed, but the men never fought better."

Again I wrote:

MARTINSBURG, July 15, 1863.

"Let me tell you not to believe the stories in the Northern papers about the rout and demoralization of our army. We remained in Maryland ten days after the battle, and yet our enemy dared not attack us, though we lay in line of battle three days within half a mile of him. Our loss was not as heavy as theirs according to their own account, either in killed or prisoners. The men are in good discipline and spirits, and ready to teach our foes a lesson when they meet them again."

In the same letter I said:

"My heart bleeds when I think of the bitter disappointment you have all experienced in the retreat of our army from Maryland. To us who have thought the hopes, for two long years deferred, were about to be realized, and have suddenly been so grievously disappointed — to *us* it is a heavy blow, and our hearts are bowed with the greatness of our grief — but to you, brave, noble women of Maryland, it must be far more bitter and more crushing. Our deepest sympathies go out to you, but still we say, Hope on! Do not despair!"

And in my diary:

"Saturday, July 11. This morning formed in line of battle, left resting a mile or two from Hagerstown. . . . The Potomac is still unfordable, but if the enemy only will attack us, we don't want to cross the river.[1] May the Lord be on our side and show Himself our Helper and our Defense. Our trust is in his right hand, and in His holy arm. Our own strength will not save us. . . . I went into the last battle feeling that victory *must* be ours — that such an army could not be foiled, and that God would certainly declare Himself on our side. *Now* I feel that unless He sees fit to bless our arms, our valor will not avail."

When General Lee did cross the Potomac (the night of July 13th), the passage was effected successfully, without the loss of a single piece of artillery — and scarcely a wagon. That was a trying march for Lee's army from Gettysburg to Hagerstown.

"During the whole march it rained hard, and the men had not one day's rations in the three. Consequently depredations were committed [such as pig sticking, chicken taking, etc.] Fence rails were burned for the first time in Pennsylvania, and by permission. I have seldom suffered as much on any march. Want of food and sleep, and the

[1] The following entry the Thursday previous shows we were not at all nervous about the proximity of the enemy. "Dr. Johnson, Johnnie Boyle, and I went out to see Mr. Berry and took dinner. Returning, supped with Mr. Rogan. Made sick by the good things." Next day, "Rode in the ambulance for the first time since I've been a soldier."

tediousness of movement, together with the inclemency of the weather and the roughness of the roads."

Reverting to the story of the battle, there are one or two things I wish to mention of a personal nature. As we were on the march to the field, on July 1st, the distant booming of the cannon in our ears, one of the privates of Murray's company came up to me, during a brief halt by the roadside, and said he wanted to speak to me. It was James Iglehart, of Annapolis. We stepped aside, and I said, "What is it, Iglehart?" He answered, "Lieutenant, I want to ask your pardon." "My pardon!" said I. "Why, what on earth do you mean?" "I've done you an injustice," he said, "and before we go into this battle, I want to tell you so, and have your forgiveness." I told him I could not imagine what he meant, and he then said that he had thought from my bearing toward him that I was "proud and stuck up," because I was an officer and he only a private in the ranks, but now he saw that he was entirely mistaken and he wanted to wipe out the unspoken injustice he had done me. The next time I heard his voice was in that last terrible charge on Culp's Hill, when our column had been dashed back like a wave breaking in spray against a rock. "McKim," he cried, "McKim, for God's sake, help me!" I turned and saw him prostrate on the ground, shot through both thighs. I went back a few yards, and putting my arm round him, dragged him to the shelter of a great rock and laid him down to die. There are two things that rise in my thought when I think of this incident. One is that if he hadn't come to me two days before and relieved his mind as he did, the gallant fellow would not have asked my help. And the other is that the men in blue in that breastwork must have been touched with pity when they saw me trying to help poor Iglehart. It took some minutes to go back and get him behind that rock, and they could have shot us both down with perfect ease if they had chosen to do it.

In my *Narrative* I have referred to that tremendous artillery duel which shook the earth for two hours on the afternoon of the second day of the battle. I now set down the fact that I held my watch in my hand and counted the number of discharges in one minute: it was one hundred and eighty. "It was a beautiful sight, but an awful one." I think it was before this that I went, first to the Tenth Virginia, and then to the Second Maryland Regiment, and conducted religious services. There was a peculiar solemnity in thus appealing to the Almighty for His protection on the battle field itself, just before rushing forward to assault the lines of the enemy. The men were lying on their arms, momentarily expecting to be ordered to the charge, and they seemed thankful for the opportunity of joining in divine worship. It was for many a poor fellow his last service on earth.

In talking with survivors of this great battle, I have sometimes remarked that I thought I had performed an exploit at Gettysburg that none of them could match. "What is that?" "Why," said I, "I went sound asleep in the very midst of the heaviest firing, lying in the Federal breastworks!" And I did, in very deed and truth. I had taken three men, at the crisis of the conflict, when word had come to General Steuart that our ammunition was almost exhausted, and had gone on foot to the ammunition wagons about a mile distant and brought three boxes of ammunition in

blankets swung to rails through the burning sun up
Culp's Hill to our men.   When I at length dropped my
precious burden in the breastworks, I fell over utterly
exhausted with the exertion, and with the loss of sleep
for six days before the battle, and fell asleep.   Such
exhaustion completely banishes the sense of danger;
and the bursting shell and whistling bullets made no
impression on me whatever in those moments of utter
collapse.   Whether I slept two minutes, or five, I do
not know, but I was rudely awakened by a piece of
shell striking me painfully on the back, but its force
was spent — it did me no real hurt.

This reminds me that on one of the recent occasions
when the graves of the Confederate dead in Arlington
were being decorated with flowers, a gentleman came
up to me and said, "Dr. McKim, I am very glad to
see you again.   It is more than forty years since we
met, and we were not acquaintances then; but I can
never forget the face of the man who brought us that
ammunition in the Federal breastworks on Culp's Hill.
I claim the privilege of introducing myself to you."

Very few men in that battle in our brigade but were
touched by shot or shell, even if they escaped being
wounded.   I myself was touched four times without
being hurt.   A ball grazed my shoulder as I was bringing the ammunition up Culp's Hill.   Another went
through my haversack and ripped the back off a New
Testament I had in my pocket.   Then the piece of
shell rebounded from a tree and struck me in the back
as I have mentioned.   But the most remarkable escape
I had was from a ball which struck me on the wrist
as I was forming the line for the last charge on Culp's
Hill.   The pain was sharp for a moment and my arm

was thrown out violently by the blow, but no bone was broken, and not a drop of blood drawn — only a large lump over the wrist-bone, red and angry looking. "Your arm is broken, is it not, Lieutenant?" said Colonel Warren of the Tenth Virginia. "I don't know yet," said I, as I drew off my gauntlet; while inwardly I said, "I hope it is. I'd be glad to compromise with the loss of an arm to get out of this hopeless charge." But I had no excuse for not going forward. The ball had struck a brass button on my gauntlet and had glanced aside; and the reason I wore gauntlets with brass buttons was that I had exchanged mine, which had none, for those of my cousin, Major W. Duncan McKim, who preferred mine to his!

I would like here to pay a tribute to the splendid fortitude of the Third Brigade, and especially of the Second Maryland Regiment, on Culp's Hill on July 3d. And I refer not so much to that last magnificent charge, in which that regiment was conspicuous above others, but to the steadiness with which the brigade obeyed the order to evacuate the intrenchments and retire to the foot of the hill. As I have said elsewhere, "To rush forward in the fire and fury of battle does not test a soldier's mettle as it does to retreat, under such circumstances, in good order. And I point to that column, after that night and day of battle, after their terrible losses, after that fatal repulse in the bayonet charge, their nerves shaken by all that they had endured, — I point to it marching steadily down that hill of death, while the heroic Capt. Geo. Williamson and another staff officer, with drawn swords, walked backward (face to the enemy) to steady them — never breaking into a run, never losing their order, — and

I say, 'Then and there was the supreme exhibition of their soldierly qualities!'"

I extract from my diary the following passage. Referring to the night of the 2d, I wrote:

"General Steuart ordered me again to the hospital to bring up the ambulances. I did not return till half past three in the morning and so got no sleep. [I remember that I had just lain down with my bridle over my arm when the first shell of the Federal artillery came crashing over our heads.] At four this morning the enemy opened fire, contrary to our expectations. We had heard the rumbling of wagons and artillery all night and supposed they were leaving." [Instead they were massing their artillery to drive us out.]

Swinton says, "During the night a powerful artillery was accumulated against the point entered by the enemy." He further says, "The troops of the 12th Corps had returned from the left, and the divisions of Williams and Gray, aided by Shaler's brigade, of the Sixth Corps, entered upon the severe struggle to regain the lost position of the line." Thus not less than seven brigades were launched against that one small brigade of Steuart. Had Longstreet attacked on the right at daybreak as ordered, this could not have been done. Was there any heroism displayed in that tremendous battle greater than that exhibited by those 2,200 men of the Third Brigade?[1]

Let it be remembered, too, that while we were pounded for hours by that powerful artillery, we had not a single piece on that hill to make reply. They marvelled that we did not return their artillery fire. Resuming the extract from my diary:

[1] By that time their number was less than 2,000.

"This hill [on our right] commanded the breastworks which we held, and we were exposed to an enfilading fire of musketry and artillery from four A.M. till eleven A.M."

Referring to the charge ordered by Major-General Johnson, and disapproved by Steuart and Daniels:

"The men were mowed down with fearful rapidity, by two lines in front and a force on the left flank, besides an artillery fire from the left rear. It was the most fearful fire I ever encountered, and my heart was sickened with the sight of so many gallant men sacrificed. The greatest confusion ensued, — regiments were reduced to companies and everything mixed up. It came very near being a rout."

Again:

"We were next formed on the breastwork [of the enemy] and exposed to a terrific fire exceeding, by the testimony of all, any engagement the army has been in. I never felt so miserable in my life — the possibility of defeat, the slaughter of the men, the retreat from the breastworks, and the consequent confusion, and the almost certain expectation of being killed or wounded, and the vivid foresight of the grief of my poor wife — all made me feel more miserable than I have ever been before. But I strengthened my heart by prayer and was enabled to be perfectly calm. The storm of shot and shell was terrible, yet I went to sleep in the midst of it several times, so weary was I. We formed again at the foot of the hill and remained till evening, when new troops were brought on and fighting continued till now (five P.M.)."

This shows that my notes were made on the battle field. The fighting after that hour was only sharp-shooting — no volley firing — no charges or counter-charging. It is amazing that the Federals made no attempt to drive us across the creek. It shows how badly they were punished and how seriously their morale was shaken.

"At 1.30 A.M. [July 4] the order was given to retire, and it was executed so quietly that though the enemy's pickets were only fifty yards from ours they did not discover it till day broke and we had formed in line of battle along a ridge beyond the town. [Seminary Ridge.] Here we threw up a hasty breastwork and awaited the attack of the enemy all day, but night came without developing any such intention. During the morning the baggage trains were sent off toward Williamsport, and we followed very slowly late in the night [eleven P.M.]."

One of the officers killed on Culp's Hill was Major Benjamin Watkins Leigh, of the staff of Major-Gen. Edward Johnson. Nothing was known at the time of the manner or place of his death; but many years afterward I had a letter from a Federal officer in Massachusetts telling how it occurred. It seems that Major Leigh, seeing a group of Confederates in a very exposed position raise a white flag in order to surrender to the enemy, gallantly rode into their midst to prevent the execution of their purpose. While so engaged he met his death, and my correspondent said that the day after the battle he was found lying on the field *still in the saddle,* his horse dead with him as if a part of him — horse and rider having been killed at the same moment. It was, my correspondent said, a strange spectacle. Stranger perhaps it was that I should receive the story of his death a quarter of a century after it occurred, from one whom I did not know, and of whom I had never heard.

At Williamsport the following amusing incident occurred. While the wagon-trains were massed there waiting for the river to fall, the enemy's cavalry approached and shelled the banks of the river. There is a deep hollow or depression there on the north side of the Potomac, and here the wagons were parked. A Confederate quartermaster officer approached the spot during the artillery fire and was amazed to observe that not a single teamster was to be seen. He could not account for it, until he happened to look toward the river, and there saw hundreds of black heads just showing above the water. The negro teamsters with one accord had plunged into the river to escape the shells, and were submerged to the neck!

During an artillery duel at or near Williamsport the negro servant of one of our officers appeared on the scene, close to the artillery while it was in action. "Cæsar," said the officer, "what are you doing here? Have I not ordered you always to keep in the rear when fighting is going on?" "Yes, Marster," said the negro, "I know you is told me dat. But I declar' fo' God, I'se look ebery whar on dis here battle field dis day, and I cyarnt find no rear." The river was the rear of the Confederate line, and the Federals were shelling it vigorously to prevent a crossing.

I have mentioned on a previous page the chaplain of the Third North Carolina Regiment, Rev. Geo. Patterson. The following incident well illustrates the character of the man. One of the officers of the brigade was desperately wounded in the battle of the third day, and Mr. Patterson was promptly by his side to minister to him. He took a lantern and went out alone on the battle field and found him. It had become known that we had orders to withdraw, and the good chaplain told the wounded young man that he would be obliged to leave him and march with his regiment, whereupon the officer asked him to read the burial service over him before he left, "for," said he, "I know I'm as good as dead." To this request Mr. Patterson gave a cheerful assent, and there on the battle field, in the darkness of the night, by the light of a lantern, the solemn service was read, and Mr. Patterson bade the dying officer farewell.

But the colonel did not die, but recovered his health, and many years afterwards, in the year 1886, in a Western town, he met Rev. Mr. Patterson and cordially greeted him. That gentleman, however, did not recognize him, and shading his eyes with his hand, looked at him intently a moment and then shook his head, saying, "I don't know you. Who are you?" The officer replied, "I am Colonel B., of — North Carolina Regiment." To which Patterson promptly replied, "Now I know you are lying, for I buried him at Gettysburg!"

CHAPTER XVI

STEUART'S BRIGADE AT GETTYSBURG — A NARRATIVE[1]

INTRODUCTORY NOTE

NEW YORK, March 4, 1878.

REV. J. WM. JONES, D.D.,
  Secretary Southern Historical Society.

DEAR SIR: The sketch which I send herewith has been prepared at the urgent request of several of the survivors of the Third Brigade (Second Corps, A. N. V.), who think that justice to the memory of the heroic men of that command who gave up their lives at Gettysburg demands a more extended notice than has yet appeared of the part borne by them on that bloody field. (Owing to the fact that on the 3d of July I was occupied chiefly on the right of the line, my narrative relates principally to the deeds of the regiments on the right.) In preparing the narrative my memory has been assisted by pocket memoranda, made on the field, and by letters written immediately after the events related. This enables me to hope that in all substantial points this account may be relied on as accurate.

It is proper to add that I was attached as aide-de-camp to the staff of the brigadier-general commanding the brigade, so that I had excellent opportunities of informing myself of its condition and its deeds.

Very respectfully, your obedient servant,

RANDOLPH H. McKIM.

THE third brigade of Johnson's division entered the battle of Gettysburg very much jaded by the hard marching which fell to its lot the week previous. It

---

[1] Reprinted from "Southern Historical Society Papers," June, 1878.

formed part of an expeditionary force of infantry, cavalry, and artillery which was detached from the Second Corps on the 24th of June, under the command of Brig.-Gen. George H. Steuart, and ordered to Mercersburg and McConnellsburg.   In the execution of the duty assigned it was required to perform some heavy marching, as the following itinerary record will show:

Tuesday, June 23, 1863. — Broke camp near Sharpsburg, and, passing through Hagerstown, halted five miles beyond at three o'clock.   Distance, seventeen miles.

Wednesday, June 24. — Moved at 4.30 A.M.   At Greencastle filed to the left on the road to Mercersburg.   Entered McConnellsburg about nine P.M. after a march of twenty-four miles.

Friday, June 26. — Marched from McConnellsburg to Chambersburg, twenty miles, through a steady rain.   The cavalry under Major Gilmor captured sixty head of cattle, forty horses, a few mules, and some militia.

Saturday, June 27. — Column moved at 7.30 A.M., through Shippensburg, to Springfield.   Men much broken down, having marched nineteen miles, many of them barefooted.

Sunday, June 28. — After a short march of six or seven miles made camp at two P.M., about five miles south of Carlisle.   Rejoined our division to-day.

Monday, June 29. — About nine A.M. received orders to march back to Chambersburg.   Great surprise expressed.   Marched eleven miles and camped one mile south of Stoughstown.

Tuesday, June 30. — Column moved at five A.M.   Passed through Shippensburg, to Green Village, where we took left road to Fayetteville.

Wednesday, July 1. — Column moved at seven A.M. Passed through Fayetteville.   On top of mountain heard rapid cannonading.   Soon saw the smoke of the battle, and then of burning houses.   Hurried to the front, but the battle was over.   Distance from our camp on Monday to Gettysburg, thirty-five miles.   This was marched by the brigade on Tuesday and Wednesday.   It may have been a greater distance; it was not less.   Our camp on the night of the 30th must have been not far east or west of Greenwood.

Thus it appears that the men of the Third Brigade had marched, within the nine days preceding the battle, at least 133, perhaps as many as 138 miles. But, though weary and footsore, they moved forward with alacrity to take part in the great conflict which had already begun.   In the first day's action they were not engaged, the enemy having been driven from the field by A. P. Hill, Rodes, and Early before their arrival. The time of their arrival may be fixed by the circumstance which I distinctly remember, viz., the arrival of General Lee upon the field, his survey of the enemy's position on Cemetery Hill with his glass, and the despatch of one of his staff immediately in the direction of the town.

Passing over the scene of conflict, where the line of battle could be in some places distinctly traced by the ranks of dead Federal soldiers, they entered the town of Gettysburg a little before dusk.   (The time of our entering the town I fix by the fact that I easily read a letter handed me by Major Douglass.)   After considerable delay the brigade moved to the east and southeast of the town and halted for the night, the men lying down upon their arms in confident expectation of engaging the enemy with the morning light.

Greatly did officers and men marvel as morning, noon, and afternoon passed in inaction — on our part, not on the enemy's, for, as we well knew, he was plying axe and pick and shovel in fortifying a position which

was already sufficiently formidable.   Meanwhile one of
our staff conducted religious services, first in the Tenth
Virginia, then in the Second Maryland Regiment,
the men gladly joining in the solemn services, which
they knew would be for many of their number the last
they should ever engage in on earth.   At length, after
the conclusion of that tremendous artillery duel which
for two hours shook the earth, the infantry began to
move.   It was past six P.M. before our brigade was
ordered forward — *nearly twenty-four hours after we had
gotten into position*.   We were to storm the eastern
face of Culp's Hill, a rough and rugged eminence on
the southeast of the town, which formed the key to
the enemy's right centre.   Passing first through a
small skirt of woods, we advanced rapidly in line of
battle across a corn field which lay between us and the
base of the hill, the enemy opening upon us briskly
as soon as we were unmasked.   Rock creek, waist-
deep in some places, was waded, and now the whole
line, except the First North Carolina, held in reserve
on our left flank, pressed up the steep acclivity through
the darkness, and was soon hotly engaged with the
enemy.   After the conflict had been going on for some
time, I ventured to urge the brigadier-general commanding to send forward the First North Carolina to
reinforce their struggling comrades.[1]   Receiving orders
to that effect, I led the regiment up the hill, guided

---

[1] It was dark, and General Steuart detained one regiment in the
field mentioned to prevent our flank being turned.   The firing in the
woods now became very rapid, and volley after volley echoed and re-
echoed among the hills.   I felt very anxious about our boys in front,
and several times urged General Steuart to send the reserve regiment
to the support of the remainder of the brigade. — *Extract from letter
written after the battle.*

only by the flashes of the muskets, until I reached a position abreast of our line of fire on the right. In front, a hundred yards or so, I saw another line of fire, but owing to the thick foliage could not determine whether the musket flashes were *up* or *down* the hill. Finding that bullets were whistling over our heads, I concluded the force in our front must be the enemy, and seeing, as I thought, an admirable chance of turning their flank, I urged Colonel Brown to move rapidly forward and fire. When we reached what I supposed the proper position, I shouted, "Fire on them, boys; fire on them!" At that moment Major Parsley, the gallant officer in command of the Third North Carolina, rushed up and shouted, "They are our own men." Owing to the din of battle the command to fire had not been heard except by those nearest to me, and I believe no injury resulted from my mistake. I mention it only to assume the responsibility for the order. Soon after this the works[1] were gallantly charged and taken about 9.30 P.M., after a hard conflict of two hours, in which the Second Maryland and the Third North Carolina were the chief sufferers.[2] Among those who fell severely wounded was Col. James R. Herbert, of the Second Maryland. The losses in the two regiments named were heavy, but the men were eager to press on to the *crest* of the hill. This, owing to the darkness

---

[1] Let me tell you the character of their works. They were built of heavy logs, with earth piled against them to the thickness of five feet, and abattis in front. — *Extract from a letter.*

[2] Bates (author of "The History of the Battle of Gettysburg") shows his ignorance of the real state of the conflict when he says, "*the fast-coming darkness* drew its curtains around the vulnerable parts everywhere spread out." It was 9 or 9.30 P.M. before the works to which he refers were taken by our brigade two hours after dark.

and the lateness of the hour, it was resolved not to do.[1]
A Federal historian (B. J. Lossing, in his "Pictorial History of the Civil War") gives the following account
of this night conflict: "Johnson moved under cover of
the woods and deepening twilight, and expected an
easy conquest by which a way would be opened for the
remainder of Ewell's corps to the National rear; but
he found a formidable antagonist in Greene's brigade.
The assault was made with great vigor, but for more than
two hours Greene, assisted by a part of Wadsworth's
command, fought the assailants, strewing the wooded
slope in front of the works with the Confederate dead
and wounded, and holding his position firmly. Finally,
his antagonist penetrated the works near Spangler's
Spring, from which the troops had been temporarily
withdrawn."   (Vol. III, p. 691.)   This statement
needs correction.   There is no doubt of the fact that
the works taken by Steuart's brigade that night were
occupied by Federal troops and that they poured a
deadly fire into its ranks. After this fire had been
kept up for two hours those troops were indeed "withdrawn" — *but the orders came from the men of Steuart's
brigade, and they were delivered at the point of the
bayonet.*[2]

---

[1] Again and again did the rebels attack in front and flank; but as
often as they approached they were stricken down and disappeared.
(Bates' "Gettysburg," p. 139.) This is one of his many misstatements.
I say of my own knowledge that the only troops in position to assault
this work *on the flank* were those of the Third Brigade, and they made
no attempt to take it until the next day. This is, unhappily, too
true. An assault then would have promised success.

[2] I find a similar statement in Swinton's "Army of the Potomac,"
p. 355, in a pamphlet by Dr. Jacobs, and in an article by General
Howard in the *Atlantic Monthly*, July, 1876. I was at a loss to account
for it until I observed that General Howard describes the vacated

It is sufficient answer to this statement of the
Federal historian to quote the language of General
Lee's official report (*Southern Historical Society Papers*
for July, 1876, p. 42): "The troops of the former
(Johnson) moved steadily up the steep and rugged
ascent under heavy fire, driving the enemy into his
intrenchments, part of which were carried by Steuart's
brigade, and a number of prisoners taken."

The position thus so hardly [1] won and at so dear a
cost was one of great importance. It was within a

works as situated between McAllister's Mill and Culp's Hill. *From
these works* part of the 12th Corps had been withdrawn to reinforce
Meade's left. *But these were not the works occupied by Steuart's brigade,
whose charge was made on Culp's Hill itself, to the north of Spangler's
Spring.* Bates says: "Passing over the abandoned breastworks further
to the right, the enemy found nothing to oppose him, and pushed out
through the woods in their rear over the stone fences that skirt the
fields farther to the south, and had nearly gained the Baltimore pike.
Indeed, the reserve artillery and ammunition, and the headquarters
of General Slocum, the commander of the right wing of the army,
were within musket range of his farthest advance." (Page 140.)
This statement, if true at all, must have reference to the movements of
troops on our left. Steuart's men did not advance beyond those
redoubtable works which, although *vacant*, belched forth flame and
Minie balls, which were just as fatal as though they had been occupied
by soldiers! Being dark, we cannot say we saw the men behind them,
but we saw the musketry flashes and we *felt* the balls that came thick
into our ranks, and some of the private soldiers who survive testify
that when they leaped the works they saw dead and wounded Federal
soldiers on the other side.

[1] Bates himself, on another page (147), makes an admission fatal
to his former assertion: "On the extreme Union right he had effected
a lodgment [this, remember, General Lee says was done by Steuart's
brigade], and had pushed forward in dangerous proximity to the very
vitals of the army; . . . the night was sure to give opportunity for
dispositions which would oust him FROM HIS ALREADY DEAR-BOUGHT
ADVANTAGE." How was it "dear-bought" if occupied *without opposition?* Verily, unoccupied breastworks must have been fatal spots
in that battle.

few hundred yards of the Baltimore turnpike, which I think it commanded. Its capture was a breach in the enemy's lines through which troops might have been poured and the strong positions of Cemetery Hill rendered untenable. General Howard says: "The ground was rough, and the woods so thick that their generals did not realize till morning what they had gained." Dr. Jacobs says: "This might have proved disastrous to us had it not occurred at so late an hour." And Swinton declares it was "*a position which, if held by him, would enable him to take Meade's entire line in reverse.*" ("Army of the Potomac," p. 355.[1])

It is only in keeping with the haphazard character of the whole battle that the capture of a point of such strategic importance should not have been taken advantage of by the Confederates. It remains, however, no less a proud memory for the officers and men of the Third Brigade that their prowess gained for the Confederate general a position where "Meade's entire line might have been taken in reverse."

But if the Confederates did not realize what they had gained, the Federals were fully aware what *they* had lost. Accordingly, they spent the night massing troops and artillery for an effort to regain their works. "During the night," says Swinton (page 356), "a powerful artillery was accumulated against the point entered by the enemy." Through the long hours of the night we heard the rumbling of their guns, and thought they were evacuating the hill. The first streak of day-

---

[1] Bates is of the same opinion: "Had he known the advantage which was open to him, and all that we now know, he might, with the troops he had, have played havoc with the trains, and set the whole army in retreat; but he was ignorant of the prize which was within his grasp." — Page 140.

light revealed our mistake. It was scarcely dawn (the writer of this had just lain down to sleep after a night in the saddle) when their artillery opened upon us, at a range of about 500 yards, a terrific and galling fire, to which we had no means of replying, as our guns could not be dragged up that steep and rugged ascent.[1] Then, a little after sunrise, their infantry moved forward in heavy force to attack us. "The troops of the 12th Corps," says Swinton, "had returned from the left, and the divisions of Williams and Geary, aided by Shaler's brigade, of the Sixth Corps, entered upon a severe struggle to regain the lost position of the line."[2] They drove in our skirmishers, but could not dislodge us from the works we had captured, although these were commanded in part by the works on the crest of the hill to our right, whence a galling fire was poured into our ranks. Next a strong effort was made to take us in flank, and I well remember that at one time our line resembled three sides of a pentagon, the left side being composed of some other brigade, centre and right composed of our own brigade, which thus occupied the most advanced position toward the crest of the hill.[3] About this time, I think,

[1] "To one conversant with the ground, it is now apparent why the enemy did not reply. The creek, the forest, and the steep acclivities made it utterly impossible for him to move up his guns, and this circumstance contributed to the weakness of his position and the futility of his occupation of this part of the line. . . . But, though he fought with a determined bravery well worthy the name of the old-time leader, yet he gained no ground and had sustained terrible losses."

[2] The enemy was evidently before us in immense numbers, and posted behind two lines of breastworks. To resist them we had but one division, which was subsequently strengthened by the brigades of Smith and Daniel. — *Extract from a letter.*

[3] "The crest of the hill to the right was still more difficult of approach,

word came to General Steuart that the men's ammunition was almost exhausted. One of his staff immediately took three men and went on foot to the wagons, distant about a mile and a quarter, and brought up two boxes of cartridges. "We emptied each box into a blanket and swung the blanket on a rail, and so carried it to the front." It was now, I think, about half-past nine, and ever since four o'clock the fire of the enemy had been almost continuous, at times tremendous.[1] Professor Jacobs says, "The battle raged furiously, and was maintained with desperate obstinacy on both sides." He goes on to speak of the "terrible slaughter" of our men. General Howard says: "I went over the ground five years after the battle, and marks of the struggle were still to be observed — the moss on the rocks was discolored in hundreds of places where the bullets had struck; the trees, as cut off, lopped down, or shivered, were still there; stumps and trees were

and from it the enemy were able to enfilade our whole line. . . . The struggle for the hill now became more and more fierce. The enemy endeavored to drive us out of the works. They attacked us in front and in flank, and opened a terrific cannonading upon us from a battery posted about 500 yards off. . . . On the right and left flank, where our lines were almost perpendicular to the front line, there were no breastworks, and the struggle was very fierce and bloody. Our men maintained their position, however, and received reinforcements." (*Extract from a letter.*)   The Third North Carolina was on the right, and suffered most heavily during this part of the battle, so that but a handful were left to participate in the final charge.

[1] "As the day wore on, the heat from the fire and smoke of battle, and the scorching of the July sun, became so intense as to be almost past endurance. Men were completely exhausted in the progress of the struggle, and had to be often relieved; but revived by fresh air and a little period of rest, again returned to the front." (Bates, p. 142.) No such refreshing rest had our brave men. They were never relieved for a moment during all that seven-hours' unintermitting fire of which General Kane speaks.

perforated with holes where leaden balls had since been dug out, and remnants of the rough breastworks remained. I did not wonder that General Geary, who was in the thickest of this fight, thought the main battle of Gettysburg must have been fought there." [1] (*Atlantic Monthly*, July, 1876, p. 66.)

But all the efforts of the enemy failed to dislodge us. Unassisted, the Third Brigade held the position they had won the night before. Several writers speak of Johnson being heavily reinforced. It may be. But I feel sure that that far-advanced line of earthworks into which Steuart had driven his brigade like a wedge the night before was held by him alone through all those terrible hours on the morning of the 3d of July. The reinforcements which came to Johnson must have been employed on the flanks or on some other portion of the line than that occupied by us.[2]

[1] Whitelaw Reid wrote as follows: "From 4 to 5 there was heavy cannonading also from our batteries nearest the contested points. . . . The rebels made no reply. . . . The musketry crash continued with unparalleled tenacity and vehemence." (Bates, p. 142.) Later in the morning he says: "The batteries began to open again on points along our outer line. They were evidently playing on what had been Slocum's line of yesterday. The rebels then were still in our rifle-pits. Presently the battery on Slocum's Hill . . . opened too, *aiming apparently in the same direction.* Other batteries along the inner line, just to the left of the Baltimore pike [McAllister's Hill] followed the signal, and one after another opened up, till every little crest between Slocum's headquarters and Cemetery Hill began belching its thunder. . . . *Still no artillery response from the rebels.*" — Page 143.

[2] My diary says that Johnson was "*subsequently*" reinforced by the brigades of Smith and Daniel. Probably this was just before the last fatal charge. I remember the latter brigade coming up at that time. I did not see it before, and I did not see Smith's brigade at all. Or both brigades may have been employed on the right and left flanks at an earlier hour. I would only state it as my conviction that the *captured works were held by the men who captured them from*

Then came General Ewell's order to assume the offensive and assail the crest of Culp's Hill, on our right. My diary says that both General Steuart and General Daniel, who now came up with his brigade to support the movement, strongly disapproved of making the assault. And well might they despair of success in the face of such difficulties. The works to be stormed ran almost at right angles to those we occupied.[1] Moreover, there was a double line of entrenchments, one above the other, and each filled with troops. In moving to the attack we were exposed to enfilading fire from the woods on our left flank, besides the double line of fire which we had to face in front, and a battery of artillery posted on a hill to our left rear opened upon us at short range.[2] What wonder, then, if Steuart was reluctant to lead his men into such a slaughter-pen, from which he saw there could be no issue but death and defeat! But though he remonstrated, he gallantly obeyed without delay the orders he received, giving the command, "Left face," and afterwards, "File right." He made his men leap the breastworks and form in line of battle on the other side at right angles, nearly, to their previous position, galled all the

9 *P.M., July 2d, to* 10 *A.M., July 3d, and by none others.* During the last hour of their occupation (10 to 11) the *right* of the works was held by the brigade of General Daniel.

[1] They were confident of their ability to sweep him away and take the whole Union line in reverse. Fortunately, Greene had caused his flank to be fortified by a very heavy work, which the make of the ground favored, extending some distance at right angles to his main line. — Bates' " Gettysburg," p. 139.

[2] Professor Jacobs seems to allude to this when he says: "In this work of death, a battery of artillery placed on a hill to the right of the Baltimore turnpike, and some distance south of the cemetery, was found to have performed a prominent part." — Page 40.

time by a brisk fire from the enemy.   Then drawing his sword, he gave the command, "Charge bayonets!" and moved forward on foot with his men into the jaws of death.   On swept the gallant little brigade, the Third North Carolina on the right of the line, next the Second Maryland, then the three Virginia regiments (10th, 23d, and 37th), with the First North Carolina on the extreme left.   Its ranks had been sadly thinned, and its energies greatly depleted by those six fearful hours of battle that morning; but its nerve and spirit were undiminished.   Soon, however, the left and centre were checked and then repulsed, probably by the severe flank fire from the woods; and the small remnant of the Third North Carolina, with the stronger Second Maryland (I do not recall the banners of any other regiment), were far in advance of the rest of the line.   On they pressed to within about twenty or thirty paces of the works— a small but gallant band of heroes daring to attempt what could not be done by flesh and blood.[1]

The end soon came.   We were beaten back to the line from which we had advanced with terrible loss, and in much confusion, but the enemy did not make a

[1] Since writing the above I have met with the following account of this memorable charge in Bates' book (page 144): "Suddenly the quiet was broken by a yell bursting from thousands of lungs, and the next instant their gray lines emerged in sight dashing madly on. . . . They had scarcely come into easy musket range when the men in blue along the line sprang to their feet and poured in a deliberate volley. The shock was terrible.   The on-coming force was staggered, and for a moment sought shelter behind trees and rocks; but obedient to the voices of their officers, they struggled on, *some of the most desperate coming within twenty paces of the Union front.*   'It cannot be denied,' says Kane, 'that they behaved courageously.'   They did what the most resolute could do, but it was all in vain. . . . Broken and well-nigh annihilated, the survivors of the charge staggered back, leaving the ground strewn with their dead and desperately wounded."

counter charge. By the strenuous efforts of the officers of the line and of the staff, order was restored,
and we re-formed in the breastworks from which we
had emerged, there to be again exposed to an artillery
fire exceeding in violence that of the early morning.
It remains only to say that, like Pickett's men later
in the day, this single brigade was hurled unsupported
against the enemy's works. Daniel's brigade remained
in the breastworks during and after the charge, and
neither from that command nor from any other had we
any support. Of course it is to be presumed that
General Daniel acted in obedience to orders.[1] We

[1] "As soon as we were unmasked a most terrific fire was opened
upon us from three directions. In front, on a rising ground heavily
wooded, the enemy were posted in two lines behind breastworks, one
above the other, so that both lines fired upon us at once. On the left
was a piece of woods, from which the enemy's sharpshooters opened a
very galling fire, raking our whole line. This decided the failure of
our attempt to storm their works, for the regiments of the left first
halted (while the right of the line advanced), and then fell back. . . .
Still we pressed on. General Steuart, Captain Williamson, and I
were all on the right centre, where were the Second Maryland and eight
men of the Third North Carolina. Oh! it was a gallant band. We had
our sabres drawn, and were cheering on the men, but there was little
need of it. Their gallantry did not avail, and their noble blood was
spilled in vain. . . . It was as if the sickle of Death had passed along the
line and mown down the noblest and the bravest. Major Goldsborough fell (as we supposed), mortally wounded. That brave officer
and noble gentleman, Captain Murray, fell dead. Friends dropped
all around me, and lay writhing on the ground. . . . It was more than
men could endure, and reluctantly they commenced falling back.
Then our task was to prevent a rout, for the brigade was terribly
cut up and the men much demoralized. Behind some rocks we rallied
the scattered regiments and made a stand. Finally we took our old
position behind the breastworks, supported by Daniel's brigade.
Here we lay for about an hour under the most furious infantry and
artillery fire I have ever experienced, but without much loss." (*Extract
from a letter describing the battle.*) I give it just as I find it, adding that
if the tattered battle flag of the Third North Carolina was followed by

remained in this breastwork after the charge about an hour before we finally abandoned the Federal entrenchments and retired to the foot of the hill. The Federal historians say we were *driven* from our position. Thus Swinton affirms that "it was carried by a charge of Geary's division." This statement I deny as an eyewitness and sharer in the conflict to the close, and as one of the staff who assisted in carrying out the order withdrawing the troops to the base of the hill. It was a very difficult thing to withdraw the fragments of a shattered brigade down a steep hill in the face of the enemy, and I have a vivid recollection of our apprehensions of the result of such a movement. But it was done, not before a charge of the enemy, but in obedience to orders, and we were not pursued, nor were the works occupied by the Federals until we reached Rock creek, at the base of the hill.

A few of our men on our left, rather than incur the danger of retiring down the hill under that very heavy fire, remained behind in the entrenchments and gave themselves up. The base of the hill reached, skirmishers were thrown out, and we remained on the west side of Rock creek till 11.30 P.M., when we retired silently and unmolested. I find the following record in my diary referring to the time when we retired to the foot of the hill: "New troops were brought on, and fighting continued until now (five P.M.)." This must refer to picket firing.

It only remains that I give such statement of our losses as my materials enable me to make. Unfortunately, I have returns only from three regiments re-

only a handful, it was because they had already suffered more heavily than any other regiment.

corded. In the Tenth Virginia (which I think was very small) the loss was (killed, wounded, and missing) 64. This I have not been able to verify. The Third North Carolina lost, according to my memoranda (killed, wounded, and missing) 207 out of 312 men. Dr. Wood, of that regiment, writes that this corresponds very nearly to statistics in his possession. The Second Maryland lost, according to my notes, 206 men. Other estimates (by Colonel Herbert and Major Goldsborough) put their loss, one at 250, the other at 222. One company, that of the lamented William H. Murray, carried into battle 92 men and lost 18 killed, 37 wounded; total 55. Another estimate (by the orderly sergeant of Company A) puts it at 62. My diary states that the brigade mustered about 2,200 before the battle. At Hagerstown, on the 8th of July, about 1,200 men reported for duty. It is probable that others subsequently came in, as I cannot think the loss was so great as 1,000 men, in the face of the following entry in my diary, July 4th: "Total loss in the brigade (killed, wounded, and missing), 680."

There were probably many stragglers on the march to Williamsport, some of whom may have been taken prisoners; but many no doubt afterward came in. The entire loss might be put at 800.[1]

---

[1] "What a field was this! For three hours of the previous evening, and seven of the morning, had the most terrible elements of destruction known to modern warfare been wielded with a might and dexterity rarely if ever paralleled. The woods in which the battle had been fought was torn and rent with shells and solid shot and pierced with innumerable Minie balls. Trees were broken off and splintered, and that entire forest, where the battle raged most furiously, was, on the following year, leafless, the stately but mute occupants having yielded up their lives with those whom they overshadowed." (Bates' "Gettysburg," p. 145.) And speaking of the state of the hill on the 4th:

These fearful losses sufficiently indicate the character of the work those brave men were called on to do. The Light Brigade at Balaklava lost about one-third of their number (247 men out of 673 officers and men) in their famous charge. That, indeed, was over in twenty minutes, while these two regiments sustained their loss of one-half and two-thirds during a conflict of ten hours duration. But at least we may claim for the men of the Third Brigade that they maintained a long and unequal contest with a valor and a constancy worthy of the best troops.

"We came upon numberless forms clad in gray, either stark and stiff or else still weltering in their blood. . . . Turning whichever way we chose, the eye rested upon human forms lying in all imaginable positions. . . . We were surprised at the accuracy as well as the bloody results of our fire. It was indeed dreadful to witness." — Id. p. 145.

CHAPTER XVII

IN the autumn of 1863, I tendered my resignation
as first lieutenant and aide-de-camp, in order to prepare myself for ordination to the ministry of the Protestant Episcopal Church. This was in fulfilment of
a resolution recorded in my diary, Jan. 1, 1863, that
if the war did not terminate in the approaching campaign, I would not feel justified in longer delaying my
preparation for the ministry, to which I had devoted
myself when I was sixteen years of age. My action
was stimulated by my deep sense of the pressing need
of chaplains in the army, and my conviction that
the opportunities for usefulness therein were very
great.

In tendering my resignation to Gen. S. Cooper,
adjutant and inspector-general, at Richmond, I stated
that I had been "looking forward to the Christian
ministry for the last five years, and for several months
had been a candidate for orders in the Protestant
Episcopal Church." I added that it was "my desire
to commence my studies at once at the seminary in
order to be prepared for ordination the ensuing spring,
at which time it is my purpose to reënter the service
in the capacity of chaplain." And I further stated
that I was not "actuated by a desire to avoid duty in
the field, but by the wish to fit myself for a position

in which I shall be able to render the army more efficient service than at present."

Brigadier-General Steuart, my chief, endorsed my
application in the following terms:

"Approved and respectfully forwarded. I appointed
Lieutenant McKim my A. D. C. on account of the faithful
and efficient manner in which he performed his duty as a
soldier in the First Maryland Regiment. He acted most
gallantly at Cross Keys, Winchester, and Gettysburg, and
has always discharged his duties faithfully. I regret to lose
his services, but consider the reasons he assigns sufficient,
having been cognizant of the facts.

" (Signed)
"GEO. H. STEUART,
"Brig.- Gen."

Major-General Johnson also approved my application, and finally General Lee himself, and accordingly
it was accepted by the President, to take effect Sept. 1,
1863.

I left the army with a heavy heart. Though the
step I had taken was dictated by a high sense of duty,
it cost me a painful effort. Indeed I can truly say that
it was a severer test of my courage to turn my back
on my general and my brother officers, and those brave
soldiers whom I had led, than to face the Federal breastworks on Culp's Hill. I had, however, every evidence
that both officers and men respected my motives and
understood my purpose. It had been generally known
among them that I was a candidate for orders, and I
had so often conducted religious service in camp and
even on the battle field that it was no surprise to them
that I should now go forward to the consummation of
my purpose to enter the ministry. But, in spite of this,

I could not overcome the thought that my retirement from the army looked like the desertion of my comrades and of the cause.[1]

My studies were conducted at Staunton, Virginia, under the Rev. Wm. Sparrow, D.D., dean of the Theological Seminary of Virginia. He was the only professor, but he was a host in himself — a fine Greek and Hebrew scholar, a theologian of great learning, and a profound and original thinker, to whom Phillips Brooks felt deeply indebted. In Greek and Latin I had graduated at the University of Virginia; also in moral philosophy; so that Hebrew and apologetics, with church history and theology proper, were now my chief concern. The previous winter I had studied alone Horne's "Introduction to the Bible." Under these circumstances and under such an inspiring teacher as Dr. Sparrow, I was able, by diligence, to fit myself to pass my examinations for deacon's orders, after eight months study, and was ordered deacon by Bishop John Johns, of Virginia, May 11th, 1864, in Trinity

[1] In a letter to my mother about this time I wrote: "Though I shrank from the imputation which *some* would probably cast upon such a course at *such a crisis*, — duty was imperative even more than *honor!* — God has made the way easy for me, and instead of opposition and misconstruction, I have been astonished to find how generally my course has been approved and my motives appreciated by my friends. General Steuart in his endorsement of my resignation gives me the credit of 'having performed my duties faithfully.' . . . .

"It was approved by my division commander and by Lieutenant-General Ewell, and also by General Lee, and finally by the President, to take effect September 1, 1863. I tell you this, my mother, that you may know that, though your son has left the field, his escutcheon is still untarnished by the imputation of fear. Tell papa that I recollect that he did not use to think me a brave boy. I do not think I am naturally so, but I have moral courage at least, and my confidence in God has taken away all fear of death, when in the discharge of my duty."

Church, Staunton, Virginia. I had several fellow-students, Wm. F. Gardner, Edward H. Ingle, and Horace Hayden. During the winter I gave lessons in French and Latin to the daughters of the Rev. Richard H. Phillips, my father-in-law.

Such spare time as I could command was largely spent in the hospitals in work among the sick and wounded soldiers. That was before the discovery of antiseptic surgery, and consequently the sufferings of the wounded were far greater than would now be the case, and the atmosphere of the hospitals was often painfully offensive, making work there very trying to the nerves. The devotion of the women of the South to the sick and the wounded was sublimely beautiful. They never flinched or wearied in their blessed labors to alleviate the sufferings of the poor fellows who were wounded or stricken with disease. Indeed the community was like one family. Such was the unity of feeling, such the common devotion to the cause, that it was like the communal life in the early Church. Whatever the people had, of means, or of comforts, or of luxuries, was freely poured out for the brave fellows who were suffering in the hospitals (many of which were churches or chapels converted to that use) for the Confederacy. It might almost have been said, "The multitude were of one heart and one soul; and none of them said that aught of the things which he possessed was his own, but they had all things common." History will hardly show a nearer approximation to that primitive communal unity than was seen in the South, and perhaps especially in Virginia, which was the chief theatre of the war. In this unity and solidarity there was large compensation for the suffering and the destitution which became more and more acute as the war dragged its slow length along.

On the 10th of Feb., 1864, I was licensed by Bishop Johns "to perform the service and deliver addresses and exhortations as authorized by Canon III, § 3, Title I, of the Protestant Episcopal Church in the Confederate States."

Under this authority I did service in the hospitals and elsewhere, and had practice in extempore speaking, which was a useful preparation for my work in the army.

I find the following list of some of the text-books which we used under Dr. Sparrow's direction:

Conant's Gesenius Hebrew Grammar.

Gesenius Hebrew Lexicon.

Hebrew Bible.

Greek Testament.

Paley's Evidences.

Butler's Analogy and Sermons.

D'Aubigné's History of the Reformation.

Mosheim's Ecclesiastical History.

Schaff's Church History.

I had the use of the excellent library of the Rev. Richard H. Phillips, my wife's father, and the great advantage of his counsel and experience.   Dr. Sparrow required of us an essay on some topic, assigned by him once in two weeks, and later we began the composition of sermons, of which I had a store of, I think, twelve, when I began my duties as chaplain.   This was a very small "barrel," but it was of little consequence because *written* sermons were not the proper "ammunition" for use in the army.   "The paper" was found to be a non-conductor, and words straight from the heart were the only "arrows" that seemed to go to the mark.

I may here set down an anecdote relating to Dr. Sparrow's preaching. After a sermon by him in Trinity Church, Staunton, three gentlemen stood in the church yard and discussed the preacher. One of them, I think Judge Sheffey, said, "Well, Dr. Sparrow can certainly dive down deeper—" "Yes," interrupted Col. John Baldwin, "and stay under longer" — "Yes," added Bishop Wilmer, "and come up drier!"

Nevertheless, all thoughtful men found him an inspiring and stimulating preacher.

As soon as possible after my ordination, I set out for the army, having received what I supposed were satisfactory assurances that I would be appointed chaplain of Major Chew's battalion of artillery, which was camped at that time near Richmond.

I left Staunton May 30th, mounted on a beautiful little blooded bay horse, "Charlie," of the then famous "Messenger" stock. He had previous to the war belonged to my wife, but had joined the army, like all good Virginians, and I had discovered him by accident, and had persuaded his owner to trade him for my "war-horse" Roy, a showy animal of "Morgan" stock. He agreed to the exchange on condition that I would not ride him in the army, but send him home to my wife. That was just what I wished to do, as I had so often heard her regret that she had consented to part with him. So on our return from Gettysburg, I found a soldier who had gone barefooted through the campaign, and obtaining a furlough for him to visit his family in Augusta County, sent the horse by him to Staunton. Weeks passed before "Charlie" was delivered in Staunton, and when he arrived he was in such a deplorable condition that none of the family recognized him. The soldier had taken him home and hitched him to the plough, and so overworked and misused the beautiful little animal that he was unfit for use for many months, and when at length he was partially restored to condition it was found that he was almost totally blind.

This unfitted him for my wife's use, but I thought I could manage to ride him in the army, for the reason that he had such splendid action that the risk of stumbling was reduced to a minimum.

He carried me well to the army, making twenty-three miles a day the first two days, and thirty-three miles a day the third and fourth day. Unfortunately, as my diary states, he "shied into the canal," but I managed to avoid going in with him. I have no recollection of how I got him out. At length on June 5th I rode into the camp of Major Chew's battalion artillery. The same day, in the evening, I held service "and had a large and attentive audience and made an address suggested by the hymn, "A charge to keep I have."

I was now happy in the belief that I had achieved my ambition, — I was commissioned and equipped for my work as a minister of Jesus Christ in the army that I loved so well. I had made a propitious beginning of my service as chaplain, and could now go forward and, by God's blessing, preach and live the Gospel to good purpose.

But I was to be disappointed. I learned on investigation that formal application for my appointment as chaplain of the battalion had never been made, and Major Chew informed me that until I received the appointment, I could not draw rations or forage. He proceeded at once to make the formal application to the Department, but, pending its action, I had no *status* in the army, and was obliged with great chagrin to leave camp and await my commission as chaplain. More than a month elapsed before I heard from the Department, and the answer was that Mr. Seddon, Secretary of War, decided that the law made no provision for the appointment of chaplains to battalions, but only to regiments, and therefore the application of Major Chew could not be granted.

Col. Thomas Munford, of the Second Virginia Cavalry, Fitz Lee's brigade, now made application for my appointment as chaplain of his regiment, but it was not till August 23d that I finally received my commission, and was qualified to join Colonel Munford's command.

During the interim, however, between my ordination and my entrance on my duties as chaplain I was not idle. I preached frequently in Trinity Church, Staunton, and elsewhere. For example, my diary notes that on August 4th, August 5th, August 6th, August 7th, and August 8th, I preached at the Virginia Hospital, Staunton, to the sick and wounded soldiers. And again, at Rawley Springs, I preached four times in one week.

At this time it was my habit to translate daily one chapter of the Epistle to the Romans, and then render ten verses back from English into Greek.[1]

I will here note an event of painful interest to my

---

[1] It may be amusing to note the following:

"June 24, 1864—Hired servant girl Milly till December 25th, agreeing to furnish her one linsey dress, one cotton dress, one pair shoes, etc., etc., together with board and medical attendance."

immediate family. About June 12th, my father-in-law, Rev. Richard H. Phillips, for so many years the highly esteemed and beloved principal of the Virginia Female Institute, was captured in the mountains of Nelson County, Virginia, and carried off a prisoner with Hunter's army to Ohio. When the Institute closed the first year of the war, Mr. Phillips had devoted himself to the work of supplying the army with cloth made in local mills, and had been commissioned captain in the Commissary Department. Upon the approach of Major-General Hunter's army he had packed up the commissary stores in wagons and sought safety for them across the Blue Ridge in Nelson County. Here he was captured, together with all the stores under his charge. I suffered, too, a loss there, for he had taken my uniform which I had worn as Steuart's aide, "for safe keeping," and this was carried off by Hunter's raiders. I had also left with him a pair of saddle-bags, which contained about half of my little store of sermons,—a precious commodity in my eyes. My friend Rev. Dr. Norton suffered a similar loss by the same raiding army when it visited Lexington. Some years after the war he attended service in some Western city, and heard one of his own sermons delivered from the pulpit by the rector of the parish. It must have been a great temptation to the clergyman who had become possessed of those sermons to use them, for Dr. Geo. Norton was a pungent and powerful preacher. I never heard that my sermons received a similar compliment, — but none the less I mourned the loss of a considerable part of my small capital.

Rev. Mr. Phillips was compelled by his captors to march on foot all the long way from Arrington through

Virginia and West Virginia to the Ohio River. It was a forced march, for General Hunter was hastening to make good his escape. The weather was very hot and oppressive, and the fatigue told seriously on a man of Mr. Phillips' age. He was obliged to subsist much of the way on parched corn, and was at one time so famished that he was fain to pick up the green onion tops thrown away by the Federal soldiers. He was kept a prisoner in Camp Chase for ten months, and there endured much unnecessary hardship, gratuitously inflicted by the prison authorities in retaliation for alleged cruelties on Northern prisoners of war in the South. When he was exchanged and returned home, he had aged twenty years and was scarcely recognized by his family.

During his confinement in prison Rev. Mr. Phillips did very effective spiritual work among his fellow prisoners both by preaching and by private personal influence. He was able to state, in a letter written about Christmas, that swearing among the men had ceased entirely. To his high character as a Christian man, he added the charm of culture and great geniality.

As instances of the rigorous treatment alluded to above, I recall his telling me that the rations issued to the prisoners were so scant that he had repeatedly known some of the men to cook three days rations and consume it all at one meal, and go without anything the rest of the three days. He also mentioned that spoiled fish were issued to the prisoners on more than one occasion.

No doubt the personality of the particular officer in command of the prisons, both North and South, was often the determining factor in the treatment meted out to the prisoners.

FIRST EXPERIENCE AS CHAPLAIN IN THE FIELD

It was on August 30th, 1864, that I left Staunton to report for duty to Col. Thomas T. Munford, as chaplain of the Second Virginia Cavalry, then camped near Winchester. My beautiful little bay, blind though he was, carried me at a good pace down the valley, 25 miles the first day, 32 the second, 35 the third. So on September 2d I found myself at last installed in my new duties, so eagerly looked forward to.

The very next day the brigade of Gen. Fitz Lee was ordered out to meet the enemy. I mounted my horse, and took my place as a matter of course in the column as it marched. This was a surprise to many of the men, and one called out to me, "Hello, Parson, are you going with us into battle?" "Oh, yes," I replied with a laugh, "I'm an old infantry soldier, — I don't mind these little cavalry skirmishes." Then rose in his stirrups a rough trooper from the backwoods, and brandishing his sabre over his head exclaimed, "That's right, Paason. You stick to us, and we'll stick to you!" I recall his appearance to this day; he had long yellow hair almost to his shoulders, his complexion was sallow, and his eyes were so light that they almost looked white. From that moment he was my fast friend. Often when he returned from picket he would bring me something in his haversack, a peach, or a pear, or some other unusual delicacy.

It was a fine body of men, that Second Virginia Cavalry, made up as follows: Co. A from Bedford County; Co. B from Lynchburg; Co. C from Botetourt County; Co. D from Franklin County; Co. E from Amherst County; Co. F and Co. G from Bedford County; Co. H from Appomattox County; Co. I from Campbell County; Co. K from Albemarle County.

I found among the officers some very congenial spirits, and the rank and file were always ready to respond to my efforts. Very soon our relations were established on a cordial basis. Plenty of marching, plenty of common hardships, and not a little fighting, quickly made us good friends. There was some fighting that first day of our acquaintance. Somewhere on the field of expected battle, I conducted a religious service ("after a severe struggle with my diffidence") and "addressed the men on the spur of the moment on God's providence and the necessity of depending on Him." It was on Friday, September 3d.

My diary shows that I established the rule of having prayers in the regiment daily, both morning and evening, and that I generally made a short address. This would be prevented by a heavy rain, but a "drizzling rain" appears to have been no obstacle. "Throwing up breastworks" would hinder the service, but it was held even on days when the regiment was on the march, — of course after making camp or bivouack. It appears also that the attendance was "very good." I rose regularly about five, sometimes half an hour earlier, groomed and fed my horse, and was early ready for any duty. If the regiment went on picket, prayers would first be held, unless it was very early. I believe the morning service was usually before breakfast and the evening service at sunset, though sometimes, especially on Sunday, it would be after dark, for I well remember once, while I was speaking, the fire died down and went out, and I could no longer see the faces of the men, and for that reason my address came to a speedy end.

GEN. THOMAS T. MUNFORD

I was fortunate in having the sympathy and active aid, in all this, of our colonel, Tom Munford, a gallant and skilful officer (who served the cause with unwavering fidelity to the last day and the last shot at Appomattox), and also of his adjutant, Samuel Griffin, — "Tip," as we always called him.

As soon as practicable after joining the regiment, I secured lists of the men in each company who were communicants of any church. I then had a mass meeting of communicants, and sought to strengthen their resolution to be faithful to their profession, and steadfast in their religious duties, and active in Christian work among their comrades. I prepared a series of resolutions along those lines and they were adopted by the meeting. My next effort was to build up a choir for the better rendering of the hymns at our services, and I had choir meetings when possible.

The following extracts illustrate our life at this period:

"Thursday, Sept. 15th. — Morning prayers at seven: large attendance. Preached at sunset on the Fall and its Consequences. Very large audience." "Friday, 16th. — Evening service at sunset and address on Abraham's Intercession for Sodom as inciting Christians to pray for the country. Very large attendance. Singing improved." "Sept. 17th, Saturday. — Held meeting of Christians at nine and after prayer and deliberation appointed committee to report to-morrow (Sunday) at three o'clock. As chairman I was appointed to draft resolutions. . . . Usual large attendance at evening prayer."

And this extract shows how willing the men were to attend service under difficulties:

"Sunday, Sept. 18. — Ordered off at daylight. Held

11 o'clock service and preached on John iii. 5 [apparently after the regiment had reached its destination]. Hughes, our blacksmith, came to me for advice and comfort. Presented claims of the Episcopal Church at some length to Cunningham of Co. D, who has never joined any church, being a recent convert. Returned to old camp at 3.30 P.M. Preached again at night on John iii. 5. Committee approved my resolutions."

(Two services, two sermons, two marches, and two conferences in one day.)

I found these sturdy men very ready to discuss the great question of religion, and open to conviction. Even the gayest and the most seemingly thoughtless would listen with deep attention. Danger and death were at their right hand very often, and this gave emphasis to the counsels and warnings I addressed to them both in public and private.

CHAPTER XVIII

WITHIN a little more than two weeks after I joined Colonel Munford's regiment, the army under Major-General Early entered upon a very active campaign in the valley of Virginia. That officer had moved into Maryland in July and had pushed his advance to the very suburbs of Washington, creating great alarm among the authorities there. It was thought at the time by many that a commander with more dash than Early — Stonewall Jackson, for example — would have attempted the capture of the city, and with much probability of success. But it is doubtful if General Lee's instructions to his lieutenant contemplated so bold an enterprise with a force no larger than that which he had under his command. The purpose of the expedition was to threaten Washington and draw off troops from Lee's front for its protection.

Gen. Phil Sheridan had accordingly been sent into the valley with a strong and well equipped army to oppose any further advance by Early. These able officers were thus pitted against each other, but the Federal general had greatly the advantage in numbers and in the armament and equipment of his troops. His cavalry, for instance, was armed with the repeating Spenser rifle, while the Confederate cavalry had only the Sharp's rifle at best. Often during this campaign did I keenly feel the inequality of the conflict between our brave fellows and their antagonists in this respect. It was hard to see the Bluecoats firing eight rounds without reloading, while the boys in gray could fire but one. But this was not the worst. Some of Early's force were armed with only the long cumbrous sporting rifle — utterly unsuited for mounted men. This circumstance was to produce disastrous results at a critical moment, as we shall see.

Between the 19th of September and the 18th of October — less than a month — Munford's regiment participated in eleven engagements, three of which were pitched battles, viz., Winchester, Fisher's Hill, and Cedar Creek.

The third battle of Winchester was fought on Sept. 19th, 1864. Fitz Lee's cavalry brigade was employed first on one flank, then on the other, and did some very effective work, especially in covering General Early's retreat. The defeat was a great surprise to us, for we had seen the enemy driven back along a great part of the line. I particularly recall a brilliant charge of Rodes' division, which seemed at the time to be the *coup de grace*. Ordered just then over to the right flank, we were astonished later to learn that our left had given way, and that the disorder had extended so far that a retreat was ordered. This was about sunset, the battle having continued all day. Seeking the cause of this sudden change in the aspect of affairs, I learned that a part of General Imboden's mounted command, armed with those long, cumbrous, muzzle-loading rifles, utterly unfit for mounted men, had given way in disorder and rushed back pell-mell through our infantry line, which was thus broken and thrown into confusion, not by the enemy, but by that mass of ill-armed and half-organized men. The Federals, taking advantage of this breach in our line, charged vigorously, and so our almost victory was turned into defeat.

It was now that Fitz Lee's cavalry did very important service in checking the Federal pursuit and covering Early's retreat. On the left flank we were dismounted and charged on foot, "driving the enemy's cavalry in confusion." On the retreat they tried to outflank us at Hollingsworth's Mills, "but our brigade charged beautifully with sabres and discomfited them." At one time during the day our men were in breastworks, under circumstances which I do not now distinctly recall, but I think it was when checkmating an attempt to turn our right. I think they must have been light intrenchments thrown up in haste, and occupied by our men dismounted. After remaining there some time with our men under the enemy's shelling, I withdrew to the place where the led horses were, one hundred yards in the rear, and there ministered as best I could to one of our poor fellows, who was almost cut in two by a shell. It was one of the most awful sights I ever witnessed during the war.

This was the first time the Confederates had been defeated at Winchester. Twice previously, in 1862 and in 1863, victory perched on their banners here. It was a discouraging blow, especially when success had seemed in their grasp till the unfortunate occurrence I have related late in the day. After a very harassing and fatiguing night march, we reached Front Royal at eight A.M. of the 20th, having had one hour's sleep, and no food for twenty-four hours. In the battle of the day previous I had discovered that it took a good deal more nerve to go through a fight as a non-combatant than as a soldier. As a staff officer in battle I had always had plenty to do to occupy my mind, and very little time to reflect on the danger of the situation. As a chaplain on the firing line with the men, I had nothing to do but to sit on my horse and be shot at (unarmed, of course), waiting for a call to attend some wounded man. Having passed through both experiences, I can say that the role of a chaplain at the fiery front takes more nerve "by a jugful" than that of a staff officer. Yet I am certain that the chaplain who sticks to his men through thick and thin will have tenfold influence over them for that reason.

In this connection I am reminded of an amusing occurrence. One of our chaplains, Rev. Dr. L——, who had fallen heir to Gen. Stonewall Jackson's sorrel mare, was riding at the head of our column as we marched down the valley, when suddenly we ran into the enemy's pickets, and the rifles began to crack at a very lively rate, whereupon the aforesaid chaplain turned the sorrel's head the other way, and began to pace rapidly to the rear. Just then General Early appeared, and seeing Dr. L——, he called out in that high-pitched drawling voice which was peculiar to him, "Hello, Parson L——, where are you going? You've been praying for forty years to get to heaven, and right down this road there's a first-rate chance to go there quick, and you won't take it!"

After an interval of one day active operations were resumed. September 21st, at Front Royal, our cavalry had quite a severe engagement with the enemy. There were charges and countercharges made gallantly on both sides. Several of our men were killed and a number wounded, among them the captain of Co. A and the captain of Co. K. At length our brigade retired before superior force. All through this campaign it was most aggravating to see the Federal troopers using their repeating carbines, while our brave fellows must reload after each shot, — eight shots to our one they had. The same day, at eventide, five miles from Front Royal, there was an artillery duel, in which the gunners of our brigade "did beautiful practice — blew up one of their caissons, and silenced one of their batteries."

We were slowly retreating down the valley, and on the 22d we had taken up a position at Milford, twelve miles from Luray. The enemy attacked us, but we held him off all day, losing some of our men in the fight. We were so early and so busily engaged that we had "neither breakfast nor dinner" that day. However, we had a "good supper."

This was another *dies nefasta* for our little army, for General Early was again defeated at Fisher's Hill.

Once more I suffered a great personal loss, for my dear friend Capt. George Williamson, serving on General Gordon's staff, was killed at Fisher's Hill, while bravely, but, as it seems, rashly, exposing himself on the picket line.

This gallant soldier and accomplished gentleman was the son of Gen. Geo. W. Williamson, a resident at that time of the city of New York, where his other son, David B. Williamson, was engaged in the practice of law. His uncle, Mr. Chas. A. Williamson, was a resident of Baltimore. There were few young men in the Southern Army possessed of such talents and such personal charm as George Williamson. He was widely read, and his culture was refined and broadened by travel and by intercourse with the world. Yet he was unspoiled and "unspotted by the world," — a man of inflexible principle, governed in all his actions by a high sense of duty, gracious, courteous, knightly in bearing, one of whom it could be truly said,

> "His strength was as the strength of ten
> Because his heart was pure."

To all these virtues was added the crown of a Christian faith and a Christian life.

I have just been reading again with reverential emotion a letter which he addressed to me on August 1st, seven weeks before he fell. On the envelope are written these words, "To be opened only after my death." He had a strong presentiment that he would not survive the campaign. In the intimacy of our circle of friends he would say that officers in the Confederate Army must not spare themselves — they must inspire the men by their example — more and more this was demanded of them now that the struggle was becoming more difficult and more desperate, — it was our only hope of success. Noble gentleman! He lived up to his faith and died a victim to it.

In the letter he entrusted to me the fulfilment of his last wishes and the administration of his affairs. To his father and to his brother he sent this message, "Tell them I endeavored to live as I trust I shall die, a Christian soldier and gentleman, leaving them little cause of sorrow in my death." In closing he said,

"Bury me, if possible, at Duncan's side, if my death entitles me to a place beside the brave dead."

I was proud then — I am proud to-day — that this superb man, this most noble and gallant gentleman, addressed me in this his last testament as "his best and dearest friend." I could have no higher aim than to deserve to be so honored. He was that rare type of friend who would dare to tell the truth, however unwelcome it might be. He did not hesitate to point out my faults to me — even to rebuke me if he saw I was in the wrong.

September 23d, the day after the battle of Fisher's Hill, I find that our cavalry was still holding the position at Milford. "The enemy have retired from our front, finding it impossible to drive us out." On the 24th we returned toward Luray, marching through Newmarket Gap. Again my record shows that the active campaign did not stop our usual regimental religious service, for though we were engaged that day in "throwing up breastworks" at Columbia Bridge ford, I held service and "addressed the men on the Thirty-seventh Psalm in connection with the condition of our cause." That same day (Saturday) Lomax's old brigade "suffered a reverse near Luray." Our own brigade marched across the river by nine P.M., and the marching and the fortifying and the service was all done (and endured) on an empty stomach — "nothing to eat all day." The next day, Sunday, 25th, we marched to Conrad's store in Rockingham County, but again I find record of religious service, — "preached in camp in the afternoon on II Peter iii. 11 (The Day of Judgment) and had more than usual attention." This was followed by a severe night march, with only an hour's sleep. The men suffered greatly with cold. "The road was terrible." Marching and camping with officers and men, and going with them into battle, I had constant opportunities of urging upon them the claims of the religion of our Lord and Saviour Jesus Christ. Many were the long, earnest talks we had together. I found the minds and hearts of these brave fellows good soil for the word of God. To some I administered the rite of baptism. If any preferred immersion, I was ready to administer the sacrament in that mode. One such case came up in midwinter, and all things were ready for the plunge into the bitter cold water, when orders came to march, and the baptism had to be postponed. Circumstances arose which made the postponement indefinite. I confess it was no small relief, for our wardrobes were so limited that I fear we should have had no change of clothing after the ordeal was past. It was easy to appreciate that immersion might have been the natural and normal method of baptism in the River Jordan, but quite the reverse in the Shenandoah in midwinter!

During these weeks of hard marching, night and day, much of it over very rough, back roads, and in the various fights that had taken place, I had been riding my beautiful little bay "Charlie." He had been blinded, by ill usage, as I have explained, but his action was so fine, and his spirit so unconquered by adversity, that his blindness was not noticeable by the casual observer. His conduct during this hard campaign entitles him to be enrolled in the Legion of Honor of those brave horses who have borne themselves with peculiar distinction on the field of battle and on the toilsome march. If ever a blind horse went through a campaign more gallantly than my little Charlie, I have yet to hear his name. In the darkness I could not steer him clear of the rocks and other obstacles on those awful roads, but never once did he fall with me. Sometimes his feet would slip on the smooth rocks, but when I tightened my rein and sat snug in the saddle he would always spring up on to his feet again, even if he had to make two attempts. Riding across the rough fields, he made the same record. I could guide him to a fence partly let down and let him put his nose over, and if it were not more than two feet high, he would carry me over without difficulty.

Two achievements of his in particular, I think, are worthy of mention. Sheridan, after his success at Fisher's Hill, had the valley almost at his mercy, — and the "tender mercies" of General Sheridan were like "the tender mercies of the wicked," only more so! His troopers were burning and destroying, up and down that fertile region, barns, crops, farming implements, everything except the roofs over the people's heads. How my blood boiled as I saw the dense clouds of smoke ascending in different quarters of the horizon! He had penetrated to Staunton. Had he burned the town? Was that the smoke of the town that I saw in the far distance? I determined to ascertain. So, September 27th, obtaining leave of absence from the colonel, I sallied up the valley to see what the situation was. At first I kept to the back road, but surveying the pike and seeing a body of the enemy moving down the valley, away from the scene of destruction, I concluded to venture down on to the pike, arguing that the troops I saw were probably the rear of the column. I proceeded accordingly *up* the pike, but had not ridden much more than half a mile when, at a sudden turn in the road, I met a troop of Federals coming down. They were almost upon me before I saw them. Reining up sharply, I wheeled and put spurs to my horse and dashed off in a full run, pursued by the Federals, who fired, as they rode after me, many shots. It was a critical moment for me. I was confident Charlie could beat them running, but what would happen when I undertook to make the right angle turn out of the pike and back to the hill road? Could the dear blind little chap make the turn without stumbling and falling, going at that speed? Certainly it was very doubtful. But I slackened speed a bit, held him well up, and made as wide a turn as possible, and the gallant beast bore me safely away from my pursuers on to the back road. Fortunately it was an up grade. Had it been a down grade, he must have fallen. Being unarmed, as I always was since becoming a chaplain, I did not return the fire of my friends in blue.

Some weeks after this, when our cavalry had again advanced down the valley nearly to Winchester, the regiment was moving, company front, across a field, when suddenly the Federal cavalry appeared directly in our rear, and were evidently preparing to charge. Whereupon our commanding officer, ordering the column to face about, so that the rear company became the front, sounded a charge against the enemy. It was executed in fine form, and the Federals were driven back. In the charge my blind little hero had become very much excited, and continually forged ahead until I found myself neck and neck with one of the sergeants at the very head of the rushing regiment.

On we went across the open field, over rocks and fallen fences, and other obstacles, till the sergeant, turning to me, expostulated at my riding a blind horse in that reckless fashion. Just then the recall sounded, and I pulled Charlie up and we rode quietly back to the main body. Again my faithful little friend had justified my confidence.

I record these two achievements to his honor.

On September 27th, the day of my unsuccessful attempt to reach Staunton, I find a record of another fight, and among the wounded was Capt. Basil L. Gildersleeve, serving on the staff of General Gordon. This accomplished and brilliant scholar, the greatest "Grecian" of his day in America, had been my professor of Greek at the University of Virginia in 1859–60. On the closing of the University he had entered the service, and had shown that he could emulate the courage of the heroes of Hellas as successfully as he could expound the intricacies of their beautiful language. He carries to this day, in his limping gait, the witness of his gallantry in that fight forty-five years ago, but, though long past seventy years of age, his intellect marches as erect and vigorous as ever. His career may remind us that the cause of the South rallied to its support men of every rank and condition in life, the student and the scholar, not less than the man of affairs.

Another of my professors, Lewis Minor Coleman, who filled with great distinction the chair of Latin, became lieutenant-colonel of artillery and gave up his glorious life at the battle of Fredericksburg in 1862, — in the same battle in which one of his most brilliant students, Randolph Fairfax, fell, leaving behind him a shining example as a young Christian soldier. The life of this beautiful and accomplished boy (for he was not of age when he was killed) was written by Rev. Dr. Philip Slaughter, and was circulated widely in the army. I think we used to call him the young "Hedley Vickars."

Then the next day, September 28th, near Waynesboro, there was a pretty hot engagement, artillery and cavalry participating. About half past four P.M. we "attacked the enemy and after a sharp fight drove him two and a half miles" towards Staunton. I was busy after nightfall tending the wounded, a number of whom on both sides had sabre cuts, for it was what cavalrymen called "a very pretty fight," in which the columns met and fought hand to hand with the sabre — a rather rare occurrence, for the cavalry were being rapidly transformed into mounted infantry and used the carbine and the repeating rifle much more than the sword. The following morning, 29th, I had the rather unusual experience of ministering spiritually to one of the enemy. This is the record I find: "Read and prayed with Robert B. Fry, of Co. F, 18th Pennsylvania Cavalry." I think I also wrote a letter for him to his father, West Fry, at Fayetteville, Washington County, Pennsylvania. This was evidently Robert Fry's return visit to us, for we visited *his* home on the 1st of July, 1863, en route to Gettysburg!

I now had a week with my family very happily in Staunton, but found the household much troubled over the captivity and imprisonment of the Rev. R. H. Phillips. Here I replenished my supply of ammunition, — Testaments, prayer-books, and hymnals.

Our next engagement was at Cedar Creek. We

marched October 13th from our breastworks at Fisher's, eight miles down the back road, and engaged the enemy.

At one stage of the fight, a squadron of the regiment was drawn up behind a little slope, mounted and ready to charge when needed. The enemy was feeling for us with his artillery, and his shells were dropping uncomfortably near. I rode to the front of the squadron, drew out my little Psalm book, read the Twenty-seventh Psalm, and offered prayer for the divine blessing and protection, the men reverently removing their hats. When I had finished, the commanding officer moved the squadron about twenty or thirty yards to a spot which he thought less exposed. No sooner was the movement executed than a shell came hurtling through the air, struck the ground and exploded on the very spot we had just left. The men exchanged glances at this, and I heard one of the roughest of the troopers say to another, "Bill, I say, that does look like an answer to pra'ar, doesn't it?"

Two days after this I distributed among the men 150 hymnals, 50 prayer-books, and about 20 copies of the New Testament. We had our usual prayer-meeting that evening, and the next day, Sunday, October 16th, I held service in the breastworks, using the Episcopal liturgy for the first time "with encouraging success," and preaching on "the Great Alternative," I Chron. xxxiii. 9. In the afternoon held another service, and preached on Phil. iii, "forgetting the things which are behind," etc. That night the regiment went on a night expedition to surprise the enemy. In this I did not take part, my horse being unfit for the march.

Tuesday, 17th, as I was preparing for our usual

evening service, marching orders were received. We marched all night and attacked the enemy at daylight. I find almost daily in this active campaign mention of earnest conversations with officers or men on the great theme of personal religion, and I have no mention or recollection of meeting with a rebuff. The next day, October 19th, was an eventful one, for then was fought the battle of Cedar Creek, so brilliant in its beginning, so disastrous in its ending. I will not attempt to tell the story of this famous engagement, but I will remind the reader of Gen. John B. Gordon's brilliant strategy — how during the night of the 18th he carried a part of his command over a very difficult mountain pass by a rough foot-path, and fell upon the Federals like an eagle descending out of the clouds, surprising them, driving them, routing them, pursuing them through their camps; and then how the major-general with the rest of the little army came upon the scene by another route, and in an evil hour stopped the pursuit, so that the Federals had time to rally and re-form. By this time the Sixth Corps[1]— the only one which, though demoralized, was not broken — advanced and checked the retreat of the fleeing Federals; and then the Federal commander brought his vastly superior numbers into play, assumed the offensive, attacked the Confederates, and the sun, which in rising had looked down on a glorious Confederate victory, beheld, as he sank to rest, that victory turned into defeat. It was one of those bitter experiences

[1] Col. Thos. H. Carter, our chief of artillery, says: "The Sixth Corps was retiring before artillery alone, and the other two corps were in full and disorganized flight at nine o'clock in the morning." See Gen. John B. Gordon's account of this battle in his "Reminiscences," pp. 352–372.

which began now to be not uncommon, as the South became more and more exhausted and the superior numbers and resources of the North were brought into effective operation.

It was certainly the belief of the rank and file of our little army that if that glorious soldier, John B. Gordon, had been in supreme command that day, there would have been no check in the pursuit; the enemy would not have been given time to rally his routed forces; the Sixth Corps would have been swept along with the rest of the beaten army, and the magnificent beginning would have been crowned by a complete victory before the day was over.   Nothing is more clear than this, — it was not Sheridan's Ride, but Early's Halt, that wrested victory from the Confederates on that eventful day!

I have two closing notes on this day. Our regimental evening service was held in face of the enemy's pickets, and then we had another all night march back to our breastworks, only to be again in the saddle next morning (the 20th) for a march all day.   Friday, 21st, the regiment marched again and camped near Forestville, where, at nightfall, we had our prayer-meeting and I spoke on the last three verses of Heb. iv. Saturday evening's address was on the words, "Will a man rob God?   Yet ye have robbed Me."   Sunday the regiment was ordered on picket.   Nevertheless we had our service at brigade headquarters, and late in the day I joined my regiment on the picket line, after I had rebuked the sutlers for selling their merchandise on the Lord's Day and had written a letter to Colonel Morgan remonstrating with him very earnestly on the impropriety of establishing his headquarters in a church. Monday we returned to camp and had our service in the evening at brigade headquarters; Tuesday the same in the first squadron, with an address on "The Brazen Serpent."

Soon after this, on October 26th, I organized a branch of the Young Men's Christian Association in the regiment, and I find a record of its meetings from time to time through that stirring fall and winter, in spite of our constant marches. It met the second time on the following Sunday evening. At the University of Virginia I had taken active part in the Y. M. C. A., which, by the way, was the first such Association organized at any institution of learning. That was in 1858.

We kept up our choir meetings also, and this contributed to the interest in the daily services. I have mentioned that my father-in-law, Rev. Richard H. Phillips, was a prisoner in Camp Chase, Ohio. His family was greatly distressed by his captivity, and feared the consequences of the hardship and the unnecessary rigor to which he was subjected. This induced me to think of offering myself as a substitute for him, to procure his release and restoration to his family. Accordingly, on October 31st I addressed a letter to Colonel Ould, the Confederate commissioner for exchange of prisoners, asking him to propose to the Federal authorities to accept me as a prisoner in place of Mr. Phillips. On the 9th of November I wrote to two members of the Confederate Congress, Col. John B. Baldwin and Hon. Allan T. Caperton, on the same subject, but nothing ever came of it. Mr. Phillips was a prisoner for ten months, when he was exchanged in the ordinary course.

It was a hard campaign for us, marked by almost daily marches, and by frequent fights more or less important. Thus, on November 11th, we marched below Cedar Creek and had an engagement in which we lost two killed and five wounded. Again the next day there was "cavalry fighting all day." My record says that General Rosser's (Confederate) brigade was "stampeded," but "our regiment charged beautifully and drove the enemy six miles." General Lomax "whipped them too," but McCausland lost two pieces of artillery. So it would seem that honors were easy that day between the blue and the gray. The following Sunday we marched back to camp, twenty-five miles, the weather very cold, "snowing and blowing." Winter had set in early, for I noted a heavy snow on November 5th.

One of my efforts was to supply all the men who wished it with copies of the New Testament. To this end I appointed one in each company to ascertain how many were desirous of being supplied with them. I also circulated a subscription for the supply of "religious papers," and I note November 14th the receipt of $106 from Co. A for this purpose.

Apparently to supply these needs I made a visit to Staunton, November 15th, "riding all night and reaching there at nine A.M."

After a three days visit there, during which my gallant little "Charlie" had the honor of carrying his mistress again after an interval of three years, I returned to camp on the 19th of November, riding from Staunton to Newmarket between 6.30 A.M. and dusk. Two days afterward I distributed my cargo, 70 Testaments, 40 hymnals, and about 100 prayer-books. Next day,

21st, the enemy advanced with three divisions of cavalry. "We met them with one brigade and some infantry skirmishers and drove them beyond Edinburgh, a distance of six miles," losing in our regiment three killed and eight wounded, to whom I endeavored to minister the consolations of religion.

I will give here a transcript of my little diary to show how my days were spent.

"Nov. 22d. Talked with Jones of Co. G, who was dangerously wounded to-day. Nov. 23d. Went to see Jones at sunrise. Read and prayed with him with much earnestness in presence of his family and some soldiers. . . . Visited two badly wounded men of the First Regiment, talked and prayed with them. Went to Mt. Jackson hospital, and talked with Brooking and McGinness, each of whom has lost a leg. On the way back conversed with Sergeant Cleburne, who was once a professor of religion. Held prayer-meeting and spoke on 103d Psalm. Small attendance because of the cold. . . . Thursday, 24th. Rose at daylight and went to see Jones. Talked and prayed with him. Performed the burial service over W. H. Cocke of Co. G, and addressed the throng on death and its lessons. Went to see Harris, Co. A. He is a Christian. Read and prayed with him with much delight. Drew near to God in evening prayer. Held prayer-meeting and spoke on "The Sting of Death is Sin." Friday, Nov. 25th. "Rose at daylight — weather very cold — withdrew to the woods for prayer. . . . Visited Jones and talked and prayed with him. He cannot *believe* — that is his difficulty. Regiment on picket. Rode five miles to see B. W. Taylor and found him somewhat better. . . . Nov. 26th. Rose before daylight and prayed with Taylor. Rode to picket post, stopping to see Jones on my way. Sunday, Nov. 27th. Distributed papers to men at sunrise, and gave notice of services. Rode to Dr.

Meem's and returned with Dr. Mitchell (Presbyterian), of Lynchburg, who preached for me on the joy in heaven 'over one sinner that repenteth.' Rode with him to see Jones."

On another day I was occupied "cutting down two trees," visiting the hospital at Mt. Jackson, where I ministered to seven wounded men, and in the evening (December 6th) "had the largest and best attended prayer-meeting for a long time. A trooper knelt in token of his desire for the prayers of the congregation."

Our troopers were in the habit of taking corn from the fields for their horses. This was a very reprehensible practice, and I took occasion to remonstrate with the men against it. I urged that it was the duty of the quartermaster's department to supply food and forage for our animals, and that it was subversive of discipline for the men to get their own supplies. But, above all, I insisted that the unhappy valley of Virginia had been swept almost bare of subsistence by the marching and countermarching of the two armies, and that of late the Federal cavalry had been robbing the people mercilessly, so that if we took the corn and fodder that were left, we were in fact taking the bread out of the mouths of the women and children. To all my arguments some of the men opposed the absolute necessity they were in to keep their horses in condition to do service and to defend the country from the advance of the enemy. This I met by the *argumentum ad equum*. "Look at my horse," I said. "He is in as good condition as any horse in the regiment, and I have not taken an ear of corn for him since I have been in the command!" When I said this I saw a twinkle in the eye of my principal antagonist in the argument, as he replied, "That's all very well, Parson, but you don't see the men a feedin' of him while you are asleep!'' On one occasion there was more serious ground for rebuke, for some depredations had been committed which reflected on the good name of the regiment. When I heard of it, I had the church bugle call sounded, and the men assembled in considerable numbers. After a very brief religious service, I addressed them, rebuking severely the act alluded to, calling it by its right name, and unsparingly condemning the perpetrators whoever they might be. It was evident from the scowling countenances of two or three of my auditors that the shot had taken effect — the guilty parties had been hit. It was the only instance of such conduct that I remember during my connection of nearly eight months with the Second Cavalry.

CHAPTER XIX

WE were now to undertake an expedition into West Virginia, under command of General Rosser, a dashing and adventurous officer, but in my humble opinion lacking sometimes in that poise and judgment so essential to the best results in a campaign.

We set out on Dec. 7th, 1864, and the next day crossed the mountains and camped in a little valley on the south fork of the Potomac. On the 9th we reached Petersburg. Later we tore up some miles of the Baltimore and Ohio R. R.

This appears to have been the whole purpose of the expedition. It was accomplished at considerable cost — indeed, it cost very dear, for to say nothing of the intense suffering the men endured in crossing and recrossing the Alleghany in the midst of a very cold winter, horses and men were much broken down by the marches, and the brigade subsequently joined the army near Richmond "much the worse for wear," and by no means as fit for service as it had been at the beginning of the winter. One evening we reached the top of the Allegheny Mountains just before dusk, and bivouacked in the forest. We had no wagons, and of course no tents — nothing, in fact, but what each trooper carried on his saddle. Every man was supposed to have a small tent-fly rolled up behind him. These were about six feet long and perhaps eighteen inches across, — two of them buttoned together and stretched across a small pole cut from the forest and supported by two forked sticks formed a little shelter under which two men could crawl and have some protection from falling weather.

Just at dusk snow began to fall, and it was evidently to be a heavy one. Quickly then these tiny shelter tents began to spring up in the forest. But unfortunately for us, neither Adjutant Griffin nor I possessed a tent-fly. So we had no resource but to lie down and cover up with what blankets we had and a rubber overall — this as quickly as possible before the ground had become covered with the snow. This, then, we did, while our comrades, standing by the little feeble fires of brushwood, bade us good-bye, saying, "We expect to find you buried alive in the morning." This expectation was literally realized, for "Tip" Griffin and I were covered up by a blanket of snow eight inches deep, — buried, but still alive. Tip, though, had the advantage of me, for he slept soundly with his head completely covered, while I, requiring fresh air, was compelled from time to time to lift the cover, whereupon the snow would roll in (our saddles making a little mound behind our heads), and then the heat of my body would melt it, — so that I had a most miserable night, not because of the cold, for the snow kept me warm, but by loss of sleep and the discomfort of lying in a pool of melted snow — "almost suffocated with the weight of the snow on my head." Another severe experience I recall was this. We crossed one of the mountain brooks not less, I think, than twenty times in a day's march, and the weather was so cold that the water as it splashed upon the horses froze, and their legs and bellies were covered with little icicles. But the forepart of the top of one of my boots was gone, so that my sock was exposed, and it soon became a frozen mass over my foot, so that I was obliged to dismount and walk all day (sometimes to double-quick) to prevent my foot being frozen or frost-bitten. Moreover I was miserably mounted — on a little long-haired mouse-colored beast, not much larger than a large sheep. I had not ventured to take my blind Charlie on this winter expedition over frozen roads. Often these were very slippery.

When Sunday came, it was simply impossible to conduct service. I rode thirteen miles that day to procure forage for our horses. On the 12th I rode on to Petersburg (W. Va.), and had bread baked for the men. This threw me behind the column and I had hard work catching up with the regiment.

During all this march back over the mountains and to Eastern Virginia, our men had to scratch a fresh hole in the hard snow, at the end of every day's march, to bivouack for the night.

My verdict was that I had suffered more hardship in the office of chaplain than I ever did as a private soldier carrying a musket and a knapsack.

On December 17th I was ordered to the hospital at Staunton for treatment of an injury to my hand.

I returned to camp at Swope's Depot early in January, and at once resumed the daily services. On the 8th we received orders to march eastward to Waynesboro and thence over the Blue Ridge. Taking Staunton en route, I consulted a surgeon there, who said it would be dangerous to return to camp in the condition my hand was in. It was much swollen and very painful. It seemed strange to be put *hors de combat* for weeks by a trifling injury, after passing through so many battles and minor engagements scathless. I had once lost a day by indisposition — the only occasion during the war when I had to ride in the ambulance—and now I had lost three weeks and was to lose more by this accident.

On January 20th, while still in Staunton, I received news of the death of my dear father, who died at the age of sixty-five years, at his beautiful home, Belvidere, in Baltimore.

It was not till January 25th that I was able to rejoin my regiment. Starting early I rode across the Blue Ridge and made "Clover Plains" by evening — the lovely home of my aunt, Mrs. John Bolling Garrett, on the eastern slope of the mountains. Next day I dined at the dear old University from whose classic shades so many of us went forth in 1861 to join the Confederate armies; and pushed on in the afternoon to "Edge Hill," the home of Col. Thos. Jefferson Randolph, grandson of Thomas Jefferson, beautifully situated on a hill almost under the shadow of famous "Monticello."

How well I recall the giant form of Colonel Randolph, as he sat and talked of the olden days of Virginia, of his illustrious grandfather, and of the Legislature of Virginia in 1832, when the whole State was so deeply stirred by the scheme for the emancipation of the negroes. He was a member of that body, and he told me that a large majority of the members was in favor of the measure; but after careful consideration it was deemed wiser to postpone action upon it until the next session, in order that the details of the scheme might be more maturely considered.

But before the Legislature reassembled, there occurred a violent ebulition of fanaticism on the part of the Abolitionists of New England. The Southern slave-holders were held up to the scorn and detestation of mankind, and the vengeance of God and man was invoked against them for the awful crime of slavery.

The consequence was a complete reaction of public opinion in Virginia on the subject of the abolition of slavery, so that when the Legislature next assembled, the whole project was dropped. Thus was wrecked the most hopeful scheme of getting rid of the institution of slavery that had ever been proposed since its introduction in 1619. We may lament that the men of Virginia did not rise superior to the feelings naturally begotten by this unfair and fanatical assault, but, human nature being what it is, we cannot be surprised that the affair terminated as it did.

Had it been otherwise — had the gradual emancipation of the slaves been decreed by Virginia — there can be little doubt that Maryland, Kentucky, Missouri, North Carolina, and Tennessee would have followed her example; and in time the moral pressure on the cotton States would have been so strong that they, too, must have adopted some scheme of emancipation. That this blessed consummation was not realized must be set down to the account of the fanatical Abolitionists, because of their violent and unjust arraignment of the South for an institution which she did not create, but had inherited, and against which the State of Virginia had many times protested in her early history.

It is not always remembered by students of American history that the original draft of the Declaration of Independence as drawn by Thos. Jefferson arraigned the king of England for forcing the institution of slavery on the people of the colonies against their will. It is also too often forgotten that the first government on earth to abolish the slave trade was the Commonwealth of Virginia. It was one of the first acts of the Old Dominion after her independence had been established, long before old England passed her ordinance against it. And when the thirteen colonies formed the United States, in 1789, the voice of Virginia was raised in earnest advocacy of the immediate abolition of the trade in negro slaves, but owing to the opposition of New England, in alliance with some of the cotton States, the evil traffic was given a twenty years further lease of life.

From Edge Hill, after one delightful evening, I rode on to Barboursville, January 26th, suffering not a little with the cold, for the thermometer registered fourteen degrees above zero. There I spent the night with another charming Virginia gentleman, a member of the Confederate Congress, Mr. B. Johnson Barbour. He was of a younger generation than Colonel Randolph, and an active participant in the affairs of the State and the Confederacy, experienced in political life, a man of broad and generous culture, and an orator of great ability. In such delightful company and in such a charming home it would have been delightful to tarry, but I could not yield to the temptation, and so pushed on the next day, reaching camp about one P.M. On Sunday, the 28th, I resumed my duties with my regiment, preaching in the Blue Run Baptist

Church, the condition of which left much to be desired. So, next day I spent several hours "cleaning out the church." My diary shows that our daily prayer-meetings were kept up through the remainder of this hard winter and up to the evacuation of Richmond, whenever circumstances permitted, and I always made an address or preached a sermon. It is pleasant to remember now, after the lapse of forty-four years, the loyal support those brave men of the Second Virginia Cavalry gave me, young and inexperienced as I was, in my work as chaplain among them.

They gave liberally, too, out of their small means for the soldiers' paper which I was interested in circulating among the men, and for the purchase of Bibles and prayer-books and hymnals.

On Sunday, February 5th, my morning service was appointed as usual, but orders were received to march to Richmond, so that my congregation was reduced to four men, — to whom, however, I preached. Our camp was on the nine-mile road, six miles from Richmond. The next Sunday (12th) was very windy and cold, so that only fifteen men responded to bugle call at church time. Open air service in such bitter weather had its difficulties. But I find record of many personal interviews with officers and men at this period about their souls' interests. On the 19th I preached both morning and afternoon in St. Paul's, Richmond, of which Rev. Dr. Minnegerode was the rector. The President of the Southern Confederacy was a regular attendant at its services, as were many other government officials. It was a very notable congregation that assembled there those last Sundays of the life of the Confederacy. Many distinguished officers would often be seen there, and

always many of the soldiers, and the costumes of the
ladies, made up with such ingenuity out of very slender
resources, would have furnished a curious study to the
woman of to-day versed in matters pertaining to female
toilette.   There was a deep solemnity in those Sunday
services in the chief church of Virginia, when such
momentous issues hung in the balance, when often
the distant booming of the cannon reminded the wor-
shippers that a life and death struggle was even then
going on.   Not a few of those who sat listening to the
words of the preacher felt that a dark cloud of impend-
ing disaster overhung the church and the city, which
might burst at any hour and overwhelm us all.   But
others, especially the young officers and the young
women, were full of hope, and even the sacred precincts
of the sanctuary could hardly restrain the ebullition of
their gayety.   It was, on the whole, a brilliant spectacle
presented to the eye of the preacher as he ascended
the pulpit of St. Paul's and surveyed the great congregation before him.   To one as new as I then was to
the pulpit, and accustomed to audiences composed
solely of my comrades in arms, clad in their rusty uniforms, it was at first a little disconcerting.

Having found it so difficult to conduct service in the
open air in the cold and inclement weather of winter, I
set about building, by the help of the men, a chapel for
our use in winter quarters.   We built it of logs and covered it with tent-flies.   In about two weeks we were able
to occupy it, but two days later the brigade was ordered
off (March 7th), and I believe we never used it again.
I had much personal work among the men at this time
and was occupied preparing some of them for baptism
and the holy communion.   That last Sunday (March

5th) I had a large and interested congregation. It was to be my last service with the regiment, for when, on the 7th of March, it was ordered off, I could not accompany it, for my horse had completely broken down — was in fact quite unable to carry me, and so I was left behind. In about a week, being unable to procure a fresh mount near Richmond, I obtained leave to go to Staunton for the purpose.

Before I left, on Sunday, March 12th, I preached again at St. Paul's in the evening. My sermon was on "The Divine Providence in Human Affairs," and my text was,

Ps. xcvii. 1, 2: "The Lord reigneth . . . clouds and darkness are round about Him. Righteousness and judgment are the habitation of His throne."

The following extract may be of interest as illustrating the state of mind of clergy and people at that crisis in the history of the Confederacy:

In conclusion what should be our state of mind in view of the doctrine of the text? What practical effect should belief in God's universal providence have upon us?

1. We should rejoice. "The Lord reigneth, let the Earth rejoice." After all, "though the heathen rage and the people imagine a vain thing" "the Lord reigneth:" He will "make the wrath of man to praise Him" and "the remainder of wrath" He will "restrain." "Fret not thyself," timid believer, "because of evil doers, neither be thou envious against the workers of iniquity, for they shall soon be cut down like the grass, and wither as the green herb." Yes! blessed be God, the wicked shall not always triumph; Truth and Justice will assert their rightful supremacy; Innocence will be vindicated; and right will at last be might; because "the Lord reigneth."

For right is might since God is God;
   And right the day must win;
To doubt would be disloyalty,
   To falter would be sin.

Christian, are you anxious and troubled? It is your
privilege to be calm and confident. Does the future fill
you with evil forebodings? Does it seem to hang over you
like some frowning precipice? It is your privilege to "take
no thought for the morrow" and to rely on his promise
"my grace is sufficient for thee." Remember, though the
heavens may gather blackness, though thunders roll and
lightnings gleam, though the depths may yawn and the
billows mount up to the skies, — yet above all "the Lord
reigneth." The issue is in His hands. He can still the raging of
the sea, and command a great calm, and we have His promise
that "all things shall work together for good to those that
love Him." Brethren, it is more than our privilege, it is
our duty to believe His word. We live in the midst of
troublous times. The calamity is not yet overpast. *We
are arrived at the crisis in the fate of our beloved country.
Whatever the result, the Christian need not fear.* He is
in the hands of his covenant God, and he may calmly
await the issue. Calmly? Yes! but not idly; he has a work
to do, he owes a duty to his country and as a Christian he
must perform it. His country is in danger, what can he
do? Take his place among her soldiers and stand up for
her defence? Yes, this he must do; but this is not all. The
battle is not to the strong. "The Lord reigneth," his Lord
who has promised to hear his prayer, and he must take his
place upon his knees and pray for divine help.

2. The doctrine of divine providence should also make
us tremble lest we resist His will and bring down His vengeance upon our guilty heads. "The Lord reigneth, let the
people tremble!" Ah, with what awful solemnity ought
these words to fall upon the ears of a nation engaged like

ours in a struggle for existence with an enemy vastly their superior in numbers and all material resources! Let us tremble, lest in a spirit of boastfulness and self-confidence we rely upon our own valor and prowess and forget to ask help of Him in whose hands are the issues of life and death, of victory and defeat! Let us tremble, lest by persisting in our impenitence and rebellion and plunging into reckless gayety and dissipation, while on the very verge of ruin, we excite the indignation of that God upon whose favor alone we depend for success. Let us tremble, lest we harden our necks and despise the chastening of the Lord; lest in our madness we charge God with injustice; lest we exhibit in our own case an example of the prophet's words, "The people turneth not to Him that smiteth them, neither do they seek the Lord of Hosts," — therefore "His anger is not turned away, but His hand is stretched out still."

CHAPTER XX

ABOUT this time occurred the famous Hampton Roads Conference between the representatives of the Confederate Government and Mr. Lincoln. Much discussion grew out of it, and it was feared the resolution of the people and of the army to continue the struggle would be shaken. To counteract such a tendency, a meeting of our regiment was held on February 13th, and the situation of the country was discussed. I took part in the discussion, and offered a series of resolutions which were enthusiastically adopted. They were as follows:

PREAMBLE AND RESOLUTIONS

Whereas, under the influence of the reverses which have recently befallen our arms, a feeling of despondency and gloom has manifested itself among the people at home; and

Whereas, the impression seems to prevail that the soldiers in the field are likewise discouraged and disheartened — even to the point of being willing to make peace with our enemies on the basis of Reconstruction:

Thereupon, be it resolved, That we indignantly repel the charge of despondency, as a slander upon our good name as Confederate Soldiers, and as unjust to the past services we have rendered; and we do at the same time declare our determination never willingly to lay down our arms, until we have extorted from the world an acknowledgment of our right to govern ourselves.

254

Resolved, 2d, that far from considering our past reverses as just cause for despondency or despair, we look upon them as urgent appeals for more vigorous and determined efforts than we have ever yet put forth; and we deem this a fit occasion for reiterating our belief that these States are fully equal to the task they have undertaken of throwing off the yoke of Northern oppression and fanaticism, and vindicating their God-given right to be free.

Resolved, 3d, that to talk of submission or compromise at this stage of the struggle — when we have already paid the price of liberty in the blood of our best and bravest — would be the basest treachery to the memory of those who have fallen, and would prove us unworthy of freedom — unworthy the possession of this fair Southern land.

Resolved, 4th, that having entered upon this contest with the conviction that our rights and interests were no longer safe under the government of the United States; and the developments of the past four years having doubly confirmed our worst apprehensions, we cannot see any distinction between Reconstruction and subjugation, except that in the latter case, though everything else were lost, *honor* at least would remain to us.

Resolved, 5th, that we hail the accession of Gen. Robert E. Lee to the supreme leadership of our armies as an omen of victory; and we are satisfied that uncompromising firmness and self-sacrificing patriotism on the part of the army and the people in the coming campaign are all that is necessary, under the guidance and blessing of Almighty God, to secure our independence, and restore to us the halcyon days of peace.

Resolved, 6th, that the best way to incline our enemies to peace is to prepare vigorously for war; and we warn our people that the apparent willingness of the Washington government to treat for peace is a veil for hostile purposes, and is intended to paralyze our energies and sow discord and discontent among our citizens and soldiers.

The sentiments of these resolutions were those entertained by Lee's brave soldiers at this period of the tremendous struggle, when the surrender of his army and the collapse of the Southern Confederacy was so near at hand — only seven weeks away. We in the field could not realize the true situation. The fatal mistake of removing Gen. Joseph E. Johnston from the command of the Southwestern Army had destroyed the last hope of resisting Sherman's advance in that direction. After Hood's defeat the cotton States were at his mercy — and his "tender mercies" were "cruel" indeed. Even if Lee could continue to hold out against the hosts of General Grant, beleaguering Petersburg and Richmond, it was now only a question of time when he would find Sherman with a great army marching on his rear. Yet his great soul did not quail even then, and the men who had followed him with supreme devotion since June, 1862, could not believe that defeat was possible, while he was still their commander. They hailed his recent appointment to be commander-in-chief of all the Confederate armies as an omen of victory. They did not realize that this appointment came at least a twelvemonth too late. Had Lee been in supreme command in May, 1864, as Grant was of the armies of the United States, the story of the war would have been greatly different. Joseph E. Johnston would not have been removed — Sherman would perhaps have been defeated—certainly he would have been checked, and his march to the sea might never have taken place. One also may believe that the genius of Gen. Nathan Bedford Forrest would have been recognized by Lee in time to have given scope to his marvellous abilities for General Sherman's discomfiture. That brilliant plan which he vainly submitted to the Richmond authorities for cutting off Sherman's communications could hardly have failed to secure the approval of Lee.

Lord Wolseley, in his appreciation of Lee, published shortly after the death of the latter, truly said that whoever would justly estimate what Lee accomplished must take into consideration the important fact that he was never given supreme command until within a few weeks of the overthrow of the Confederacy. Even his direction of the movements of the Army of Northern Virginia was subject to the approval of the Richmond authorities. It is almost pathetic to read that when Lee was planning his campaign into Pennsylvania in 1863, he had to submit it for approval to Jas. A. Seddon, Secretary of War. One feature of his plan was, in fact, negatived by Mr. Jefferson Davis. I mean the organization of an army (however small) at Manassas under Lieutenant-General Beauregard. This would have been a menace to Washington, and might have held a portion of the Army of the Potomac in its defence, thus weakening the strength of the army which Lee was to meet at Gettysburg.

But as we see it now, the task of the Confederate generals was too great for human hands to accomplish. The South was worn out by attrition and starvation. Her resources were exhausted. Her ports were closed — hermetically sealed by the great navy of the United States — and she had not within her own territory the supplies necessary to carry on such a war against so rich and powerful a foe. The process of exhaustion had been going on till her sources of life were almost gone.

"In my opinion, as a student of war," wrote Viscount Lord Wolseley to me some years ago, "it was the blockade of your ports that killed the Southern Confederacy, not the action of the Northern armies."[1] This view was ably set forth by the Hon. Hilary A. Herbert in an address delivered while he was Secretary of the Navy; and Hon. Chas. Francis Adams, in his oration at Lexington, Va., at the centennial of General Lee's birth, presented the same view with great force.

I come now to the end of the story of my experiences as chaplain of the Second Cavalry.

On the 15th of March I left Richmond for Staunton by the Danville R. R., accompanied by my wife, who had been a guest at Westwood, the home of Col. Thos. H. Ellis, for a week or two, and my father-in-law,

---

[1] Following is the text of the letter referred to above.

FARM HOUSE, GLYNDE, LEWES,
November 12, 1904.
DEAR SIR:

It was very kind of you to send me a copy of your speech to the Confederate veterans. I have perused it with the deepest interest. It has revived my remembrance of the sympathy with which I watched the campaigns to which you so eloquently allude in "The Confederate Soldier, his Motives and Aims."

I have often pondered over the effect upon the future of the United States that a refusal on the part of Mr. Lincoln to hand us back Messrs. Mason and Slidell would have had. In my opinion, as a student of war, the Confederates must have won had the blockade of the Southern ports been removed by us, as it would have been at once if the North had been ruled by a flashy politician instead of the very able and far-seeing Mr. Abraham Lincoln.

It was the blockade of your ports that killed the Southern Confederacy, not the action of the Northern armies.

However, you are now a united people, and as such by far the greatest power in the world. I earnestly hope our two nations may always be closely united. With such a union of heart and strength firmly established, we might easily forbid all great wars in the world. What a glorious end to aim at!

I have always hoped for *such* a close alliance of the English race

Rev. Richard H. Phillips, who had returned from the military prison at Camp Chase, Ohio, where he had been confined for ten months. I have already referred to the sad change in this noble gentleman, which the privations and sufferings of his imprisonment had wrought. The train which took us out of Richmond carried also a large number of exchanged prisoners. They presented a pitiful sight — many of them emaciated to the last degree, many suffering with distressing coughs that showed they were marked for the grave. It could not be expected that one out of ten of that train load of Confederate soldiers would ever be fit for duty again. The treatment of Northern prisoners in Southern prisons has been much discussed. An important sidelight is cast on this subject by a consideration of the conditions existing in the South during the war. As regards medicines, let it be noted that quinine sold in Richmond as early as July, 1862, for $60 an ounce, while in New York it was but $5 per ounce. That was before Confederate currency had so frightfully depreciated. As regards food and clothing, I see from my diary that in February, 1864,

throughout the world, for every Christian man must realize, that whilst war is a dire scourge, peace on earth and good will toward all men is not only the highest philosophy, but the injunction of Him whose followers we all profess to be.

Again thanking you for your great kindness in sending me a copy of your great speech, allow me to subscribe myself,

Yours very faithfully,

WOLSELEY.

To THE REVD. R. H. McKIM, etc., etc.,
Washington, U. S.

P. S. — It was most kind of Mrs. Hugh Lee to ask you to send me the copy of the speech in question.

W.

The speech to which Lord Wolseley refers is given in the Appendix, p. 286.

milk was $2 per gallon; a pound of candles cost $7; a pair of boots, $140; half soling a pair of boots, $11; a roadside breakfast, $5; a box of blacking, $4; a halter, $10; butter, $5 per pound; 1 pair of shoestrings, $1.50. In December, 1864, I bought 6 pounds butter for $54, 1 turkey, $17, 1 spool cotton, $5, soap, $2 per pound. In January, 1865, 1 yard mourning crepe cost $140, putting one shoe on my horse, $5. Five dollars in gold brought $200. Soon after a pair of woman's shoes cost $200, and 3 pounds of tea and a few pounds of sugar cost $465.   It is recorded in the diary of a refugee that in Richmond, the last winter of the war, sugar was $20 per pound, meal, $40 per bushel, flour, $300 per barrel, ham, $7 per pound.   One feed for a horse cost $5, board of a horse for one month, $300.

At the table of General Lee, commander-in-chief of the Confederate armies, there was meat only twice a week, while the usual fare was boiled cabbage and sweet potatoes and corn pone.

How, then, could our prisoners be properly fed amid such scarcity of provisions?   And how could they be properly supplied with medicines when these existed in such very small quantities in the South?   Medicines had been made, by the United States authorities, contraband of war.

It ought also to be remembered that Jefferson Davis offered in the summer of 1864 to surrender the sick and wounded Federal prisoners in his hands without equivalent, but though the offer was accepted, the necessary transportation did not arrive until the following November.

Again I recall the fact that General Grant refused to carry out the cartel for the exchange of prisoners, lest the Confederate armies should be reinforced. In August, 1864, he wrote to General Butler as follows:

"It is hard on our men in Southern prisons not to exchange them, but it is humanity to those left in the ranks left to fight our battles. At this particular time, to release all rebel prisoners North would insure Sherman's defeat and would compromise our safety here."

I will not stop to observe at how much higher valuation this shows that one Southern soldier was held than one Northern soldier, but I ask, Upon whom, then, rests the responsibility for the prolongation of the suffering of Northern soldiers in Southern prisons?

I believe that as a rule the Confederate authorities did the best they could for the prisoners they held, if regard be had to the scarcity of provisions and the great paucity of medicines and hospital comforts in the South at that time.

Can the same be said for the United States authorities in their treatment of Southern prisoners of war?

But the best refutation of the charge against the South in this respect is furnished by a comparison of the statistics of the respective mortality in the prisons at the North and those at the South.

The whole number of Federal prisoners in Southern prisons was, in round numbers, 270,000, and of Confederate prisoners in Northern prisons 220,000. But the deaths of Confederates in Northern prisons were 26,436, while of Union soldiers in the Southern prisons only 22,576 died. (See Report of Mr. Stanton, Federal Secretary of War, dated July 19, 1866 — also Report of Federal Surgeon-General Barnes.) Thus the *per centum* of deaths in Southern prisons was less than nine, while the *per centum* of deaths in Northern prisons was more than twelve.[1]

[1] At the beginning of the war, May 21, 1861, the Confederate Congress passed an Act providing that

"Rations furnished prisoners of war shall be the same in quantity and quality as those furnished to enlisted men in the army of the Confederacy."

And in General Orders, No. 159, the Commissary-General ordered that —

"Hospitals for prisoners of war are placed on the same footing as other Confederate States Hospitals in all respects."

These orders were loyally obeyed.

The publication of the reports and correspondence relative to the exchange and treatment of prisoners — they fill four volumes of the "Rebellion Records" — furnishes a complete vindication of the Confederate Government from responsibility for the sufferings of Federal prisoners in the Southern prisons. They show that from the beginning to the end of the war the authorities of the Confederacy were eager to exchange the prisoners in their hands, but not till July 22, 1862, did the work of exchange begin. It continued till April 1, 1864, less than two years, when it was stopped by General Grant, and was not resumed till the latter part of January, 1865. And it was during this period that the greatest suffering and mortality of the prisoners in our hands occurred, — because of the great scarcity of food, and clothing, and medicines, and other comforts in the South at that period.

To meet this unfortunate situation and to mitigate the great suffering, Judge Ould, the Confederate commissioner on exchange for prisoners, proposed October 6, 1864, "that each government shall have the privilege of forwarding for the use and comfort of such of its prisoners as are held by the other, necessary articles of food and clothing."

It took a whole month to get the consent of the Federal authorities to this proposal. Previous to this, January 24, 1864, Judge Ould proposed that the prisoners on each side should be attended by their own surgeons, and that these "should act as Commissaries, with power to receive and distribute such contributions of money, food, clothing, and medicines as may be forwarded for the relief of prisoners." These surgeons were also to have full liberty to make reports to their respective governments of any matters relating to the welfare of prisoners.

To this humane proposal of the Confederate commission no reply was ever made. But it remains on record, pointing forever an accusing finger at the United States authorities, who would not embrace the

But to resume my narrative.   We had a long and laborious journey.   The first Sunday after our departure, March 19th, we had arrived in Lynchburg, where I preached in St. Paul's morning and evening. From that place we proceeded in an open wagon, on the 22d, reaching Lexington on the evening of the 23d.

opportunity of relieving the sufferings of the unfortunates in the prisons, North and South.

By a stroke of his pen General Grant could have emptied the prisons at Richmond, Andersonville, and other Southern places; but he would not do it.   Why?   Because, as we now know, "he preferred that the Confederates should be burdened with caring for these Federal prisoners when living, and charged with their death, should they die."

To any reader who is under the impression that the conditions existing in Libby Prison and at Andersonville find no parallel in any Northern prison, we commend the perusal of the report of Dr. Wm. H. Van Buren, of New York, on behalf of the United States Sanitary Commission, May 10, 1863, in which a state of things is described at Camp Douglas and at St. Louis, among the Southern prisoners, too horrible to quote.   The physicians who investigated the condition of the prisoners at St. Louis, say:

"It surely is not the intention of our government to place these prisoners in a position which will secure their extermination by pestilence in less than a year."

To conclude, let me quote the language of Mr. Charles A. Dana, who was the Federal Assistant Secretary of War during the war. In an editorial in the New York *Sun* (in 1876) he said:

"The Confederate authorities, and especially Mr. Davis, ought not to be held responsible for the terrible privations, sufferings, and injuries which our men had to endure while they were kept in Confederate military prisons.   The fact is unquestionable, that while the Confederates desired to exchange prisoners, to send our men home, and to get back their own, General Grant steadily and persistently resisted such an exchange. . . . It was not the Confederate authorities who insisted on keeping our prisoners in distress, want, and disease, but the commander of our own armies. . . . Moreover there is no evidence whatever that it was practicable for the Confederate authorities to feed our prisoners any better than they were fed, or to give them any better care and attention than they received."

See "Official Report of the History Committee of the Grand Camp, C. V., Department of Virginia, by Hon. Geo. L. Christian."

There we rested till Monday, 27th, and on the 26th I preached for Dr. Norton, then in charge of the church there,—its rector, Rev. Dr. Pendleton (a graduate of West Point) being an artillery officer in Lee's army. After a tedious wagon journey we at length arrived in Staunton on the 27th at eleven P.M. As soon as possible I procured a fresh horse — a beautiful bay mare, the best mount I had during the war — and set out to rejoin my regiment.

But it was too late. As I approached Richmond, I learned it had been evacuated, and soon found the enemy were between me and our army. After several futile attempts, I at length reached a point nine miles from Appomattox, only to learn that General Lee had that day, April 9th, surrendered what remained of the Army of Northern Virginia. It was impossible to believe it, until I saw some of the men who had been included in the surrender and been paroled. To say that I was not prepared for such an issue feebly expresses what I felt. Such was the confidence of Lee's soldiers in his supreme ability that, spite of all the evidences of the exhaustion of the Confederacy and the depletion of its armies, we could not for a moment entertain the thought that the Army of Northern Virginia could be compelled to lay down its arms and give up the struggle. The fact is that army was starved out — or rather the South was starved out, and could no longer feed its people or its soldiers. The number of desertions from the ranks during the previous month was ominous of the end that was preparing. And the reason was to be sought, not in the weakening of the resolution or the devotion of the men, but in the pleadings of the women at home. The distress existing in the farmhouses and cabins, where dwelt the wives and children of the soldiers of Lee's army, had become so acute that it could no longer be borne in silence; and every mail brought letters to the men, telling the hard conditions of life — the desperate straits to which their families were reduced — and appealing to them to come home and help keep them from starvation. These appeals were heart-rending, and if the men, by hundreds and thousands, responded by deserting the ranks and hastening to the relief of their wives and children, who will throw the first stone of condemnation at the course they took? That they meant to return to the colors, when they had put in a crop, or made some provision for the wants of their families, I do not doubt.

I will here set down the substance of a conversation I had many years afterward with Gen. Custis Lee, the eldest son of our commader-in-chief. The facts he related are surely most important to the right understanding of this last act in the great drama of the Civil War.

Gen. Custis Lee was captured at the battle of Sailor's Creek, together with many other Confederate officers. There followed kindly greetings between the Union and the Southern soldiers, some of whom had been associated in the old Federal army. While this was going on, Gen. Custis Lee says one of the Union officers (it was General Benham) said to one of the Confederates, "Oh, you could not get away. We knew beforehand every move you were going to make!" Asked to explain his meaning, he said that when the Union Army entered Richmond, one of the first places they made for was the executive mansion, and there in a scrap basket a soldier picked up a document which proved to be a communication from General Lee to the Secretary of War, containing information of the most important character. It seems that the Confederate Congress (one or both houses, I do not remember which) had requested General Lee to inform the President what his plans were, in the event of its becoming necessary to evacuate Richmond; and General Lee (always obedient to the civil authority) had sent to Mr. Davis a confidential statement, indicating the lines by which he would withdraw his army, and the points where he wished supplies to be accumulated for its use.

The officer to whom this document was shown at once recognized its great importance, and took immediate steps to have it forwarded, post haste, to General Grant, so that within twenty-four hours after Lee began his retreat, his whole plan of operations was laid before the Union commander.

Gen. Custis Lee told me that some time after the conclusion of the war he was in his father's office going over some papers with him, and then for the first time narrated to him what General Benham of the Union Army had said on that occasion. When General Lee heard the story he was greatly moved, and exclaimed, "Well, Custis, that explains it! I could never, till now, understand why I failed to extricate that army. I never worked harder than I did to accomplish it, yet every move I made was at once checkmated. It also explains why General Grant, who, the first day after the evacuation of Petersburg seemed hesitating and uncertain in his movements, became suddenly very vigorous and displayed more energy, skill, and judgment in his movements than I ever knew him to display before."

This extraordinary incident is of the deepest interest to the student of that campaign, and explains to us, who were Lee's soldiers, how it came to pass that his army was so soon and so hopelessly hemmed in.[1]

The most candid of the Federal historians, Dr. James Ford Rhodes, expresses the opinion that "in these final operations Grant outgeneralled Lee. The conditions," he says, "were not unequal: 49,000 men opposed 113,000, and the game was escape or surrender. He also intimates that some Confederate writers have admitted that "if everything had been managed properly the Army of Northern Virginia might have eluded surrender and protracted the war."

In reply let it first be said that if the Confederate officers responsible for the conduct of affairs at the

[1] I append a copy of a letter on this subject addressed to Major Walthall, and printed in the Memoirs of Jefferson Davis by his wife (1890), Vol. II, p. 595. But I have preferred to give in the text the incident as related to me orally by Gen. G. W. C. Lee on the occasion referred to.

"After I was taken prisoner at Sailor's Creek, with the greater part of the commands of General Ewell and General Dick Anderson, and was on my way to Petersburg with the officers of the three commands, we met the United States engineer brigade under command of General Benham, whom I knew prior to the breaking out of the war as one of the captains of my own corps — the engineers.

"He did not apparently recognize me, and I did not make myself known to him; but he began talking to General Ewell, in a loud tone of voice which could be distinctly heard by all around.

"I heard General Benham say, among other things, that 'General Weitzel had found, soon after his entrance into Richmond, a letter from General Lee, giving the condition of the Army of Northern Virginia and what he proposed to do should it become necessary to withdraw from the lines before Richmond and Petersburg, and that the letter was immediately sent to General Grant. In answer to some battle of Five Forks had "managed properly" — if they had carried out the plans of their great chief with a fair degree of fidelity — that battle would have been a Confederate victory, and Sheridan, as he testified himself, would have been captured. But there was grievous neglect — there was inexcusable dereliction of duty — and, as a consequence, Lee's lines were broken and he was forced to retreat. If evidence of the truth of this statement is demanded, the fact that the Confederate general officer, whose name has been always associated with the most superb feat of arms at Gettysburg, was relieved of his command by General Lee while on the retreat to Appomattox may serve as sufficient confirmation at least of the opinion of the commander of the Army of Northern Virginia.

So much for the direct cause that compelled the retreat. And for the rest, the extraordinary fact related by Gen. G. W. C. Lee is entirely sufficient to dispose of the statement that Grant outgeneralled Lee in the retreat to Appomattox. When the lion is caught in the net, it does not require the skill of a mighty hunter to slay him.

doubt expressed by General Ewell or someone else, General Benham replied, 'Oh, there is no doubt about the letter, for I saw it myself.'

"I received the impression at the time, or afterward, that this letter was a confidential communication to the Secretary of War in answer to a resolution of the Confederate Congress asking for information in 1865. When I mentioned this statement of General Benham to General Lee, some time afterward, the latter said, 'This accounts for the energy of the enemy's pursuit. The first day after we left the lines he seemed to be entirely at sea with regard to our movements; after that, though I never worked so hard in my life to withdraw our army in safety, he displayed more energy, skill, and judgment in his movements than I ever knew him to display before.'

[A true copy]   "G. W. C. LEE."

Dr. Rhodes, it is true, in the passage just quoted wrote in ignorance of the fact that chance had put General Grant in possession of the plans of General Lee. But it is strange that so careful a writer should have committed himself to the statement that "the conditions" between the two armies "were not unequal." He sees only the naked fact of 49,000 Confederates against 113,000 — which, by the way, is a quite exaggerated estimate of Lee's forces when the retreat began. He has no eyes for the enormous difference in the equipment of the two armies, — the one "armed, clothed, equipped, fed, and sheltered as no similar force in the world's history had ever been before," — the other almost starved, having been long on greatly reduced rations, scantily clothed, its vitality lowered by exposure to cold and hail and sleet, and by overwork in the trenches, consequent on the smallness of their numbers. Nor has the Federal historian any recollection of the difference between the condition of the mounts of the cavalry of the two armies. He forgets that the horses in Lee's army had long been, like the men, on starvation rations. Surely, when we consider these facts, one must say that if ever two armies faced each other under unequal conditions, it was when the soldiers of Lee and Grant grappled with each other in those last days before Appomattox. The true estimate of the situation was given by Mr. Charles Francis Adams when he said in his oration at Lexington:

"Finally, when in April the summons to conflict came, the Army of Northern Virginia seemed to stagger to its feet, and, gaunt and grim, shivering with cold and emaciated with hunger, worn down by hard, unceasing attrition, it faced its enemy, formidable still."

I will not dwell upon the affecting scenes that were witnessed when the terrible fact became known that the remnant of the Army of Northern Virginia was to be surrendered to General Grant and the mighty host under his command. Those heroes of more than a hundred battles wept like children when the news came. To the very last they were unconquered. That very morning they had fought with all their old intrepidity and resolution. And they would have fought on, had their beloved commander bid them, till the last man had fallen face to the foe; but when Lee told them to sheathe their swords and stack their muskets, they obeyed him, though with breaking hearts.

This, his last act as the commander of the Confederate armies, was every way worthy of his heroic character. How much easier to have put himself at the head of his surviving soldiers and died with them in one last splendid but desperate charge! Or again, how much easier to have yielded to the counsels of some of his captains, and, having cut his way through the encircling Federal host, to have. continued the struggle in a guerilla warfare that might have been prolonged indefinitely!

Both of these temptations he put aside, and rose to the height of the supreme sacrifice which duty to his people demanded. "The question is," he said to his officers, "Is it right to surrender this army? If it is right, then I will take all the responsibility." He asked no man to share with him that awful responsibility — to bear any part of the burden of that tremendous decision. He took it all — he bore it all, on his own heroic shoulders. Is there in history any finer spectacle of self-devotion for duty's sake than this? Is it any wonder his soldiers idolized him, and were ready to die for him? Were they not justified in looking to him as

"The great prince and man of men."

As I draw the curtain over this scene at Appomattox I would pay my tribute of admiration to that superb army whose history closed that day. My own words would to some extent be discounted by the fact that I served myself in its ranks. I will therefore rather refer to the opinions of some of its illustrious opponents, — to "Fighting Joe" Hooker's testimony that "it exhibited a discipline and efficiency which the Army of the Potomac had vainly striven to emulate," — to the words of Swinton, "that incomparable Southern Infantry, which, tempered by two years of battle, and habituated to victory, equalled any soldiers that ever followed the eagles to conquest," — to the generous tribute of Major Jas. F. Huntington, "the indomitable courage, the patient endurance of privations, the supreme devotion of the Southern soldiers, will stand on the pages of history, as engraven on a monument more enduring than brass," — to the acknowledgment of another Federal commander that the army of Lee "was the finest army that ever marched on this continent."

To all these tributes I add the generous acknowledgment of Mr. Chas. Francis Adams "that Lee and the Army of Northern Virginia never sustained defeat. Finally succumbing to exhaustion, to the end they were not overthrown in fight."

And for myself I can only repeat what I have said elsewhere on a public occasion: "These men were heroes, if ever heroes were. What hardships did they not uncomplainingly endure, on the march, in the bivouac,

in the trenches! What sacrifices did they not cheerfully make for a cause dearer than life itself! What
dangers did they not face with unquailing front! Who
that ever saw them can forget those hardy battalions
that followed Stonewall Jackson in his weird marches
in the great valley campaign? Rusty and ragged
were their uniforms, but bright were their muskets
and their bayonets, and they moved like the very
whirlwind of war! . . . They were private soldiers —
fame will not herald their names to posterity. They
fought without reward, and they died without distinction. It was enough for them to hear the voice of duty,
and to follow it, though it led them by a rugged path
to a bloody grave. . . . They were not soldiers of fortune, but soldiers of conscience, who dared all that
men can dare, and endured all that men can endure in
obedience to what they believed the call of their country. If ever men lived of whom it could be truly said
that their hearts echoed the sentiment,

"Dulce et decorum est pro patria mori"

these were the men. They loved their State. They
loved their homes and their firesides. They were no
politicians. Most of them knew little of the warring
theories of constitutional interpretation. But one
thing they knew — armed legions were marching upon
their homes, and it was their duty to hurl them back
at any cost. For this, not we only who shared their
perils and hardships do them honor — not the Southern people only — but all brave men everywhere.

"Nameless they may be on the page of history,
but the name of the soldier of the Army of Northern
Virginia will echo round the world through the ages

to come, and everywhere it will be accepted as the synonym of valor, of constancy, and of loyalty to the sternest call of duty."

As I have stated, I was not present at the surrender, but having found the enemy between me and our army, had made a wide détour, and was still nine miles away when the news came to me that all was over.

As soon as I was assured beyond doubt of the overwhelming fact, I turned Lady Grey's head back toward Staunton, and that day we covered together sixty-five miles,—the longest ride I had ever made. When, the second day after, I reached Staunton, night had set in, and I hoped to get home without being observed or recognized. But it was moonlight, and as I rode through the main street, I was soon surrounded by a group of men eager for news from the army. I said, "There is news, but I prefer not to tell you what it is, for I know you will not believe it." The answer was a chorus of demands to tell what it was. Again I demurred and asked to be excused — only to meet the same reply. So at last I said, "Well, if you will have it — General Lee has surrendered to General Grant!" This, as I anticipated, was greeted with derisive laughter, and I was told I was demoralized and had accepted a groundless rumor as the truth.

In fact, the people could not believe it possible. The disaster was too utterly overwhelming to be accepted on the testimony of one man.

When our idolized leader sheathed his sword at Appomattox the world grew dark to us. We felt as if the sun had set in blood to rise no more. It was as if the foundations of the earth were sinking beneath our feet.

I recall saying to Dr. Sparrow soon after my arrival

in Staunton, "I feel as if I had nothing left to live for!"
— only to receive from the dear old man a tender but
well-deserved rebuke for such an unchristian sentiment.

In closing my narrative, I wish to put on record in
these pages that my regiment, the Second Virginia Cavalry, under the command of that gallant gentleman,
Col. Cary Breckinridge, performed valiant service during the closing days of the great drama. It acted with
its accustomed gallantry, and more cannot be said.
General Munford did not consider that his cavalry
was included in the surrender of General Lee's army,
for reasons which it is not necessary here to explain.
Col. Cary Breckinridge gives the following account of
the course pursued by the Second Virginia Cavalry; he
says, "After leaving Appomattox Court House, we
made a détour to the right through woods and fields
and roads, over hills and valleys, bearing to the left.
After going perhaps a mile, were reached the Lynchburg road, at the top of a considerable hill, a few miles
west of Appomattox Court House. In making this
move there were some lively encounters with the Federal Cavalry, more particularly on our left, where
General Rosser and W. H. F. Lee were fighting. . . .
Almost simultaneously with the arrival of the Second
Virginia Cavalry in the road, certainly the last to reach
it, as we neared the rear of the enemy, a small force
of their cavalry came charging up the road, and attacked
us in the rear. We wheeled about and a squadron or
two was ordered to charge them, which was done in
good style, the enemy retreating in the direction of
the Court House. Holding our position on the hill,
the enemy came our way the second time, and were
again driven back.

"This was done handsomely by the First Maryland Cavalry, under the following circumstances: When the enemy, in full charge, was seen coming at them, not over a hundred yards distant, Capt. W. J. Raisin, commanding the first squadron and riding with Colonel Dorsey, at the head of his regiment, remarked, 'Colonel, we must charge them, it is the only chance,' and the words had not left his lips when Dorsey, who had perceived the necessity, gave the command, 'Draw sabre! Gallop! Charge!' And this little band of Marylanders hurled themselves against the heavy column of the enemy and drove them back. This was the last blow struck by the Army of Northern Virginia."

" This was the last action in which the Second Virginia Cavalry had a part, and with the charge of the First Maryland Cavalry may be said to have been the last effort made by any portion of Lee's army in behalf of the Southern cause."

General Munford held that as his command was outside of the lines, he did not consider that he was included in the terms of the surrender, and hence he felt at liberty to withdraw his skirmishers, having already gained the Lynchburg road. Accordingly, he marched the regiment to Lynchburg and there it was disbanded, on the very spot where it had been organized in 1861, — disbanded "subject to reassemble for the continuance of the struggle." It had made for itself an honorable record; it left June 1, 1861, with 700 men upon it rolls, and it is shown that 7 of its captains were killed and 10 wounded; 10 of its lieutenants were killed and 22 wounded; 2 sergeants were killed; 1 adjutant killed; 138 men were killed; 362 wounded; 89 died in service; 75 were captured; making an aggregate accounted for 654. I may here mention that Lieut.-Col. Cary Breckinridge received five sabre cuts in one engagement. Its blood was spilt from the first Manassas to Appomattox. About ten days later General Munford received a communication from the President of the Confederate States, ordering him to join the army of Gen. Joe Johnston, and there lies before me an order dated Headquarters Munford's Cavalry Brigade, April 21, 1865, in which General Munford makes a stirring appeal to his soldiers to rally once more to his banner and continue the struggle. This order concludes as follows:

"We have still a country, a flag, an army, and a government. Then to horse! A circular will be sent to each of your officers, designating the time and place of assembly. Hold yourselves in instant readiness, and bring all true men with you from this command who will go, and let us who struck the last blow, as a part of the Army of Northern Virginia, strike the first with that victorious army which, by the blessing of our gracious God, will yet come to redeem her hallowed soil.

"Thos. T. Munford, Brigadier-general
"Commanding Division."

A few days after the issuance of this order General Munford learned that Gen. Joe Johnston was negotiating to surrender his army. This put an end to his project, designated in the said general order. In the meantime, however, it had reached Colonel Dorsey of the First Maryland Cavalry and that officer immediately rallied his command and was proceeding to join General Munford, but he, on the 28th of April, wrote Colonel Dorsey, informing him of General Johnston's approaching surrender and of the abandonment of the design.

CONCLUSION

SOME four or five years ago, while attending a reunion of Confederate veterans at Nashville, I made the acquaintance of Colonel ———, who told me the following story.

At the outbreak of the war in 1861, he, then a very young man and resident in Tennessee, went to his father and said, "Father, I have thought over the issue between the North and the South and have decided that it is my duty to join the Southern Army." To which his father, also a Tennesseean, replied, "All right, my son, you must of course act as your conscience dictates, but I must tell you that I also have earnestly reflected on the situation and have decided that it is *my* duty to join the Union Army." And so they parted in all kindness, to serve in the opposing armies.

Now it happened that in one of the battles in the southwest the father and the son, each in command of a regiment, the one under the Stars and Stripes, the other under the Stars and Bars, met in deadly conflict, neither being aware of the identity of his antagonist; and the son took the father prisoner, not knowing it was his father. This was a remarkable experience not often paralleled, but what was more remarkable still was the statement made to me by Colonel ——— that the fact that he and his father were fighting on opposite sides in that tremendous

277

conflict made no difference in their feelings toward each other. So absolutely did father and son respect each other's conviction of duty that their mutual affection remained unchanged.

In bringing to a close my fragmentary record of experiences and observations as a Confederate soldier, I would like to say that I hope nothing I have written will seem inconsistent with the respect I feel for the honest convictions of the brave men who fought against the South, under the same constraint of duty as that which actuated us in the opposite ranks. Good and true men reached different conclusions in that supreme issue presented in 1861. It was inevitable. As Mr. Charles Francis Adams has said, "In case of direct and insoluble issue between sovereign State and sovereign Nation, every man was not only free to decide, but *had* to decide the question of ultimate allegiance for himself; and whichever way he decided he was right." Brave men respect each other. Men who draw the sword for conscience' sake should, and will, sooner or later, recognize the equal right of their antagonists who are also in arms for conscience' sake.

This was finely expressed a quarter of a century ago by a brave Union soldier, now a justice of the Supreme Court.[1]

"We believed that it was most desirable that the North should win; we believed in the principle that the Union is indissoluble; but we equally believed that those who stood against us held just as sacred convictions that were the opposite of ours, and we respected them, as every man with a heart must respect those who gave all for their belief."

[1] Justice O. W. Holmes.

But that same profound respect for the convictions which conscience enforces makes it impossible for us who stood for the South in 1861 to profess any repentance, or any regret, for the course we then took. A man cannot repent of an act done in the fear of God and under the behest of conscience. We did what we believed in our hearts was right. We gave all for our belief. We cannot regret obeying the most solemn and sacred dictates of duty as we saw it.

We would not do aught to perpetuate the angry passions of the Civil War, or to foster any feeling of hostility to our fellow citizens of other parts of the Union. But we must forevermore do honor to our heroic dead. We must forevermore cherish the sacred memories of those four terrible but glorious years of unequal strife. We must forevermore consecrate in our hearts our old battle flag of the Southern Cross — not now as a political symbol, but as the consecrated emblem of an heroic epoch. The people that forgets its heroic dead is already dying at the heart, and we believe we shall be truer and better citizens of the United States if we are true to our past.

The Southern people have already shown the world how the defeats of war may be turned into the victories of peace. They have given mankind an example of how a brave and proud race may sustain disaster, and endure long years of humiliation, yet rise again to power and glory.

I have said elsewhere two things of the Confederate soldier which I wish to repeat here.

The first is that the supreme issue in his mind in all that great struggle was not, as is generally supposed, the dissolution of the Union. No, the dissolution of the Union was not what the Confederate soldier had chiefly at heart. Nor was the establishment of the Southern Confederacy what he had chiefly at heart. Both the one and the other were secondary to the preservation of the supreme and sacred right of self-government. They were means to the end, not the end itself.

And the second thing I wish to say is that I do not believe the valor and devotion of the armies of the South were so lavishly poured out in vain. By their all-sacrificing patriotism they arraigned before the world the usurpation of powers and functions which by the Constitution were reserved to the States — and their arraignment has not been in vain. Silently, as the years have rolled by since Appomattox, its accusing voice has been heard, and its protest has become effective, until to-day the rights of the States — of all the States — are recognized as inviolate by both the executive, the legislative, and the judicial departments of the Government. And therefore I hold that just as surely as the enemies of the North saved the Union from dissolution, so surely did the armies of the South save the rights of the States within the Union. So that, if it is due to the valor of the Northern Army and Navy that we have to-day an indissoluble Union, it is equally due to the valor of the Confederate soldiers and sailors that that indissoluble Union is composed of indestructible States.

Thus victor and vanquished will both be crowned with the laurel of victory by the future historian.

I will add one other conviction which I deeply cherish. The Confederate soldier has left a legacy of valor and of liberty to his fellow countrymen, North and South, which is destined to be recognized as a part of the national inheritance.

A recent historian of "The Greatness and Decline of Rome" [1] has remarked that the whole course of ancient history proves the tenacity and depth of republican ideas and traditions in the little Greek or Italian republics, and the difficulty of abolishing their liberties. He tells us that the republicanism of ancient Rome which the empire *seemed* to crush and destroy has still been mighty in modern Europe. It has inspired Europe to fight for her great ideals of liberty, without which European history would have been a counterpart of Oriental history, a continuous succession of despotisms, rising one upon the ruins of another.

It is thus that I believe the heroic spirit of liberty which animated the soldiers of the Confederacy, though it *seemed* to be crushed and destroyed at Appomattox, will in generations to come inspire Americans to fight for the high ideals of freedom and self-government which the men of the North and the men of the South have alike inherited from their forefathers. It will be recognized that the men who followed the battle flags of the Confederacy at such cost of hardship and trial and peril — exhibiting a devotion, a fortitude, a valor, and a self-sacrifice never surpassed — were animated by motives as pure and unselfish as ever stirred the hearts and nerved the arms of patriots. And so it will come to pass that the glorious valor and steadfast devotion to liberty which characterized the Confederate soldier will be acknowledged as a part of the national inheritance, to be treasured and guarded by every American who loves his country and values

[1] Professor Ferrero.

the traditions of her glory. The fact that he did not succeed in his enterprise will abate no jot or tittle from the honor paid to his memory; for I dare to believe that the American of the future will recognize the eternal truth that it is not success which ennobles, but duty well done — manhood illustriously displayed, whether in victory or defeat.

Thus the fame of the Confederate soldier will shine with imperishable lustre:

"Immota manet, sæcula vincit."

APPENDIX

THE MOTIVES AND AIMS

OF

THE SOLDIERS OF THE SOUTH IN THE CIVIL WAR

AN ORATION

DELIVERED BEFORE THE UNITED CONFEDERATE
VETERANS AT THEIR FOURTEENTH ANNUAL
REUNION AT NASHVILLE, TENN.
JUNE 14, 1904

BY

RANDOLPH HARRISON McKIM, D.D., LL.D., D.C.L.
RECTOR OF THE CHURCH OF THE EPIPHANY, WASHINGTON, D.C.

Τίς γὰρ ἢ τῶν ποιεῖν δυναμένων ἢ τῶν λέγειν ἐπισταμένων οὐ πονήσει
καὶ φιλοσοφήσει βουλόμενος ἅμα τε τῆς αὑτοῦ διανοίας καὶ τῆς ἐκεί͵ _ν
ἀρετῆς μνημεῖον εἰς ἅπαντα τὸν χρονὸν καταλιπεῖν. — *Isocrates*

ORIGINALLY PUBLISHED
BY ORDER OF THE UNITED CONFEDERATE VETERANS

THE REV. RANDOLPH H. McKIM, D.D. 1904

ORATION

Ladies and Gentlemen, Comrades and Fellow-citizens:

It is with deep emotion that I rise to address you to-day. When I look over this vast concourse of the brave men and the noble women of the South — representing every one of the eleven sovereign States once associated in the Southern Confederacy — and when I look into the faces of the veteran survivors of that incomparable army that fought with such magnificent valor and constancy for four long years under those tattered battle flags, now furled forever, I am overwhelmed at once by the dignity and the difficulty of the task assigned me. There is such a vast disproportion between the powers which the occasion demands and those which I possess, that I should not dare to essay the task but for my confidence in your generosity and forbearance to a speaker who at least can say: "I too loved the Lost Cause and marched and fought under the banner of the Southern Cross."

There are two unique features which must arrest the attention of every observer of this scene to-day. The first is the fact that all this pageantry, all this enthusiasm, is a tribute to a lost cause. The second is the fact that we assemble under the victorious banner to pay our reverend homage to the conquered one.

A stranger coming into our midst and observing our proceedings might suppose that we were met here to celebrate the foundation of a State, or to acclaim the triumph of armies, or to exult in the victory of a great cause. But no! Nine and thirty years ago our new republic sank to rise no more; our armies were defeated; our banner went down in blood!

What then?   Are we here to indulge in vain regrets, to lament over our defeat, or to conspire for the reëstablishment of our fallen cause? No! The love and loyalty which we give to the Lost Cause, and to the defeated banner, is a demonstration of the deep hold that cause had upon the hearts of the Southern people, and of the absolute sincerity and the complete devotion with which they supported it; but it is no evidence of unmanly and fruitless repining over defeat, nor of any lurking disloyalty to the Union, in which now, thank God, the Southern States have equal rights and privileges with all the other States of our broad land. We saw our banner go down, with breaking hearts. When our idolized leader sheathed his sword at Appomattox the world grew dark to us. We felt as if the sun had set in blood to rise no more. It was as if the foundations of the earth were sinking beneath our feet. But that same stainless hero whom we had followed with unquestioning devotion taught us not to despair. He told us it was the part of brave men to accept defeat without repining. "Human virtue," he said, "should be equal to human calamity." He pointed upward to the star of duty, and bade us follow it as bravely in peace as we had followed it in war.   Henceforth it should be our consecrated task, by the help of God, to rebuild the fallen walls of our prosperity.

And so we accepted the result of the war in good faith. We abide the arbitrament of the sword. We subscribe as sincerely as the men who fought against us to the sentiment: *"One Flag, one Country, one Constitution, one Destiny."* This is now for us an indissoluble Union of indestructible States. We are loyal to that starry banner. We remember that it was baptized with Southern blood when our forefathers first unfurled it to the breeze. We remember that it was a Southern poet, Francis Scott Key, who immortalized it in the "Star Spangled Banner." We remember that it was the genius of a Southern soldier and statesman, George Washington, that finally established it in triumph.

Southern blood has again flowed in its defence in the Spanish war, and should occasion require, we pledge our lives and our sacred honor to defend it against foreign aggression, as bravely as will the descendants of the Puritans. And yet, to-day, while that banner of the Union floats over us, we bring the offering of our love and loyalty to the memory of the flag of the Southern Confederacy! Strange as it may seem to one who does not understand our people; inconsistent and incomprehensible as it may appear; we salute yonder flag — the banner of the Stars and Stripes — as the symbol of our reunited country, at the same moment that we come together to do homage to the memory of the Stars and Bars. There is in our hearts a double loyalty to-day; a loyalty to the present, and a loyalty to the dear, dead past. We still love our old battle flag with the Southern cross upon its fiery folds! We have wrapped it round our hearts! We have enshrined it in the sacred ark of our love; and we will honor it and cherish it evermore, — not now as a political symbol, but as the consecrated emblem of an heroic epoch; as the sacred memento of a day that is dead; as the embodiment of memories that will be tender and holy as long as life shall last.

Let not our fellow-countrymen of the North mistake the spirit of this great occasion. If Daniel Webster could say that the Bunker Hill monument was not erected "to perpetuate hostility to Great Britain," much more can we say that the monuments we have erected, and will yet erect, in our Southland, to the memory of our dead heroes, are not intended to perpetuate the angry passions of the Civil War, or to foster or keep alive any feeling of hostility to our brethren of other parts of the Union. No; but these monuments are erected, and these great assemblages of our surviving veterans are held, in simple loyalty to the best and purest dictates of the human heart. The people that forgets its heroic dead is already dying at the heart; and we believe it will make for the strength and the glory of the

United States if the sentiments that animate us to-day shall be perpetuated, generation after generation. Yes, we honor, and we bid our children honor, the loyalty to duty — to conscience — to fatherland — that inspired the men of '61, and it is our prayer and our hope that, as the years and the generations pass, the rising and the setting sun, the moon and the stars, winter and summer, spring and autumn, will see the people of the South loyal to the memories of those four terrible but glorious years of strife; loyally worshipping at the shrine of the splendid manhood of our heroic citizen soldiers, and the even more splendid womanhood, whose fortitude and whose endurance have challenged the admiration of the world. Then, when the united republic, in years to come, shall call, "To arms!" our children, and our children's children, will rally to the call, and, emulating the fidelity and the supreme devotion of the soldiers of the Confederacy, will gird the Stars and Stripes with an impenetrable rampart of steel.

But it is not the dead alone whom we honor here to-day. We hail the presence of the survivors of that tremendous conflict. Veterans of more than forty years! you have come from all over the South — from the Patapsco and the Potomac, the James and the Rappahannock, the Cumberland and the Tennessee, the Mississippi and the Rio Grande — from the sea-shore — from the Gulf — from the Blue Ridge and the Alleghanies, and some of you even from the shores of the Pacific Ocean — to pay your tribute to the dead cause and the dead heroes who laid down their lives for it. May I, on behalf of this great assembly — on behalf of the whole South — offer *you* a tribute of respect and veneration to-day? We hail you as the honored survivors of a great epoch and a glorious struggle. We welcome you as the men whom, above all others, the South delights to honor.

It is indeed a matter of course that we, your comrades and your fellow Southrons, should honor you. But we are not alone. Your brave antagonists of the Northern armies begin at last to recognize the purity of your motives, as they have always recognized the splendor of your valor. The dispassionate historian, even though his sympathy is given to the North, no longer denies the sincerity of your belief in the sacredness of your cause. The world itself confesses the honesty of your purpose, and the glory of your gallant struggle against superior numbers and resources. Most of you that survive have no insignia of rank, no title of distinction. You were private soldiers,— but I see round your brows the aureole of a soldier's glory. You are transfigured by the battles you have fought: Nashville, Franklin, Perryville, Murfreesboro, Shiloh, Chickamauga, in the West; and Manassas, Seven Pines, Mechanicsville, Sharpsburg, Fredericksburg, Chancellorsville, Gettysburg, the Wilderness, and Cold Harbor, in the East.

But you have done more than bare your breast to the foeman's steel. You have shown to the world how the defeats of war may be turned into the victories of peace. You have taught mankind how a proud race may sustain disaster and yet survive and win the applause of the world. In those terrible years of Reconstruction — how much more bitter than the four years of war! — you splendidly exemplified the sentiment,

"Mergas profundo, pulchrior exilit!"

Out of the depths of the bitter flood of Reconstruction the South emerged, through your fortitude, through your patience, through your courage, more beautiful than ever.

For all this your people honor you in your old age. They cherish the memory of your deeds, and will hand it down a priceless heirloom to their children's children. You are not pensioners on the bounty of the Union, thank God! Your manhood is not sapped by eating the bread of dependence. You have faced poverty as bravely as you faced the cannon's mouth, and so I salute you as the aristocracy of the South!

Your deeds have carved for you a place in the temple of her fame. They will not be forgotten — the world will not forget them. Your campaigns are studied to-day in the military schools of Europe; yes, and at West Point, itself.

But, alas! your ranks are thinned. Each year the artillery of the great destroyer of human life mows down hundreds of the men in gray. One after another of our great captains has said "*Adsum*," as the angel of God has called the roll beyond the river. Since you last met, two of those illustrious leaders have passed from our sight — Longstreet, the brave, and Gordon, the superb — Gordon, whose white plume, like the plume of Henry of Navarre, was ever in the forefront of the charging line — Gordon, of whom we may say — and what could be higher praise? — that he was worthy to be the lieutenant of Lee, and the successor of Stonewall Jackson in the confidence and affection of the Army of Northern Virginia — Gordon, who, at Appomattox, taught us not to lose faith in God, and for a quarter of a century before his death taught us to have faith in our fellow-citizens of the North. As we think of those superb leaders, now gone from our gaze, we are tempted to say: Alas! the stars by which we have guided our course have set, one by one, beneath the horizon. But no! Let us rather say that death has only placed them higher in the firmament, as fixed stars, whose deathless light shall never fail us in the generations to come. Dead? Are these our heroes dead? No, they yet live as live the heroes of old; as Leonidas lives in the firmament of patriotism; as Shakespeare lives in the firmament of intellect; as Newton and Bacon live in the realm of science; as Jefferson and Madison and Marshall live in the realm of statesmanship; as Washington lives in the realm of pure and steadfast love of liberty. Veterans, when I say this I am not giving utterance to the partial and prejudiced view of a Southern soldier; I am but echoing the judgment of the world.

The ablest military critic in the British army in this generation has placed Lee and Stonewall Jackson in the same group with Washington and Wellington and Marlborough, the five greatest generals, in his opinion, of the English-speaking race; and the President of the United States, Mr. Roosevelt, has said in his "Life of Thomas H. Benton": "The world has never seen better soldiers than those who followed Lee; and their leader will undoubtedly rank, as without any exception, the very greatest of all the great captains that the English-speaking peoples have brought forth; and this, although the last and chief of his antagonists, may himself claim to stand as the full equal of Wellington and Marlborough." As to the rank and file, General Hooker of the Union Army has said that "for steadiness and efficiency" Lee's army was unsurpassed in ancient or modern times, — "We have not been able to rival it." And Gen. Chas. A. Whittier of Massachusetts has said, "The Army of Northern Virginia will deservedly rank as the best army which has existed in this continent, suffering privations unknown to its opponent. The North sent no such army to the field." It is, then, not the extravagance of hyperbole, but the sober utterance of truth, to say that these heroic leaders and the heroic men who followed them — sublime in their devotion to duty; magnificently unregardful of the possibility of waging successful war against such vast odds of numbers and resources — have raised a monument more lasting than brass or marble; higher and grander than the great pyramid of Egypt; more splendid than the tomb of Napoleon at the Hôtel des Invalides; more sublime than Westminster Abbey itself — a monument which will rivet the gaze of generations yet unborn — a monument at whose feet mankind will bow in reverence so long as freedom survives on earth. It is a shaft not made with hands — a spiritual obelisk — on which all men will read: "*Sacred to the memory of men who laid down their lives, their fortunes, and their sacred honor in loyal obedience to the call of duty as they understood it.*"

Comrades, standing here at the foot of that unseen column, reared by the valor and the virtue of the citizen soldiers of the Armies of the South, I feel that a duty is laid upon me, which I may not refuse to perform. From the hills and valleys of more than a thousand battle fields, where sleep the silent battalions in gray, there rises to my ear a solemn voice of command which I dare not disobey. It bids me vindicate to the men of this generation the course which the men of the South followed in the crisis of 1861. It is not enough that their valor is recognized. It is not enough that their honesty is confessed. We ask of our Northern brethren — we ask of the world — a recognition of their patriotism and their love of liberty. We cannot be silent as long as any aspersion is cast by the pen of the historian, or by the tongue of the orator, upon their patriotic motives, or upon the loftiness of the object they had in view through all that tremendous conflict. We make no half-hearted apology for their act. It is justice for which we plead, not charity.

The view of the origin and character of the course of action followed by the Southern States in 1861, which has so widely impressed itself upon the popular mind, may be summed up in four propositions. First, that the Secession of the cotton States was the result of a conspiracy on the part of a few of their leaders, and that it was not the genuine expression of the mind of the people. Second, that the act whereby the Southern States withdrew from the Union was an act of disloyalty to the Constitution, and of treason to the United States government. Third, that the people of the South were not attached to the Union and were eager to seize upon an excuse for its dissolution. Fourth, that the South plunged into a desperate war for the purpose of perpetuating slavery, and made that institution the cornerstone of the new confederacy which it sought to establish.

I propose briefly to examine these propositions, and shall endeavor to show that every one of them, when scrutinized under the impartial light of history, must be pronounced essentially erroneous. Believing that they are erroneous and that they do grave injustice to the memory and the motives of the men of the South in that great crisis, it becomes a sacred duty to expose the unsubstantial foundation upon which these opinions rest, lest our children and our children's children should misread and misunderstand the acts of their fathers.

1. I need not spend much time upon the first of these propositions. The evidence at the disposal of the historian is conclusive that the action taken by the cotton States in withdrawing from the Union had the support of an overwhelming majority of the people of those States. There was no conspiracy. The people were in advance of their leaders. The most recent, and perhaps the ablest, of the Northern historians, acknowledges this, and says that had not Davis, Toombs, and Benjamin led in Secession, the people would have chosen other leaders. The number of unconditional Union men in the seven States that first seceded, he declares, was insignificant, and he makes the remarkable admission that "had the North thoroughly understood the problem, had it known that the people of the cotton States were practically unanimous and that the action of Virginia, North Carolina, and Tennessee was backed by a large and genuine majority, it might have refused to undertake the seemingly unachievable task." [1] There can be no question, then, that the impartial historian of the future will recognize that, whether right or wrong, the establishment of the Southern Confederacy was the result of a popular movement — was the act, not of a band of conspirators, but of the whole people, with a unanimity never surpassed in the history of revolutions.

2. I come now to the question whether the act of the Southern States in withdrawing from the Union was an act

---

[1] Rhodes' History of the United States, Vol. III, p. 404.

of disloyalty to the Constitution and of treason to the government of the United States. This once burning question may now be discussed without heat. It is no longer a practical, but a thoroughly academic, question. The right of Secession, if it ever existed, exists no longer. The Fourteenth Amendment to the Constitution has changed the character of our political fabric. When we surrendered at Appomattox, the right of Secession was surrendered forever.

But when we say that right does not exist to-day, we do not acknowledge that it did not exist in 1861. On the contrary, we maintain that it did exist, and that those who maintained its existence had upon their side, logically and historically, the overwhelming weight of evidence. Our late antagonists, who are now our brethren and our fellow-citizens, cannot be expected to agree with us in this proposition, but we put it to their candor and their sense of justice to say whether the South had not as good a right to her opinion of the meaning of the Constitution as the North had to hers. There were in 1860 two interpretations of that instrument, there were two views of the nature of the government which was established. On what principle and by what authority can it be claimed that the view taken by the South was certainly wrong, and that the view taken by the North was certainly right? Or, waiving the question which view was really right, we ask our Northern friends to tell us why the South was not justified in following that interpretation which she believed to be the true one? She had helped to build — nay, she was the chief builder of — the fabric of the Constitution. A Massachusetts historian [1] has said that, of the five great men who molded the nation, four were men of the South — Washington, Jefferson, Madison, and Marshall; and though these great men differed in political opinion, yet three, at least, Washington, Jefferson,

---

[1] Mr. John Fiske.

and Madison, are on record as declaring that the Constitution was a compact between the States, and that those thirteen States were thirteen independent sovereignties.[1]

[1] Even Marshall might be appealed to in support of that view; for in the debate on the adoption of the Constitution he used the following language: "Can they [the Congress] go beyond the delegated powers? If they were to make a law not warranted by any of the powers enumerated, it would be considered by the judges [of the Supreme Court] as an infringement of the Constitution which they are to guard. . . . They would declare it void." — Magruder's "Life of Marshall," p. 82.

Whatever he may have thought of the nature of the government at a later period, he here stands forth as an advocate of that view which confines the government to the exercise of such powers as are distinctly "enumerated." He was then (1788) in his thirty-third year.

In the same debate, referring to Virginia's right to resume "her powers, if abused," he said, "it is a maxim that those who give may take away. It is the people that give power, and can take it back. Who shall restrain them? They are the masters who give it." (Elliott's "Debates," III, p. 227, quoted in "The Republic of Republics," p. 109.) Words could not more plainly avow the right of the people of a State to resume the powers delegated to the General Government.

As to Mr. Madison's opinion, it is enough to quote his declaration that in adopting the Constitution they were making "a government of a federal nature, consisting of many co-equal sovereignties."

As to Washington's views, when he said of the proposed Union under the Constitution, "Is it best for the States to unite?" he clearly recognized that it was the people of each State who were to form the Union. The United States would be, when formed, the creature of the States. He often speaks of the accession of the individual States to the proposed government, which he calls "*the New Confederacy.*" (Letter to General Pinckney, June 28, 1788.)

This new Union was in his eyes "a compact." In a letter to Madison, August 3, 1788, he uses this language: "*Till the States begin to act under the new compact.*" (See on this "The Republic of Republics," pp. 222–230.)

In the letter written by Washington, by order of the Convention, to accompany the copy of the proposed Constitution sent to each State, the following passage occurs:

"It is obviously impracticable in the Federal Government of these States to secure all rights of independent sovereignty to each, and yet provide for the interest and safety of all." This certainly implies

Let the young men of the New South remember the part the Old South took in the planting and training of Anglo-Saxon civilization on these western shores.

Our New England brethren have been so diligent in exploiting the voyage of the *Mayflower*, and the landing of the Pilgrims, and their services to morality and civilization and liberty in the new world, that they seem to have persuaded themselves, and would fain persuade the world, that American liberty is a plant chiefly of New England growth, and that America owes its ideas of political independence and representative government, and its reverence for conscience, to the sturdy settlers of our northeastern coasts. Her orators and her poets, year after year, on Fore-fathers' Day, not only glorify — as is meet — the deeds of their ancestors, but seem to put forward the claim, in amazing forgetfulness of history, that it is to New England that the great republic of the West owes the genesis of its free institutions, the inspirations of its love of civil and religious liberty, and its high ideals of character.[1]

It is then not amiss to remind the Southern men of this generation that thirteen years before the *Mayflower* landed her pilgrims at Plymouth Rock, three English ships, the *Susan Constant*, the *Godspeed*, and the *Discovery*, came to anchor in the James River, Virginia; and that the vine of English civilization and English liberty was first planted, not on Plymouth Rock, in 1620, but at Jamestown Island, Virginia, on the 13th of May, 1607. What Webster so nobly said of. the *Mayflower* may be as truly said of these three ships that bore the first Virginia colony. "The stars that guided them were the unobscured constellations of civil and religious liberty. Their decks were the altars of the living

that each State entering the Union was an independent sovereign, which surrendered *some* of its rights for the good of all.

[1] Rev. Dr. Coyle in a recent sermon before the Presbyterian General Assembly refers to "the Puritan Conscience which put rock foundations under this Republic."

God." Let me also recall the fact that on July 30, 1619, eighteen months before the Pilgrims set foot on American soil, the vine of liberty had so deeply taken root in the colony of Virginia that there was assembled in the church at Jamestown a free representative body (the first on American soil) — the House of Burgesses — to deliberate for the welfare of the people. There also, more than a century before the Revolution, when Oliver Cromwell's fleet appeared to whip the rebellious Old Dominion into obedience, Virginia demanded and obtained recognition of the principle "*No taxation without representation*"; and there, in 1676, just one hundred years before the revolt of the Colonies, that remarkable man, Nathaniel Bacon, "soldier, orator, leader," raised the standard of revolt against the oppressions of the British Crown.

But this is not all. That spot on Jamestown Island, marked to-day by a ruined, ivy-clad, church tower and a group of moss-covered tombstones, is the sacred ground whence sprang that stream of genius and power which contributed most to the achievement of American independence, and to the organization of American liberty. That first colony, planted in tidewater Virginia, was, in the revolutionary period, prolific in men of genius and force and intense devotion to liberty never perhaps equalled, in modern times, in any region of equal size and of so small a population. This is acknowledged by careful and candid historians to-day, among whom I may mention Senator Lodge, of Massachusetts. It was a Southern orator, Patrick Henry, who gave to the colonists in his matchless eloquence the slogan, "Give me liberty or give me death!" It was a Southerner, Richard Henry Lee, who brought forward in the first Congress the motion that "these colonies are, and by right ought to be, free and independent states." It was a Southerner, Thomas Jefferson, who drafted the immortal Declaration of Independence! It was a Southerner, George Mason, who had earlier drawn the Virginia Bill of Rights, a docu-

ment of even profounder political statesmanship, and which
was taken by Massachusetts as the model of her own bill
of rights! It was a Southerner, George Washington, who
made good the Declaration of Independence by his sword
after seven years of war! It was a Southerner, James Madison, who earned the title "Father of the Constitution"!
It was a Southerner, John Marshall, who became its most
illustrious interpreter!

I ask, then, in view of all this, whether the South was not
justified in believing that the views of constitutional interpretation which she had inherited from such a political ancestry were not the true views? Let our Northern friends
answer, in all candor, whether the South, with such an heredity as this, with such glorious memories of achievement,
with such splendid traditions of the part her philosophers
and statesmen and soldiers had taken, both in the winning
of independence, and in the building of the temple of the
Constitution, had not good reason for saying, "We will
follow that interpretation of the Constitution, which we
received from our fathers — from Jefferson and Madison
and Washington — rather than that which can claim no
older, or greater, names than those of Story and Webster."
For be it remembered that for forty years after the adoption
of the Constitution, there was approximate unanimity in
its interpretation upon the great issue on which the South
took her stand in 1861. In truth Webster and Story apostatized from the New England interpretation of the Constitution. It is an historical fact that the Constitution was
regarded as a compact between the States for a long period
(not less than forty years after its adoption) by the leaders
of opinion in the New England States. Moreover, in the
same quarter, the sovereignty of the States was broadly
affirmed; and also the right of the States to resume, if need
be, the powers granted under the Constitution.[1]

[1] Samuel Adams objected to the preamble to the Constitution.
"I stumble at the threshold," he said; "I meet a National Government

These statements will no doubt be received by many with surprise, possibly with incredulity. Permit me then briefly to justify them by the unquestionable facts of history. The impartial historian of the future will recall the fact that the first threat of Secession did not come from the men of the South, but from the men of New England. Four times before the Secession of South Carolina, the threat of Secession was heard in the North — in 1802–03, in 1811–12, in 1814, and in 1844–45. The first time it came from Col. Timothy Pickering, of Massachusetts, a friend of Washington and a member of his Cabinet; the second time from Josiah Quincy, another distinguished citizen of Massachusetts; the third time from the Hartford Convention, in which five States were represented; the fourth time from the Legislature of Massachusetts.[1]

---

instead of a federal Union of sovereign States." To overcome this, Governor Hancock brought in the Tenth Amendment as to the reservation to the States of all powers not expressly delegated to the General Government.

The Websterian dogmas had then no advocates in New England. Hancock, Adams, Parsons, Bowdoin, Ames, were all for State sovereignty.

[1] The statement in the text might be made even stronger, as the following facts will show:

January 14, 1811, Josiah Quincy, of Massachusetts, in the debate on the admission of Louisiana, declared his "deliberate opinion that, if the bill passes, the bonds of the Union are virtually dissolved; . . . that as it will be the right of all [the States], so it will be the duty of some to prepare definitely for a separation — amicably, if they can, violently, if they must."

In 1812 "pulpit, press, and rostrum" of New England advocated Secession. In 1839 ex-President John Quincy Adams urged publicly that it would be better for the States to "part in friendship from each other than to be held together by constraint," and declared that "the people of each State have the right to secede from the confederated Union." In 1842 Mr. Adams presented a petition to Congress, from a town in Massachusetts, praying that it would "immediately adopt measures peaceably to dissolve the Union of these States." In 1844, and again in 1845, the Legislature of Massachusetts avowed the right

And what were the occasions calling forth these declarations of the purpose of dissolving the Union? The first was the acquisition of Louisiana; the second was the proposed admission of Louisiana as a State into the Union; the third was dissatisfaction occasioned by the war with Great Britain; the fourth was the proposed annexation of Texas. These measures were all believed by the New England States to be adverse to their interests. The addition of the new States would, it was thought, destroy the equilibrium of power, and give the South a preponderance; and therefore these stalwart voices were raised declaring that there was in the last resort a remedy, and that was the dissolution of the Union. This was the language held by the legislature of the leading New England State in 1844:

"The Commonwealth of Massachusetts, faithful to the compact between the people of the United States, according to the plain meaning and intent in which it was understood by them, is sincerely anxious for its preservation, but it is determined, as it doubts not the other States are, to submit to undelegated powers in no body of men on earth."

This stalwart utterance of the great State of Massachusetts expresses exactly the attitude of the seceding States in 1861. They believed that "the compact between the people of the United States" had been violated, and that they could no longer enjoy equal rights within the Union, and therefore they refused to submit to the exercise of "undelegated powers" on the part of the National Government.

Thus the North and the South, at these different epochs,

of Secession and threatened to secede if Texas was admitted to the Union.

Alexander Hamilton threatened Jefferson with the Secession of New England "unless the debts of the States were assumed by the General Government." February 1, 1850, Mr. Hale offered in the Senate a petition and resolutions, asking that body to devise, "without delay some plan for the immediate peaceful dissolution of the American Union." And Chase and Seward voted for its reception. (See "Oration of Mr. Leigh Robinson, December 13, 1892," p. 32.)

held the same view of the right of withdrawal from the Union. When New England became alarmed lest the South should gain a preponderance of power in the Union, she declared, through the potent voice of the Legislature of Massachusetts, that she would dissolve the Union rather than submit to the exercise, by the government, of undelegated powers.

The South held with great unanimity to the doctrine of State Sovereignty, and that that sovereignty was inviolable by the General Government. She had good right and reason to believe it, for it had been the faith of her greatest statesmen from the very foundation of the republic. Mr. Madison, the Father of the Constitution, held to that faith; and when Patrick Henry opposed the adoption of the Constitution upon the ground that the words, "we, the people," seemed to imply a "consolidated government" and not "a compact between States," he replied that it was not "we, the people," as composing one great body, but "the people as composing thirteen sovereignties." [1]

In fact, the original language of the preamble was: "We, the people of the States of New Hampshire, Massachusetts, Rhode Island, Connecticut, New York, New Jersey, Pennsylvania, Delaware, Maryland, Virginia, North Carolina, South Carolina, and Georgia, do ordain, declare, and establish the following Constitution." This preamble was passed unanimously; nor was there any change of opinion upon this point, but when it was seen that unanimous ratification by all the States could not be expected, it was decided that the consent of nine States should be sufficient to establish the new Confederacy, and as it could not be known beforehand which nine of the thirteen would ratify the instrument, the names of the States had to be omitted from the preamble. Mr. Madison further says: "Each State, in ratifying the Constitution, is considered as a sovereign body, independ-

[1] Elliott's "Debates," Ed. 1836, Vol. III, pp. 114, 115.

ent of all others, and only to be bound by its own voluntary act." [1]

Daniel Webster, in his great speech in reply to Mr. Hayne, in 1830, and again, in 1833, in his reply to Calhoun, argued that the Constitution was not a "compact," not a "confederacy," and that the acts of ratification were not "acts of accession." These terms, he said, *would imply the right of Secession*, but they were terms unknown to the fathers; they formed a "new vocabulary," invented to uphold the theory of State Sovereignty.

But in fact all these terms were in familiar use in the great debates on the formation of the Constitution. In 1787 Mr. Gerry, of Massachusetts, speaking in the Constitutional Convention, said: "If nine out of thirteen States can dissolve the compact (he was speaking of the Articles of Confederation) six out of nine will be just as able to dissolve the new one hereafter." Gouverneur Morris, of Pennsylvania, in the same debates, repeatedly described the Constitution as a compact. Alexander Hamilton speaks of the new government as "a confederate republic" a "confederacy," and calls the Constitution a "compact." General Washington writes of the Constitution as a compact, and repeatedly uses the terms "accede" and "accession," and once the term "secession." If any further proof were needed, it is furnished by the form in which both Massachusetts and New Hampshire ratified the Constitution. Both of these States, in their acts of ratification, refer to that instrument as "an explicit and solemn *compact*."

The proof, then, is overwhelming that the fathers and the conventions of the States used those very terms which Mr. Webster declared in 1830 and 1833 implied the right of Secession, and which he had himself used in 1819, and used again in 1850 and 1851. As to the independent sovereignty of the States, it was certainly held by the Federalists as well

---

[1] *Federalist*, No. XXXIX.

as by their opponents.[1] Thus Alexander Hamilton defends the constitutional exemption of the States from suit in the courts, on the ground that it was "one of the attributes of sovereignty," "enjoyed by the government of every State in the Union." Elsewhere he speaks of the States of the Union as "thirteen independent States." Benjamin Franklin, Gouverneur Morris, and Roger Sherman held similar language. And John Marshall, afterward Chief Justice, denying that a State can be called to the bar of a Federal Court, said: "Is it rational to suppose that the *sovereign power* shall be dragged before a court?" [2]

As to the right of dissolving the compact, as a last resort, in defence of its rights by any State, let our children and our children's children never forget that it was a right frequently asserted in the earliest period of our constitutional history. [3] Thus the people of Virginia, in their act of ratification, "declare and make known that the powers granted under the Constitution, being derived from the people of the United States, *may be resumed* by them, whensoever the same shall be perverted to their injury or oppression,"

---

[1] Charles Francis Adams in his Phi Beta Kappa Oration, 1902, said, "It does not lie in the mouths of the descendants of the New England Federalists of the first two decennials of the nineteenth century to 'invoke the avenging pen of history' to record an adverse verdict in the case of any son of Virginia who threw in his lot with his State in 1861." (Page 34.)

Governor Randolph of Virginia, in the Virginia Ratifying Convention, urged that the rights of the States were safeguarded in the Constitution, and added, "If you say that notwithstanding the most express restrictions, they [the government] may sacrifice the right of the States, then you establish another doctrine — that the creature can destroy the creator, which is the most absurd and ridiculous of all doctrines." (Elliott's "Debates," Vol. III, p. 363.) (See "The Republic of Republics," (p. 396.)

John Dickinson and Ellsworth speak in the same strain of the independent sovereignty of the States.

[2] Elliott's "Debates," Vol. III, p. 503.

[3] Elliott's "Debates," Vol. I, pp. 360, 361, 369.

and New York and Rhode Island went even farther and declared "that the powers of government *may be reassumed by the people* whenever it shall become necessary to their happiness." [1] Thus the right of Secession was solemnly asserted in the very acts by which these States ratified the Constitution. That assertion was part of the ratification. The ratification was conditioned by it. And the acceptance of the States as members of the Union carried with it the acceptance of the condition and the recognition of the right of Secession.

Mr. Webster, in his maturer years, in fact in the very last year of his illustrious life, distinctly recognized the right of Secession. In his speech at Capon Springs, Va., in 1851, he said:

"If the South were to violate any part of the Constitution intentionally and systematically, and persist in so doing, year after year, and no remedy could be had, would the North be any longer bound by the rest of it? And if the North were deliberately, habitually, and of fixed purpose, to disregard one part of it, would the South be bound any longer to observe its other obligations? . . . I have not hesitated to say, and I repeat, that if the Northern States refuse, wilfully and deliberately, to carry into effect that part of the Constitution which respects the restoration of fugitive slaves, and Congress provide no remedy, the South would no longer be bound to observe the compact. A bargain cannot be broken on one side, and still bind the other side." [2]

Looking back then to-day, my comrades, over the four and

---

[1] In 1898, Mr. Madison, in a report to the Virginia Legislature, said:

"The States, being the parties to the constitutional compact, and in their sovereign capacity, it follows of necessity that there can be no tribunal above their authority to decide in the last resort whether the compact made by them be violated."

[2] Curtis's "Life of Webster," Vol. II, pp. 518, 519.

forty years which separate us from the acts of Secession passed by the Southern States, we say to the men of this generation, and to those who will come after us, that the opprobrium heaped upon those who then asserted the right of Secession is undeserved. That right had not been then authoritatively denied. On the contrary, it had been again and again asserted North and South by eminent statesmen for nearly sixty years after the formation of the Union. Those who held it had as good right to their opinion as those who denied it. The weight of argument was overwhelmingly in their favor. So clear was this, that the United States government wisely decided, after the fall of the Confederacy, that it was not prudent to put Jefferson Davis upon his trial for treason. Let it be remembered that the formation of the United States, in 1788, was accomplished by nine of the States seceding from the Confederacy which had existed for eleven years, and which had bound the States entering into it to "a perpetual Union." *Thus the Union itself was the child of Secession!*

These arguments appeared to us convincing then. They are no less convincing to-day. They may not appear so to some of our friends in the North; but we appeal to them in all candor, and I do not believe our appeal will be in vain, to say whether the South, believing *as* she did, was not justified in the forum of conscience in doing *what* she did. The eminent Northern historian, to whom allusion has already been made, acknowledges that "a large majority of the people in the South believed in the constitutional right of Secession," and as a consequence that the war on the part of the National Government "seemed to them a war of subjugation." [1] Again he says it was "in their eyes a fight for their property and their liberty against spoliation and conquest." But if so, was not their resistance justified? Is it not the act of patriotism to resist spoliation and con-

---

[1] Rhodes' History of the United States, Vol. III, pp. 400, 401.

quest, and were not those dead heroes of ours, whose consecrated memories we honor to-day, patriots in the noblest
sense of the word? Upon every recurring Fourth of July
for eighty-five years the Southern men had been reminded,
by the reading of the Declaration of Independence, that
"governments derive their just powers from the consent
of the governed." Is it surprising, then, that when the
people of the South, *en masse*, deliberately refused their consent to the government of the United States, they should
have felt themselves justified in what they did by the principles of the Declaration of Independence? Our argument
for the independent sovereignty of the States may not appear
conclusive to many of our Northern friends, but at least
they cannot deny to the men of '61 the same right of revolution that their patriot sires and ours asserted in 1776.
But, if so, then we claim the assent even of those who most
stoutly deny the right of Secession, to the assertion that the
armies of the South were composed, not of traitors, but of
patriots. They will, they must, agree with us, that no man
can be a traitor if his heart is pure and his motives patriotic.

There was a time, during those dark years of Reconstruction, when public opinion in the North demanded that we
who had fought under the Southern flag should prove the
sincerity of our acceptance of the results of the war by
acknowledging the unrighteousness of our cause, and by
confessing contrition for our deeds.

But could we acknowledge our cause to be unrighteous
when we still believed it just? Could we repent of an act
done in obedience to the dictates of conscience? The men
of the North may claim that our judgment was at fault;
that our action was not justified by reason; that the fears
that goaded us to withdraw from the Union were not well
grounded; but, so long as it is admitted that we followed
duty as we understood it, they cannot ask us to repent. A
man can only repent, I repeat, of what he is ashamed, and it
will not be claimed that we should be ashamed of obeying

the dictates of conscience, in the face of hardship and danger and death.

That able and honest, though biassed, historian to whom I have just referred, speaking of Robert E. Lee, confesses that "censure's voice upon the action of such a noble soul is hushed," and he declares that the time will come when the whole American people will "recognize in him one of the finest products of American life, for surely as the years go on we shall see that such a life can be judged by no partisan measure, and we shall come to look upon him as the English of our day regard Washington, whom little more than a century ago they delighted to call a rebel." [1]   Most true a testimony, but, my comrades, what is here so nobly acknowledged of our glorious chieftain, must be seen to be true also of the gallant men who followed him; and we feel sure that the time is coming, if it has not already come, when it will be recognized all over the land of which that starry flag is the emblem, that the soldiers who fought under those tattered battle flags of the Southern Cross were animated by as pure a patriotism and as high a devotion to liberty as any men who ever fought, on any field, in any age of the world. That acknowledgment indeed has already been made, and made nearly a generation ago, by two of the most gallant sons of New England who were our foemen in the great strife — I mean General Francis Bartlett and Captain Oliver Wendell Holmes of Massachusetts. Captain Holmes now occupies a seat upon the Supreme Bench of the United States. Let me ask you to listen to the generous words which he uttered nearly a quarter of a century ago:

"We believed that it was most desirable that the North should win; we believed in the principle that the Union is indissoluble, but we equally believed that those who stood against us held just as sacred convictions that were the opposite of ours, and we respected them as every man

---

[1] Rhodes, *Ib.*, p. 413.

with a heart must respect those who give all for their belief." [1]

All honor to the valiant soldier and accomplished scholar who uttered those words! All honor, too, to another noble son of New England, Charles Francis Adams, who has more recently declared, recognizing the same principle, that both the North and the South were right in the great struggle of the Civil War, because each believed itself right.[2]

3. I come now to the third proposition which I engaged to consider. It is said, and widely believed, that the people of the South were not attached to the Union and were eager to seize upon an excuse for its dissolution. Even if it were conceded that the South had the right of Secession, or at any rate the right of revolution, we are told that if she loved the Union as she ought to have loved it, she would not have exercised that right.

In considering this assertion it will be necessary to distinguish in our reply between the States that first seceded and the border States of Virginia, Tennessee, North Carolina, and Arkansas, which later gave in their adhesion to the Southern Confederacy. As to the former — the cotton States — if it be true, as candid historians acknowledge, that their people "*all* held that the North was unconstitutionally and unjustly attempting to coerce the sovereign States" [3]; if it be true, as we have seen is now conceded, that the people of those States solemnly believed that their liberties were assailed, and that the war waged against them was a war of subjugation, then I submit that they were

[1] Address at Keene, N. H., on Memorial Day.

[2] When Jefferson Davis and Robert E. Lee were cadets at West Point the text-books in use on political science were by St. George Tucker, a Southern writer, and William Rawle, a Northern writer, and both taught the right of a State to secede. (See "Republic of Republics," by W. J. Sage, p. 32.) Can these illustrious men be attainted as traitors because they put in practice the principles taught them by the authority of the government of the United States?

[3] Rhodes, *Ib.*, p. 402.

constrained to choose between their love of the Union and their love of liberty; and I do not believe that any brave and candid patriot of any Northern State will condemn them because, holding that belief, they made the choice they did. The judgment of the South may be impeached,[1] but not her patriotism; not her love for the Union; if, shut up to such an alternative, she preferred liberty without Union to Union without liberty.

The case of the border States is somewhat different. Maryland, Virginia, North Carolina, Kentucky, Missouri, Tennessee, were all opposed to Secession. They refused to follow the lead of South Carolina. For example, as late as April 4 Virginia voted by eighty-nine to forty-five against the ordinance of Secession. They believed the Southern States had just grievances against the North, and that there was much to justify the fears which they entertained, but they were not prepared to dissolve the Union. They still hoped for redress within the Union by constitutional means. Moreover, the men who became our greatest generals, and our most illustrious and determined leaders in the Southern Confederacy, were, a majority of them, earnest Union men.

---

[1] Yet her judgment was sustained by some of the most illustrious men of the North. Millard Fillmore had said, in 1856, referring to the possible election of Frémont, as a sectional President, "Can they have the madness or folly to believe that our Southern brethren would submit to be governed by such a chief magistrate?" And Rufus Choate, the same year, wrote that if the Republican party "accomplishes its objects and gives the government to the North, I turn my eyes from the consequences. To the fifteen States of the South that government will appear an alien government. It will appear worse. It will appear a hostile government. It will represent to their eye a vast region of States organized upon anti-slavery, flushed by triumph, cheered onward by the voices of the pulpit, tribune, and press; its mission to inaugurate freedom and put down the oligarchy; its constitution the glittering and sounding generalities of natural right."

If this was true in 1856, how much more in 1860, after the John Brown raid, and when the hostility between the North and the South had reached such an acute stage!

I think it may be said, too, that the States which furnished most of the munitions of war and most of the fighting men were opposed to Secession. The Union which their forefathers had done so much to create,[1] first by the sword and then by the pen and the tongue, was dear to their hearts.

But there came a cruel issue. On the 15th of April, 1861, President Lincoln issued a proclamation calling for 75,000 men to coerce the seceded States back into the Union. The border States were called upon to furnish their quota of armed men to march against their Southern brethren. Thus an issue was forced upon them which the future historian, however antagonistic to the South, must ponder with sympathy and emotion. The men of these border States were compelled to decide either to send soldiers to fight against their brethren, or to say, "We will throw in our lot with them and resist military coercion." Now, whatever division of sentiment existed in regard to the policy, or even the right, of Secession, there was almost complete unanimity in these States in repudiating the right of coercion. That right had been vehemently repudiated in the discussions in the Constitutional Convention by James Madison, Alexander Hamilton, and Edmund Randolph. The South remained true to the doctrine of the fathers on this point.[2]

It is vain to ask at this date what would have happened

[1] When, after the Revolution, it became apparent that jealousy of the preponderance of Virginia, resulting from the vastness of her domain, would prevent the formation of the Union, that State, with truly queenly generosity, gave to the Union her Northwestern Territory, out of which the States of Ohio, Indiana, Illinois, Michigan, Wisconsin, and part of Minnesota, were afterward carved. This was in 1787. Has any other State, or group of States, done as much in proof of attachment to the Union? Moreover she dedicated this vast territory as free soil, by the ordinance of 1787.

[2] Mr. Madison opposed the motion to incorporate in the Constitution the power of coercing a State to its duty, and by unanimous consent the project was abandoned. Alexander Hamilton denounced the proposal to coerce a State as "one of the maddest projects ever devised." Edmund Randolph said it meant "civil war."

if that fatal proclamation of April 15 had never been issued, but it is impossible to repress the thought that perhaps, after all, the truest statesmanship rested with those who, like Edward Everett, and Horace Greeley, and William H. Seward, and General Scott, believed that the policy of coercion was a political error. Certain it is that but for that policy those great States just enumerated would not have thrown in their lot with the Southern Confederacy, and it is a supposition by no means destitute of rational foundation that without their support the seven States which had already seceded would have ultimately sought readmission to the Union, and that the Union might have been saved, and slavery ultimately abolished, without the dreadful cost of a fratricidal war and without the unspeakable horrors of that Reconstruction period, when the star of liberty sank as if to rise no more on the Southern States,[1] and without that act — the quintessence of injustice to the whites, and of unkindness to the blacks themselves — I mean the act which conferred the right of suffrage indiscriminately on the newly emancipated slaves.

But, waiving all this, I come back to the question, Can any blame attach to the people of the border States for choosing as they chose in the face of the cruel alternative, which was forced upon them by Mr. Lincoln's proclamation, to abandon the Union, or to draw their swords against their Southern brethren?

It has been well and wisely said by a recent historian (Mr. Rhodes) that "the political reason of Virginia, Maryland, and Kentucky inclined them to the North, their heartstrings drew them to the South." I put it to any man with a heart to say, whether, when the bayonet is directed against the bosom of a member of one's own household, he is to blame

---

[1] Out of that horror of great darkness the heroic soul of Robert Edward Lee cried aloud in agony: "Had I foreseen these results of subjugation, I would have preferred to die at Appomattox with my brave men, my sword in this right hand."

for throwing himself into the breach in his defence, even though the bayonet be in the hand of the officer of the law? I affirm that the ties of blood and kindred are more sacred even than those which bind a man to the government of his country. Could the men of Virginia and North Carolina and Tennessee be expected to raise their hands against their family altars and firesides, whatever view they might have taken of the constitutional questions at issue? But the men of those States believed with great unanimity that the sovereignty of a State was inviolable by the General Government. That was the faith they had received from their fathers, from a long line of illustrious statesmen and political philosophers. Of this let one decisive example suffice. Though Robert E. Lee abhorred the idea of Secession and loved the Union with a passionate devotion, yet when he was asked by a member of a committee of Congress whether he did not consider that he was guilty of treason in drawing his sword in behalf of the South, he answered: "No, I believed my allegiance was due to the State of Virginia."

The people of the South believed, as we have said, that government derives its just powers from the consent of the governed. They believed the General Government had no rightful power of coercion. Their New England brethren had for many years confirmed them in that belief. Moreover they believed a union by force not the Union which the fathers had in view. A governmental fabric pinned together by bayonets did not seem to them a republic, but a despotism.

4. I come now to consider the opinion, so widely held, that the South plunged into a desperate war for the purpose of perpetuating slavery, and made that institution the corner-stone of the new confederacy which it sought to establish. Before dealing directly with this, however, a little history upon the subject of the relation of the South to slavery will be salutary.

Certainly we have no tears to shed over its abolition. There is not a man in the South who would wish to see it reëstablished. But there are several facts, unknown to some, and ignored by other, historians, which are essential to a right understanding of this question. I shall hold them up to the light to-day, because I would not have the attitude of that dear, noble, old South misrepresented or misunderstood by our descendants.

In the first place let it never be forgotten that it was the government of England, and not the people of the South, which was originally responsible for the introduction of slavery. In 1760 South Carolina passed an act to prohibit further importation of slaves, but England rejected it with indignation.

The colony of Virginia again, and again, and again, protested to the British king against sending slaves to her shores, but in vain — they were forced upon her.[1] Then, too, Virginia was the first of all the States, North or South, to prohibit the slave-trade, and Georgia was the first to incorporate such a prohibition in her organic constitution. In fact, Virginia was in advance of the whole world on this subject; she abolished the slave-trade in 1778, nearly thirty years before England did, and the same period before New England was willing to consent to its abolition. Again, at the formation of the Constitution, Virginia raised her protest against the continuance of that traffic, but New England raised a voice of objection, and, uniting her influence with that of South Carolina and Georgia, secured the continuance of the slave-trade for twenty years more, by constitutional provision.[2] On the other hand the first statute establishing slavery in America was passed by Massachusetts, December, 1641, in her code entitled Body of Liberties. The first fugitive slave law was enacted by the

[1] One hundred petitions against the introduction of slaves were sent by the colonists of Virginia to the British government.

[2] "The Critical Period of American History," by John Fiske, p. 262.

same State. She made slaves of her captives in the Pequot war. Another fact to be remembered is that every Southern State legislated against the slave-trade.

Thus slavery was an inheritance which the people of the South received from the fathers; and if the States of the North, after the Revolution, sooner or later abolished the institution, it cannot be claimed that the abolition was dictated by moral considerations, but by differences of climate, soil, and industrial interests.[1]

It existed in several of the Northern States more than fifty years after the adoption of the Constitution, while the importation of slaves into the South continued to be carried on by Northern merchants and Northern ships, without interference in the traffic from any quarter, until it was prohibited by the spontaneous action of the Southern States themselves.

Note this also: The contest between the North and the South over the extension of slavery to the territories was a contest on the part of the South for equal rights under the Constitution, and it ought to be clearly understood that it did not involve the increase of slavery. Had that right been conceded, not one additional slave would have been

---

[1] The Supreme Court in 1857 held the following language: "This change had not been produced by any change of opinion in relation to this race, but because it was discovered by experience that slave labor was unsuited to the climate and productions of these States, for some of them . . . were actively engaged in the slave-trade."

Goodell's "Slavery and Anti-slavery" — an authority not friendly to the South — says (pp. 10–11) that the merchants of New England seaports "almost monopolized the immense profits of that lucrative, but detestable, trade."

The principal operation of abolition in the North, says an English authority, "was to transfer Northern slaves to Southern markets." (Ingram's "History of Slavery," London, 1895, p. 184.)

On March 26, 1788, the Legislature of Massachusetts passed a law ordering all free negroes out of the State. If they would not go voluntarily, they were to be whipped out. This confirms the view stated in the text.

added to the number existing in the country. "It was a question of the distribution or dispersion of the slaves rather than of the extension of slavery. Removal is not extension. Indeed, if emancipation was the end to be desired, the dispersion of the negroes over a wider area, among additional territories, eventually to become States, and in climates unfavorable to slave labor, instead of hindering, would have promoted this object by diminishing the difficulties in the way of ultimate emancipation." [1]

And now I call your attention to a fact of capital importance in this discussion; viz., that the sentiment in favor of emancipation was rapidly spreading in the South in the first quarter of the nineteenth century. Wilson acknowledges "there was no avowed advocate of slavery" at that time in Virginia. It is stated on high [2] authority that, in

[1] This is the language of Jefferson Davis, but the argument is Henry Clay's. In 1820 he argued that the extension of slavery was far-seeing humanity, and Mr. Jefferson agreed with him, saying that spreading the slaves over a larger surface "will dilute the evil everywhere and facilitate the means of getting finally rid of it." Mr. Madison took the same view. These three statesmen were all earnest emancipationists.

[2] Judge Temple of Tennessee. "The Covenanter, the Cavalier, and the Puritan," p. 209.

"In 1822 there were five or six abolition societies in Kentucky. In 1819 the first distinctively emancipation paper in the United States was published in Jonesboro, eastern Tennessee." There were eighteen emancipation societies in that region organized by the Covenanters, Methodists, and Quakers.

Ib., p. 208.

A Massachusetts writer, Geo. Lunt, says: "The States of Virginia, Kentucky, and Tennessee were engaged in practical movements for the gradual emancipation of their slaves. This movement continued until it was arrested by the aggressions of the Abolitionists."

The people of the South believed they were, at heart, more friendly to the Negro race than their Northern brethren, and such facts as the following appeared to justify their belief. In 1830, Senator Benton called attention to the "actual expulsion of a great body of free colored people from the State of Ohio, and not one word of objection, not one note of grief." The whole number expatriated was estimated at ten the year 1826, there were 143 emancipation societies in the whole country; and of this number 103 were established in the South. It is well known that one branch of the Legislature of Virginia gave a very large vote in favor of a law of emancipation in the year 1832, and I was assured in 1860, by Col. Thomas Jefferson Randolph, of Virginia, the grandson of Mr. Jefferson — himself an influential member of the legislature in 1832 — that emancipation would certainly have been carried the ensuing year, but for the revulsion of feeling which followed the fanatical agitation of the subject by the Abolitionists of the period. The legislature of 1832, though it defeated the emancipation bill by a small majority, yet passed a resolution postponing the consideration of the subject till public opinion had further developed.[1]

It is our belief, and we put the statement on record, that our children and children's children may remember it, that but for passions naturally roused by the violent attacks made upon the moral character of the Southern slave-holder, slavery would have been peaceably abolished in the border

thousand. He added: "This is a remarkable event, paralleled only by the expulsion of the Moors from Spain and the Huguenots from France." In 1846 the liberated slaves of John Randolph were driven by a mob away from the lands which had been purchased for them in Ohio. In 1855 the Topeka (Kansas) constitution adopted by the Free-soilers contained an article, ratified by a vote of almost three to one, forbidding any free negro to reside in the State, and this was accepted by the Republican House of Representatives. In 1860 the constitutions of thirty out of thirty-four States of the Union excluded negroes from exercising the suffrage. Facts like these did not tend to confirm the confidence of the people of the South in the sincerity of the agitation on behalf of the negro.

[1] The *Richmond Whig* of March 6, 1832, said:

"The great mass of Virginia herself triumphs that the slavery question has been taken up by the legislature, that her legislators are grappling with the monster, and they contemplate the distant but ardently desired result [emancipation] as the supreme good which a benevolent Providence could vouchsafe." — *Niles Register*, Dec. 10, 1831, p. 266 and p. 78.

States before the middle of the nineteenth century, and it cannot be doubted that the sentiment against it must ultimately have become so strong that it would also have been abolished in the cotton States without violence and without war.

This opinion is scouted by Northern historians; but let the facts be calmly weighed in the balance:

It is acknowledged that slavery was almost universally considered a great evil in the South from 1789 down to 1837.

It is further acknowledged that public opinion there underwent a revolution on this subject in the decade 1832–42; it was now spoken of by some of her writers and leaders for the first time as a blessing.[1]

It is a fact which cannot be denied in the light of history, that the sentiment in favor of emancipation was rapidly spreading in the South down to 1832. I have already quoted the statement made to me in 1860 by a member of the legislature of Virginia of 1831–32 that its members were agreed at that time on the principle of emancipation.

What, then, produced this fateful change of sentiment, which the historian records between 1832 and 1837? It is often said that the invention of the cotton-gin was the cause. But that invention came in 1793. It was forty years too early to account for this phenomenon which we seek to understand.

It is our belief that the future historian, who shall be a careful student of human nature, and of the motives which influence its action, as well as of historical facts, will see in the abolition crusade which was launched by William Lloyd Garrison, Jan. 1, 1831, the real cause of this revolution in Southern sentiment on the subject of slavery.

The violence and the virulence of that crusade produced its natural result.[2] It angered the South. It stifled dis-

[1] See Rhodes, History of United States," Vol. III, pp. 54, 68.

[2] One of these writers said the only hope for the moral improvement of the whites in the South was the amalgamation with the black race. Slave-holders were called "bloodhounds."

cussion. It checked the movement toward emancipation. It forced a more stringent policy toward the slave.

The people of the South, of whom Von Holst writes that they were as moral and as religious as any other people in the world, found themselves held up to the odium of mankind for the abominable crime of holding men in bondage, an act which holy men like Jonathan Edwards and George Whitfield had committed in the eighteenth century, without offence to the most sensitive conscience. But this was not all. The publication of Garrison's *Liberator* Jan. 1, 1831, was followed, seven months after, by Nat. Turner's negro insurrection, in which sixty-one persons, men, women, and children, were murdered in the night. The South naturally, and I think with reason, connected these two events as cause and effect,[1] and the ghastly spectre of servile insurrection, like that which desolated San Domingo, rose before the imagination of the people from the Potomac to the Rio Grande. After this the emancipation societies in the South were dissolved and all discussion of the subject ceased. As to the character of that abolition crusade, I agree with Henry Clay that its authors were reckless of consequences, ready to "hurry us down that dreadful precipice that leads to civil war and the dissolution of the Union." I agree with Rufus Choate that the Abolition party was "a party which knows one-half of America only to hate it." I agree with Edward Everett in applying to the Abolitionists the words of the poet:

> "Arouse the tiger of Hyrcanean deserts;
> Strive with the half-starved lion for its prey;
> Lesser the risk, than rouse the slumbering fire
> Of wild fanaticism."

As to its methods, it is enough to recall the fact that in 1835 President Jackson, in his message to Congress, called

---

[1] The governor of Virginia publicly expressed his belief that this insurrection "was designed and matured by fanatics in some of the neighboring States."

attention to the transmission through the mails "of inflammatory appeals addressed to the passions of the slaves, in prints and in various sorts of publications, calculated to stimulate them to insurrection, and to produce all the horrors of a servile war." Now, bearing these facts in mind, and remembering the statement quoted from Col. Thomas Jefferson Randolph, that the abolition crusade was the immediate cause of the legislature of Virginia abandoning the scheme of emancipation, which they had previously been agreed on in principle, we hold that the future historian will confirm our claim that, but for the fanaticism of the Abolitionists, slavery would certainly have been peaceably abolished in Virginia, and probably in the other Southern States.[1]

But this is not the whole story. That movement was as essentially unjust as it was violent and fanatical. It was a demand for immediate emancipation without compensation or consideration of any kind. England in 1833 abolished slavery in the West Indies, but she compensated the slave-owners, devoting $100,000,000 to that purpose. But never in all the long abolition agitation of thirty years, from 1831 to 1861, was there any proposition to remunerate the South for the loss of her slaves.[2] Her people were expected to make a sacrifice for emancipation never demanded before of any people on earth. I do not forget Mr. Lincoln's proposal, in March, 1862, but that was addressed to the border States which had not seceded, and, besides, had it been otherwise, it came too late, when flagrant war had embittered the hostility between the sections.

[1] Daniel Webster in his 7th of March speech attributed the change of sentiment in Virginia on the subject of slavery to the intemperance of the Abolitionists. Many other Northern leaders were of the same opinion.

[2] Mr. John Ford Rhodes (I, 381), indeed, says that there can be no doubt that the North would have gladly agreed to emancipation with compensation, but he is not able to adduce any evidence in support of this opinion beyond an *obiter dictum* of Mr. Seward in the Senate that he was willing "to apply the national treasure to effect the peaceful, voluntary removal of slavery itself."

It is said, however, to the reproach of the South, that her sentiments on the subject of slavery were behind the age in 1861. But how far was she behind? And why?

Let her critics remind themselves that, as late as 1821, the State of Rhode Island sent a slave-trader to represent her in the United States Senate. As late as 1833 a great English minister, Sir Robert Peel, would have nothing to do with either immediate emancipation or gradual. And Mr. Gladstone, at the same epoch, while admitting that the extinction of slavery was "a consummation devoutly to be desired and in good earnest to be forwarded," yet held that "immediate and unconditional emancipation, without a previous advance in character, must place the negro in a state where he would be his own worst enemy." It is fair to remember also that Pitt, Fox, Grenville, and Grey, while eager to bring the slave-trade to an instant end, habitually disclaimed as calumny any intention of emancipating the blacks on the sugar islands.

Again the dispassionate enquirer will reflect that it was much easier, and much less costly, to be an enthusiastic Abolitionist in old England, or New England (where slavery was not profitable), than in the Southern States, where the labor of the black was necessary to the cultivation of the great staples.

The people of the South, too, could better realize the difficulty and the danger of emancipation. She was, as Jefferson said, in the position of the man who held the wolf by the ears — she didn't want to hold on, but she was afraid to let go.

Was she to blame if she feared to repeat the mistakes and failures of the English abolition movement, of which Mr. Disraeli said: "The movement of the middle class for the abolition of slavery was virtuous, but it was not wise. It was an ignorant movement. The history of the abolition of slavery by the English, and its consequences, would be a narrative of ignorance, injustice, blundering, waste, and

havoc, not easily paralleled in the history of mankind."
If, then, we acknowledge that the South was behind the rest
of the civilized world in 1861 in her sentiment on the subject
of slavery, we think her apology is ample: *First*, that she
was interested in the perpetuation of slavery as no other
people ever was; *second*, that the difficulty and the danger
of emancipation pressed upon her as upon no other people;
and *third*, that her sentiment, which had been for a quarter
of a century moving steadily toward emancipation, was
violently turned back by the fanaticism of the abolition
crusade.[1]

But the Southern Confederacy is reproached with the fact
that it was deliberately built on slavery. Slavery, we are
told, was its corner-stone. Even that most honest historian,
Mr. Rhodes, says, "Their fight, they averred, was for liberty,
and yet they were weighted by the denial of liberty to three
and one-half million of human beings."

But if slavery was the corner-stone of the Southern Confederacy, what are we to say of the Constitution of the United
States? That instrument as originally adopted by the
thirteen colonies contained three sections which recognized
slavery.[2] And whereas the constitution of the Southern
Confederacy prohibited the slave-trade, the Constitution
of the United States prohibited *the abolition* of the slave-
trade for twenty years! And if the men of the South are
reproached for denying liberty to three and a half millions
of human beings, at the same time that they professed to
be waging a great war for their own liberty, what are we to
say of the revolting colonies of 1776, who rebelled against

---

[1] We acknowledge with sorrow that there was a painful deteriora-
tion in the attitude of many influential men in the South toward slavery between 1840 and 1860. There was even a movement of some
strength in favor of the revival of the slave-trade in the decade preceding the war. This change of view cannot be excused, but it was
undoubtedly the reaction from the violent fanaticism of the abolition movement.

[2] Article I, Sections 2 and 9, and Article IV, Section 2.

the British crown to achieve their liberty, while slavery existed in every one of the thirteen colonies unrepudiated? Cannot these historians who deny that the South fought for liberty, because they held the blacks in bondage, see, that upon the same principle they must impugn the sincerity of the signers of the Declaration of Independence? For while, in that famous instrument, they affirmed before the world that all men were created free and equal, and that "governments derive their just powers from the consent of the governed," they took no steps whatever to free the slaves which were held in every one of the thirteen colonies. No, my friends, if the corner-stone of the constitution of the Southern Confederacy was slavery, the Constitution of 1789 — the Constitution of the United States — had a worse corner-stone, since it held its ægis of protection over the slave-trade itself! We ask the candid historian then to answer this question: If the colonists of 1776 were freemen fighting for liberty, though holding men in slavery in every one of the thirteen colonies, why is the tribute of patriotism denied to the Southern men of 1861 because they too held men in bondage?

If George Washington, a slave-holder, was yet a champion of liberty, how can that title be denied to Robert E. Lee?

Slavery was not abolished in the British dominions until the year 1833. Will any man dare to say there were no champions of human liberty in England before that time?

But after all that may be said, we are told that slavery was the cause of the war, and that the citizen soldiers of the South sprang to arms in defence of slavery.

Yes, my comrades, History, or rather let us say Calumny, masquerading as History, has told the world that that battle-flag of yours was the emblem of slave power, and that you fought, not for liberty, but for the right to hold your fellow-men in bondage.

Think of it, soldiers of the Southern Cross! Think of it, followers of Lee and Jackson and Albert Sidney Johnston!

You were fighting, they say, for the privilege of holding your fellowmen in bondage! Will you for one moment acknowledge the truth of that indictment? Ah, no! that banner of the Southern Cross was studded with the stars of God's heaven, like Old Glory itself. You could not have followed a banner that was not the banner of liberty! You sprang from the loins of freemen! You drank in freedom with your mother's milk! Your revolutionary sires were not inspired by a more intense devotion to liberty than you were!

Tell me, were you thinking of your slaves when you cast all in the balance, your lives, your fortunes, your sacred honor, in order to endure the hardships of the march, and the camp, and the peril and the suffering of the battle field? Why, it was but a small minority of the men who fought in the Southern armies — hardly one in ten — that were financially interested in the institution of slavery.

There is, however, a court to which this contention may be referred for settlement — one whose decision all men ought to accept. It is composed of the three men who may be supposed to have known, if any men knew, the object for which the war was waged, — Abraham Lincoln, Jefferson Davis, and Robert E. Lee. And their decision is unanimous. Mr. Lincoln always declared that the object of the war was the restoration of the Union, and not the emancipation of the slaves. Mr. Davis as positively declared that the South was not fighting for slavery, but for independence. And Robert E. Lee expressed his opinion by setting all his slaves free Jan. 8, 1863, and then going on with the war for more than two years longer.[1]

[1] I will only add that if the North waged the war not for the Union but for the slave, then it is remarkable that Mr. Lincoln and his advisers never found out that fact. And as to the South — if, indeed, she fought not for liberty but for her property in slaves — it is still more remarkable that Jefferson Davis should have embarked on the enterprise of Secession, believing that he would as a consequence lose his slaves, for in February, 1861, he wrote to his wife in these words, "In any case our slave property will eventually be lost;" and that General Lee should

I will not apologize, my comrades, for having taxed your patience so long. You will recognize at once the importance and the difficulty of the task I set myself to perform, and you will not begrudge the consecration of even so long a time as I have detained you to-day, in order that the true story of the course pursued by the Southern States should again be set forth.

The generation which participated in that great struggle is rapidly passing away, and we believe that no fitting occasion should be neglected by those who yet survive, to vindicate the motives and to explain the principles of the actors in that great drama. Only by iteration and reiteration by the writers and speakers of the South will the real facts be rescued from oblivion, from misunderstanding, and from misrepresentation, and the conduct and characters of our leaders, and the heroic men who followed them, be understood and honored as they ought to be honored by the generation that comes after us. And, my friends, the fulfilment of this duty will make for unity and fraternity among Americans, not for sectionalism. It will strengthen, not weaken, the bonds of the Union in the years to come if the generations yet unborn are taught to recognize that the principles and the aims of the men of the South were as high and as pure as those which animated their foemen of the North. Had the men of '61, North and South, known each other, and respected each other, and each other's motives, that terrible Civil War would never have been. Let the Union of the future be founded on mutual respect, and to this end let the truth concerning the principles and acts of the old South be told — the whole truth and nothing but the truth — "nothing extenuated, nor aught set down in malice."

have emancipated every one of his slaves more than two years before the close of the war. Thus the political head of the Confederacy entered on the war foreseeing the eventual loss of his slaves, and the military head of the Confederacy actually set his slaves free before the war was half over; yet both, they say, were fighting for slavery!

Comrades and fellow-citizens, we thank God that to-day the sun shines upon a truly reunited country. Sectionalism is dead and buried. In the providence of God the Spanish War has drawn North and South together in bonds of genuine brotherhood. Their blood has watered the same soil; their common patriotism has glorified again the land of Washington. Men who faced one another in deadly conflict at Shiloh and Gettysburg rushed side by side under the Stars and Stripes up the heights of San Juan and El Caney. There was no North or South on those fields of battle, or in Santiago Harbor, or in front of Manila. Yes, and, as was well said by our own Hilary Herbert at the Peace Jubilee, "Out of the grave of sectionalism arose the triumphant spirit of Americanism." Men of the South, we have part in that spirit of Americanism. It is our heritage as well as theirs.

For one moment let us turn from the sacred past — from the memories of this day and hour — and look into the future. And what is it that we behold? Surely a Pisgah prospect of beauty and hope! A great destiny opens before America. Great are her privileges, her opportunities, her responsibilities. The God of nations has given her possibilities of power and usefulness among the peoples of the globe that are almost boundless. He has great things for this nation to do. He has given her a great part to play in the spreading of civilization and liberty and religion throughout the world. Blind indeed will the people be if they do not see it so — faithless if they do not grasp it! But I want to say that we of the South claim our part in this great destiny of America. Eagerly and joyfully we accept our share in the responsibilities, in the opportunities, in the strenuous conflicts, in the conquests, in the glory of the future of our country. To that future we turn our faces. To its duties, to its labors, to its battles we consecrate ourselves, our strength, and our manhood. We are Americans, and nothing that pertains to the honor, to the welfare, to the glory of America is, or shall be, foreign to us.

But this occasion belongs not to the future, but to the past. Let our closing thoughts then be dedicated to the memory of our dead — that mighty host of brave soldiers and sailors who fell under the banner of the Lost Cause forty years ago. The Grecian orator, whose words I have chosen as a motto for my address, speaking of the Athenians, exclaims, "Is there a poet or an author who will not do his utmost, by his eloquence and his knowledge, to immortalize such heroic valor and virtue?" Such is my feeling as I think of those now silent battalions of Southern soldiers that sleep on so many hard-fought fields. But where is the poet or the orator who can fitly eulogize them? The pen of a Thucydides, the tongue of a Pericles or a Demosthenes, the harp of a Homer, were needed justly to tell the epic story of that great struggle in which the best and bravest sons of our Southland freely laid down their lives; a struggle so gigantic in its proportions that the siege of Troy — the famous battles of the long Peloponnesian War — even the great engagements of Marathon and Leuctra, of Salamis and Chæronea — sink into insignificance in the comparison.

I will not attempt then to pronounce a fitting panegyric upon those brave men, nor upon their splendid leaders: captains whose valor, whose prowess, whose skill, whose heroic constancy were never outshone on any field, in any age, by any leaders of men; not by Agamemnon, "King of Men"; not by Achilles, the "swift-footed," "the invincible"; not by Ulysses, "the wise"; nor by Ajax, "the mighty"; not by Miltiades at Marathon; nor by Leonidas himself at Thermopylæ; nor by any of the long line of illustrious heroes and patriots who, in ancient and in modern times, have shed lustre on manhood by their valor or by their constancy. Comrades, it is my conviction that the Muse of History will write the names of some of our Southern heroes as high on her great roll of honor as those of any leaders of men

in any era. Fame herself will rise from her throne to place
the laurel with her own hands upon the immortal brows of
Robert E. Lee, and Albert Sidney Johnston, and Stonewall
Jackson. I grant, indeed, that it is not for us who were
their companions and fellow-soldiers to ask the world to
accept our estimate of their rightful place in history. We
are partial, we are biassed in our judgments, men will say.
Be it so. We are content to await the calm verdict of the
future historian, when, with philosophic impartiality, the
characters and achievements and motives of our illustrious
leaders shall have been weighed in the balances of Truth.
What that verdict will be is foreshadowed, we believe, by
the judgment expressed by Field-Marshal Lord Wolseley,
who said, "I believe General Lee will be regarded not only
as the most prominent figure of the Confederacy, but as the
great American of the nineteenth century, whose statue is
well worthy to stand on an equal pedestal with that of Washington, and whose memory is equally worthy to be enshrined in the hearts of all his countrymen." What that
verdict will be was in fact declared by Freeman himself
when he said that our Lee was worthy to stand with Washington beside Alfred the Great in the world's temple of
Fame.

What you ask of me, however, comrades, in these closing
moments is quite apart from the task of the historian or
the orator. It is simply to give honest utterance to the
love and admiration that glow in the breast of every one
of us for those our companions-in-arms who fell on the almost
countless bloody fields of that Titanic struggle in repelling
the invaders from our soil. All honor to their memory!
We cannot call their names. They are too numerous to be
told over, even if we had here the muster-rolls of all the
Confederate armies. But if their names could be called,
we could answer as was answered for that famous hero, La
Tour d'Auvergne, the "first Grenadier of France" — whose
name, though he was no more, was still borne on the muster-

roll of his regiment — "Dead on the field of honor!" Only two months ago the urn containing the heart of that illustrious soldier was removed to Paris to rest under the dome of the *Hôtel des Invalides*, and while the order rang out "*Au Drapeau*," arms were presented and the captain of the Forty-sixth Regiment, in accordance with the old tradition, called out the name, "La Tour d'Auvergne!" After a second or two of silence the answer came back in clear and ringing tones, "Dead on the field of honor."

Comrades, we make that answer to-day, forty years after the end of the war, and our children and children's children in generations to come will repeat it, as the names of our veterans shall be called, — "Dead on the field of honor!" Yes, for these men to whom we pay the tribute of our homage were heroes, if ever heroes were. What hardships did they not uncomplainingly endure, on the march, in the bivouack, in the trenches! What sacrifices did they not cheerfully make, for a cause dearer than life itself! What dangers did they not face with unquailing front! Who that ever saw them can forget those hardy battalions that followed Stonewall Jackson in his weird marches in the great Valley campaign? Rusty and ragged were their uniforms, but bright were their muskets and their bayonets, and they moved like the very whirlwind of war!

They fill, most of them, nameless graves. They were private soldiers. Fame does not, and will not, herald their names and deeds to posterity. They fought without reward — and they died without distinction. It was enough for them to hear the voice of duty, and to follow it, though it led them by a rugged path to a bloody grave. "Tell my father I tried to do my duty," was the last message of many a dying soldier boy to his comrades on the field of battle. Oh! it is for this we honor and revere their nameless memories to-day. They were not soldiers of fortune, but soldiers of duty, who dared all that men can dare, and endured all that men can endure, in obedience to what they believed the sacred call of country. If ever men lived of whom it could be truly said that their hearts echoed the sentiment, "*Dulce et decorum est pro patria mori*," these were the men. They loved their State; they loved their homes and their firesides. They were no politicians. They knew little of the warring theories of constitutional interpretation. But one thing they knew — armed legions were marching upon their homes, and it was their duty to hurl them back at any cost! For this, not we only, who shared their perils and hardships, do them honor — not the Southern people only — but all brave men everywhere. Nameless they may be, but the name of "Confederate soldier" will echo around the world through the coming years and will be accepted as the synonym of valor, of constancy, and of loyalty to the sternest call of duty.

My comrades, I have been in the Eternal City, surrounded by the deathless relics and monuments which commemorate the glorious achievements of the citizens and soldiers of ancient Rome. I have paced the aisles of that stately church in which Venice has piled up the splendid memorials in brass and in marble of the men who made her name great in Europe — who made her to sit as a queen upon her watery throne among the nations. I have stood under the dome of the *Hôtel des Invalides*, in Paris, on the spot upon which France has lavished with unstinted hand her wealth and her art to shed glory upon the name to her greatest soldier — his sarcophagus reposes upon a pavement of costly marbles gathered from all quarters of the globe, and so arranged as to represent a Sun of Glory irradiating the name of the hero of Marengo, and of the Pyramids, of Jena, and of Austerlitz. And I have meditated in awe-struck silence beneath the fretted roof of Westminster Abbey, surrounded by the almost countless memorial marbles which twenty generations of Englishmen have erected to celebrate the fame of their most illustrious kings and nobles, soldiers and patriots, jurists and statesmen, poets and historians, musicians and dramatists.

But on none of these occasions have I been so impressed with the patriotic and unselfish devotion that human nature is capable of, as when I have contemplated the character and the career of the private soldiers of the Confederacy. Not for fame or for reward, not for place or rank, not lured by ambition, or goaded by necessity, but in simple obedience to duty, as they understood it, these men suffered all, sacrificed all, dared all — and died! No stately abbey will ever cover their remains. Their dust will never repose beneath fretted or frescoed roof. No costly bronze will ever blazon their names for posterity to honor — but the Potomac and the Rappahannock, the James and the Chickahominy, the Cumberland and the Tennessee, the Mississippi and the Rio Grande, as they run their long race from the mountains to the sea, will sing of their prowess forevermore! The mountains of Virginia and Tennessee and Georgia will stand eternal witnesses of their valor, though no Thorwaldsen chisel on their solid rocks a lion like that at Lucerne, stricken to the death, but even in death, and as its life-blood ebbs away, protecting the shield committed to its defence.

As I recall the magnificent valor of those half-fed, half-clad legions of the Confederacy, the thought comes: "But after all they failed. The Confederacy fell. The banner of the Southern Cross sank to earth to rise no more. All the courage and the constancy of those heroic souls could not, or, at any rate, did not, bring success. Their cause is known to-day as 'the lost cause.'" Yes, as we remember the superb but fruitless prowess they displayed on so many fields, the words of the poet recur to our minds:

> "In vain, alas! in vain ye gallant few,
> From rank to rank your volleyed thunders flew."

But *was* it in vain? I do not believe it. It is true that their flashing bayonets did not establish the new Confederacy. It is true that those proud armies of Lee and John-ston were slowly worn away by attrition until, reduced to gaunt skeletons of what they had been, they surrendered to the vast hosts of the Union armies. But it is *not* true that those gallant Southrons suffered and died in vain. No brave battle fought for truth and right was ever in vain! The truth survives, though the soldier of the truth perishes. His death, his defeat, becomes the seed of future success. Over his dead body the armies of the truth march to victory. I might say that to have given, amid disaster and defeat, such splendid examples of what American man-hood can accomplish, was enough to prove that they did not shed their blood to no purpose. "*Being dead they yet speak.*" They tell us and our children and children's children, that courage, self-sacrifice, and loyalty to conviction are sub-lime; they are better than mere success; they carry with them their own reward. Death was not too high a price to pay for the exhibition to the world of such heroism as theirs. *That* cannot die. It shines as the stars with a deathless light above the sordid and selfish aims of men. It will inspire generations to come with noble ideals of un-selfish living. It is a new example of the profound words of Jesus: "*He that loseth his life shall find it.*"

It is said that on the spot where the three devoted patriots of the three Swiss cantons met, by the borders of Lake Lucerne, and bound themselves in a solemn league to rid Switzerland of the tyrant's yoke, three fountains afterward sprang up. The legend embodies an eternal truth. The soil trodden by a patriot is holy ground, and, though his banner may go down in disaster, and he himself perish, and his cause be overwhelmed by defeat, yet his memory and his example will remain a benediction to his people. Foun-tains of blessing spring up on the sod consecrated by the patriot's sufferings and sacrifices for his country.

Let us note, then, wherein they failed and wherein did not fail. They failed to establish the Southern Confederacy.

Why? For no other reason but this — God decreed otherwise. Yes, my comrades, the military genius of our commanders was not at fault, the valor of the Confederate armies was not at fault; but it was God's will that this country should not be divided into two rival nations, jealous of each other; armed against each other. It may be said they failed to preserve the institution of slavery. I answer again they did not draw their swords to defend slavery. It was the cause of liberty that fired their souls to do, to dare, and to die. They conceived that the Federal Government was trampling on the liberties of the States, and they rose in their defence. It was the sacred heritage of Anglo-Saxon freedom, of local self-government won at Runnymede, that they believed in peril when they flew to arms as one man from the Potomac to the Rio Grande. They may have been right, or they may have been wrong, but that was the issue they made. On that they stood. For that they died.

That, be it remembered, was the supreme issue in the mind of the Southern soldier. *The dissolution of the Union was not what he had chiefly at heart. The establishment of the Southern Confederacy was not what he had chiefly at heart. Both the one and the other were secondary to the preservation of the supreme and sacred right of self-government. They were means to the end, not the end itself.*

Did they fail then in this, their supreme and ultimate aim? I answer, they did not fail to make such a protest against the aggressions of power upon the province of liberty as has filled the world with its echo. They did not fail in successfully arraigning by the potent voice of their superb valor and their all-sacrificing patriotism the usurpation of powers and functions which, by the Constitution, were distributed to the States.

It is my belief that the close and candid student of public opinion in our country, these forty years past, will conclude that this protest of theirs has not been in vain. In spite of the historians who have misread the causes and the objects of the war on the part of the South, the fact that the Confederate soldiers and the people of the South made their superb struggle and their marvellous sacrifices for the right of local self-government, has silently impressed the minds of the American people, with the result that that right has been steadily gaining in the strength of its hold upon the people of many of the States of the Union.[1]

So convinced am I of this, that I make bold to predict that the future historian will say that while the armies of the North saved the Union from dissolution, the armies of the South saved the rights of the States within the Union. Thus victor and vanquished will both be adjudged victorious, for, if it is due to the Federal soldier that the Union is henceforth indissoluble, it is equally due to the Confederate soldier that this indissoluble Union is composed, and shall forever be composed, of indestructible States.

Comrades, when I consider these things I no longer echo, as I once did, the sentiment which Lucan puts into the mouth of a great Roman:

> "*Victrix causa diis placuit,*
> *sed victa Catoni,*"[2]

for I see that the "conquered right" has won the victory after all; the conquered banner triumphs in defeat; the lost cause is lost no longer, and God, who denied us success in the way of our own choosing, has granted it in another and better way.

Yes, ye gallant defenders of our stainless Confederate

[1] Members of Congress from the South observed a great change in this respect in the sentiments of their fellow members from the North and the West. Moreover, the limitation of the authority of the General Government to those powers distinctly delegated, and the reservation to the States of the powers not delegated, has been affirmed again and again by the Supreme Court since the war.

[2] Rendered by Dr. E. A. Washburn thus:
> "Let a conquering might
> Bribe all the gods to silence, —
> Cato's choice be with the conquered right!"

banner, ye did not die in vain! Your deeds have cast a halo of glory over our Southern land which will only grow brighter as time advances. Your memory will be a priceless heritage which we will transmit to our children's children untarnished. None shall ever write "traitor" over your graves unrebuked by us, while God gives us the power of speech! Farewell, brave comrades, farewell, till the tryst of God beyond the river. The bugle has sounded "taps" over your graves. After all these years its pathetic notes still vibrate in our ears, reminding us that we shall see your faces no more on earth.

But we clasp your dear memory to our hearts to-day once more. Ye are "our dead"; ours ye were in those stern years from 1861 to 1865, when we marched and camped and battled side by side; "ours" by the sacred bond of a common consecration to a cause which was holy to us; ye are "ours" to-day as we recall with pride your cheerful endurance of unaccustomed hardships — your heroic steadfastness in danger and disaster, your magnificent courage in the deadly trenches, or at the flaming cannon's mouth.

Ye were "our dead" when ye lay stark and stiff on the bloody fields of Manassas, of Winchester, of Shiloh, of Perryville, of Chickamauga, of Fredericksburg, of Malvern Hill, of Chancellorsville, of Sharpsburg, of Gettysburg, of the Wilderness! Ye will be "ours" again when the last great reveille shall sound, and the brothers whom the fortunes of battle divided shall be reunited in the better land!

GENERAL J. E. B. STUART IN THE GETTYSBURG CAMPAIGN

A Reply to Colonel John S. Mosby[1]

By Randolph Harrison McKim, *late First Lieutenant and A. D. C. Third Brigade, General Edward Johnson's Division, Army of Northern Virginia*

Col. John S. Mosby, the brave and able commander of a famous partisan corps in Virginia during the Civil War, has published a book in exposition of the part borne by Gen. J. E. B. Stuart's cavalry in the Gettysburg campaign, and in defence of that heroic officer from the unfavorable criticism passed on his course in that campaign.[2] The splendid services of Jeb Stuart to the Southern cause are written on the heart of the Southern people; and his superb leadership in that brilliant, though mistaken, raid round the Federal Army between June 27th and July 1st, and, later, his invaluable service on the retreat from Gettysburg, are, I think, universally acknowledged. They were long ago celebrated, among others, by General Fitzhugh Lee in his description of the Gettysburg campaign contained in his life of Gen. Robert E. Lee, pp. 265–266.[3] The most brilliant cavalry officer of the Army of Northern Virginia did not

[1] An address delivered before the Lee Camp Confederate Veterans, Richmond, Va., Jan. 21, 1910.

[2] "Stuart's Cavalry in the Gettysburg campaign," 1908. He also published in November, 1908, an article on the same subject in the "Journal of the Military Service Institution," to which I replied in the same journal, May, 1910.

[3] It is remarkable that Colonel Mosby should include Gen. Fitz Lee

have to wait for Colonel Mosby to sing his praises in the year 1908.

But there have been, and are, many of the soldiers of Lee, who, though they yield to none in their admiration of General Stuart, nevertheless are of opinion that he made several serious errors of judgment in the Gettysburg campaign, and that these contributed not a little to the Confederate failure. Unfortunately, these recent publications of Colonel Mosby are of such a character that it is necessary to reopen this painful subject, and to speak as plainly as that writer has done. This is the more necessary because his argument is so plausible, and is stated with so much dialectical skill, that only the very careful reader is likely to detect its fallacies.

Colonel Mosby first impeaches the accuracy of both of General Lee's Reports of the Battle of Gettysburg (of July 31st, 1863, and January, 1864) in several important statements made therein; viz.: 1. That General Lee was in ignorance of Hooker's movements until the night of June 28th, 1863, when General Longstreet's scout reported his army approaching South Mountain; 2. That General Lee then, and therefore, changed his plan and ordered his army to concentrate east of South Mountain; 3. That it had been Lee's intention to concentrate at Harrisburg and that he ordered Hill and Longstreet to that place after reaching Chambersburg; 4. That "the absence of the cavalry rendered it impossible to obtain accurate information" of the movements and position of the Federal Army.

This serious impeachment of General Lee's accuracy in regard to the particulars of his own campaign is largely

among those who have thrown the blame of the Gettysburg campaign on Stuart. For General Lee says: "This officer has been unjustly criticised for not being in front of Lee's army at Gettysburg, but Lee and Longstreet must be held responsible for his route." ("Life of General Lee," p. 265.)

based on a letter taken from General Lee's Official Letter
Book, and dated at Chambersburg, June 28th, 7.30 A.M.,
in which General Lee says to General Ewell:

"I wrote you *last night* stating that General Hooker was
reported to have crossed the Potomac and is advancing by
way of Middletown, the head of his column being at that
point in Frederick County. I directed you in my letter to
move your forces to this point."

Colonel Mosby declares that this letter refutes "every
word" of the statements of General Longstreet, Colonel
Marshall, General Long, Colonel Walter Taylor, General
Fitz Lee, and General Lee's own report in regard to the
campaign in the particulars above named. He further says
that General Ewell's and General Early's reports show that
the movement against Harrisburg was arrested on June
27th, and thus agree with the statements of the letter of
June 28th, which he quotes.

Now I affirm, on the contrary, that the reports of Ewell
and Early are irreconcilable with the accuracy of *the date*
of this famous letter. Nobody can reconcile this letter,
as dated (June 28th, 7.30 A.M.), with the indisputable
facts of the campaign. The genuineness of the letter is
undisputed—it is in the well-known handwriting of Colonel
Venable, of Lee's staff — but the accuracy of the date is
called in question. Suppose it to have been written on
June 29th, and it is then in complete harmony with General Lee's report, with the statements of his staff on the
points at issue, and with the reports of General Longstreet, General Ewell, and General Early.

Now this famous letter turns out to have been copied in
the letter book of General Lee *from memory*, by Col. Charles
Venable. It is marked thus: *"From memory — sketch of
a letter."*

It is not the original letter. It was copied afterward
some time before July 1st — the date of the next letter. It
cannot therefore have the same authority as the original

would have. Especially on the question of date, it is more liable to error. Let us now suppose that there was a mistake in the date, and that it should have been dated "June 29th, 7.30 A.M.," instead of June 28th, 7.30 A.M."[1] Then the first order to Ewell to march back from Carlisle written "last night" would be dated June 28th, not June 27th.

If this hypothesis harmonizes with the reports of Ewell and Lee and with the dates when the divisions of the Third Corps began their march to Cashtown, then the probability of its correctness becomes very strong.

It seems to me it does thus harmonize.

Consider that such a despatch was of supreme importance, and would therefore be sent as fast as a courier could carry it. Colonel Marshall testifies that it was long after ten P.M., June 28th, when he found General Lee in conference with the scout who brought the intelligence of Hooker's movements. Even if the despatch was not sent until midnight, General Ewell might easily have received it by six in the morning, for it is, as Colonel Mosby reminds us, only thirty miles from Chambersburg to Carlisle.

Now, if it was written on the 27th, and received by Ewell early on the morning of the 28th, why did Gen. Edward Johnson's division not receive orders to march back southward from Carlisle till nine A.M., on the 29th, as my diary proves? (I was a staff officer in Johnson's division and kept a careful diary of the campaign.) But, if it was written on the 28th, despatched at midnight, and received by Ewell by six or seven A.M., of the 29th, orders to Gen. Edward Johnson and to General Rodes might well have been issued as early as nine A.M.

Again, if Ewell received the order on the morning of the 29th, it exactly harmonizes with his statement in his report that he "was starting on the 29th" for Harrisburg "when ordered by the general commanding to join the main

[1] Since writing the above I have learned that Colonel Stribling has made a similar suggestion, but I have not yet seen his paper.

body of the army." He says, "I was starting on the 29th for that place when ordered by the general commanding to join the main body of the army at Cashtown."

Again, it appears that Johnson's reserve artillery and trains were passing through Chambersburg after midnight of the 29th. Mr. Jacob Hoke, Mosby's authority, says it was between one and two A.M. From this Colonel Mosby infers they "must have started on the evening of the 28th." But why? If they had started at nine or ten A.M., on the 29th, could not the head of the train have covered thirty miles and reached Chambersburg by one or two hours after midnight? Thirty miles in sixteen hours is not at all extraordinary, especially in an emergency. Mr. Hoke, whom Mosby cites as a witness, says the trains were moving "hurriedly" — "at a trot." This shows they were making a forced march.[1]

Turn now to Early's report. He says that on the evening of the 29th he received General Ewell's instructions to move back to the west side of South Mountain, together with a copy of Lee's order to him — evidently the *first* order. Now if my hypothesis is correct, and if Ewell received Lee's letter in the early hours of the 29th, what was to prevent Capt. Elliott Johnson from riding from Carlisle to York, a distance of thirty-six miles, as Colonel Mosby points out, between eight A.M. and five P.M.? I myself rode for Gen. Geo. H. Steuart fifty miles by daylight on June 23rd, in Pennsylvania. But on the supposition that Ewell received that famous letter and order on the morning of the 28th, how can we account for the fact that Early did not receive Ewell's order till the evening of the 29th?

I submit that these facts make it beyond contradiction that there is an error in the date of the letter as it was copied from memory. The supposition that General Lee sent

---

[1] If this was the artillery of Col. Snowden Andrews, that was camped five miles south of Carlisle, so that it had only twenty-five miles to march to Chambersburg.

that letter to Ewell on the night of June 27th bristles with improbabilities. There is the improbability that Lee would have waited till the 30th to order Hill and Longstreet to march to Cashtown. There is the improbability that an order of such importance would not be despatched with due military expedition. Its omission from Lee's letter book is suggestive of haste. It was written at night, and would seem to have been despatched at once without taking time to copy it in the letter book. This increases the improbability that it would not be sent post haste to Ewell.

Then there is the improbability that Ewell, having received so supremely important an order, should have put off its execution for twenty-four hours — from the morning of the 28th to the morning of the 29th. Again, there is the improbability that he should have waited twenty-four hours before he sent his staff officer to transmit General Lee's order to General Early at York. Then, finally, there is the improbability that General Longstreet and Colonel Taylor and Colonel Marshall and General Long and General Lee himself should all have believed and stated that the news of the proximity of Hooker should have been brought by a scout on the 28th, if the fact was really known on the 27th.

Colonel Mosby's whole argument on this point hinges on the accuracy of the date of the letter or rather "sketch of a letter" written down from memory. It appears to me immensely more likely that Colonel Venable made a mistake of date in writing that sketch of Lee's letter than that all the improbabilities I have enumerated should have occurred.

Colonel Mosby says: "Nobody can reconcile this letter with Lee's report." Neither can anybody reconcile this letter, as dated, with the facts of the campaign as reflected in the reports of Ewell and Early. Either Colonel Venable in writing the letter from memory made a mistake in dating it the 28th, or General Lee and General Longstreet and General Long and Colonel Marshall and Colonel Taylor were all mistaken in the belief that the change in the plans of the campaign was due to the arrival of a scout on the night of the 28th. Which is the more likely supposition? If it was written on the 29th, it is in complete harmony with General Lee's report. But even if it were granted that Lee knew on the 27th of June that Hooker had crossed the Potomac, that fact would not advance one step the contention of Colonel Mosby that Lee had no need of Stuart's cavalry with his army during those critical days from June 27th to July 1st.

In order to confirm his denial that General Lee intended to concentrate his army at Harrisburg, Colonel Mosby points to the fact that A. P. Hill's corps was turned eastward on its arrival at Chambersburg and camped near Fayetteville. This, he thinks, conclusive against any such intention. But General Hill in his report says ("Rebellion Records," Vol. XXVII, pt. 2, p. 606):

"On the morning of June 29th, the Third Corps ——— was encamped on the road from Chambersburg to Gettysburg, near the village of Fayetteville. I was directed to move on this road in the direction of York, and to cross the Susquehanna, menacing the communications of Harrisburg with Philadelphia, and to coöperate with General Ewell." These doubtless were the orders written by Colonel Marshall the night of the 28th of June.

General Early also in his report says it had been his intention to cross the Susquehanna by the bridge at Wrightsville and move up the left bank of that river against Harrisburg.

Thus General Early, General Hill, and General Ewell all testify that they had been ordered to move against Harrisburg; yet Colonel Mosby asserts that Lee had no such plan, though it is stated in both his reports, as well as by his staff officers.

It may be granted that there are certain inaccuracies in the reports of the battle signed by General Lee, but it is asking too much of our credulity to have us suppose that General Lee did not know when and why he changed his plan of campaign at Chambersburg. There are also inaccuracies in General Stuart's report, as when he says that General Lee informed him it was likely one column of the army would move through Gettysburg, the other through Carlisle. What General Lee wrote was that one column would move through Emmitsburg, the other through Chambersburg.

．　　．　　．　　．　　．　　．　　．　　．

And now as to the second, and main, point of Colonel Mosby's contention that Gen. J. E. B. Stuart acted in strict accordance with General Lee's instructions between the 23d of June and the 2d of July. What were General Lee's instructions to General Stuart? He wrote to Ewell that he had instructed General Stuart "to march with three brigades across the Potomac and place himself on your right and in communication with you, keep you advised of the movements of the enemy, and assist in collecting supplies for the army." To General Stuart himself Lee wrote on June 22d, "You can move with the other three (brigades) *into Maryland* and take position on General Ewell's right, place yourself in communication with him, guard his flank, keep him informed of the enemy's movements and collect all the supplies you can for the use of the army. One column of Ewell's army will probably move toward the Susquehanna by the Emmittsburg route, another by Chambersburg."

[Observe that when General Lee gave General Stuart this order to take position on General Ewell's right, that officer was just leaving Hagerstown. In his report ("Rebellion Records," Vol. XXVII, pt. 2, p. 443) he says that on June 22d he "received orders from the commanding general to take Harrisburg, and *next morning* Rodes and Johnson commenced their march into Pennsylvania."]

This order was repeated in a letter to General Stuart dated June 23, a part of which I quote:

HEADQUARTERS, ARMY OF NORTHERN VIRGINIA,
June 23, 1863, 3.30 P.M.

Major-General J. E. B. Stuart, Commanding Cavalry:
General, . . .

If General Hooker's army remains inactive you can leave two brigades to watch him, and withdraw with the three others, but should he not appear to be moving northward, I think you had better withdraw this side of the mountain to-morrow night, cross at Shepherdstown next day, and move over to Fredericktown.

You will, however, be able to judge whether you can pass around their army without hindrance, doing them all the damage you can, and cross the river east of the mountains. In either case, after crossing the river, you must move on and feel the right of Ewell's troops, collecting information, provisions, etc.

Give instructions to the commander of the brigades left behind to watch the flank and rear of the army, and (in the event of the enemy leaving their front) retire from the mountains west of the Shenandoah, leaving sufficient pickets to guard the passes, and bringing everything clean along the valley, closing upon the rear of the army.

I am very respectfully and truly yours,
(Signed)   R. E. LEE, General.

Thus, in the very last communication received by General Stuart from General Lee, the order was emphatically given that as soon as he crossed the river, he should place his command on Ewell's right and march with him toward the Susquehanna.

The commanding general indicated Frederick as Stuart's first objective, and he thought he had better cross the river at Shepherdstown, but gave him the option of crossing

east of the Blue Ridge if he could do so *without hindrance.*
General Stuart found Hooker's army in the way — a
big "hindrance" surely — but yet chose to cross east of
the Ridge, thus cutting himself off from both Ewell and
Lee.

Now, the first question is, Did General Stuart carry out
the above instruction and do these things? The history
of the campaign shows that he did *none* of these things.
He was not on Ewell's right in the march toward the Susquehanna; he did not guard his flank; he did not keep him
advised of the movements of the enemy. The second
question is, Did General Lee give Stuart discretion to take
such a route as, in the event, prevented his carrying out
these instructions? Was he allowed to cross the Potomac
east of the Blue Ridge, and pass "by the enemy's rear,"
and so find himself in such a position that he *could not* carry
out those instructions?

Now Colonel Mosby here puts a gloss on the record, and
represents that General Lee instructed General Stuart
to "move into Pennsylvania and *join Ewell on the Susquehanna.*" (Page 88.) Throughout the whole discussion he
again and again represents General Lee's order in this way,
as an order to proceed to the Susquehanna and join General
Ewell. (Pages 89, 91, 154, 180.)

But this is not what General Lee ordered him to do, but
to place himself on Ewell's right in the latter's movement
"toward the Susquehanna," to guard his flank and keep
him informed of the enemy's movement. Colonel Mosby
eliminates all this and represents the order received by
General Stuart to be to "join Ewell on the Susquehanna"
and then "act as Ewell's chief of cavalry." (Page 89.)
Again, "Lee had informed Stuart that he would find Ewell
on the Susquehanna." (Page 180.)

Lee had done nothing of the kind. I submit that this
is a complete misreading, or misstatement, of General
Lee's instructions. Though General Lee and General

Longstreet both suggested that Stuart should cross east of the Blue Ridge and pass in the rear of Hooker's army, it was evidently the intention that he should, as soon as possible, connect with General Ewell in his northward march "toward the Susquehanna." General Stuart himself says in his report that he was directed "to proceed *with all despatch* to join the right of the army in Pennsylvania."

In his zeal to justify General Stuart, Colonel Mosby has misread, and so misstated, the records. Such carelessness in a crucial point like this is inexcusable.

Here let it be noted that, in order to interpret correctly the meaning and intent of General Lee's communications to General Stuart in those critical days, June 22–24, it is essential to place before the mind's eye the situation of the two armies at the time. General Stuart in his report says:

"I submitted to the commanding general the plan of leaving a brigade or so in my present front, and, passing through Hopewell or some other gap in the Bull Run Mountains, attain the enemy's rear, passing between his main body and Washington, and cross into Maryland, joining our army north of the Potomac. The commanding general wrote me authorizing this move if I deemed it practicable."

Now, at the time of this correspondence, Ewell's corps, whose right flank Stuart was "to guard," was just beginning its march northward from Hagerstown, and General Hooker's army was in Virginia. General Stuart's plan, then, contemplated passing round General Hooker's rear, *while his army was still south* of the Potomac; and *General Lee's authorization contemplated that, and that only.* It did not authorize Stuart to carry out his plan of passing round the enemy's rear after the enemy had transferred his army to the north side of the Potomac. Colonel Mosby confirms this view, for he says (p. 212): "The orders contemplated Stuart's crossing the Potomac in advance of both armies."

And General Stuart's plan, proposed to General Lee, and to which he understood General Lee agreed, was, to use the words of his report, "to cross into Maryland, joining our army north of the Potomac." He gives no intimation that he understood that he was to join Ewell "on the Susquehanna," as Colonel Mosby states the case. General Stuart also tells us that General Lee "directed me, after crossing, to proceed with all despatch to join the right of the army in Pennsylvania."

Colonel Mosby himself says: "The object was to go the most direct route to Ewell." (Page 212.)

Precisely here was the error of judgment committed by the gallant Stuart — he did not keep in view the main object of his expedition, which was to coöperate with Ewell in his march from the Maryland line to Harrisburg. This, the first and principal duty imposed upon the chief of cavalry by the commanding general, was subordinated to the secondary and incidental object of damaging General Hooker's communications and making a raid around his army.

When General Stuart discovered that the Federal Army was moving to cross the Potomac, which it did three days before he crossed at Seneca Ford, two things should have been considered by him, *first*, that the reason given by General Longstreet for the suggestion that he should pass in the rear of the Federal Army (viz., that his passage of the Potomac by Shepherdstown "would disclose our plans") no longer existed, for evidently the enemy had discovered Lee's northern movement and were following him; and, *second*, that General Lee's permission to pass around the rear of the Federal Army did not apply to the situation now developed when the Federal Army had left Virginia. He had permission to make that movement only if there was no "hindrance" in the way. To take that course now (after June 25th) would completely prevent the main object of his expedition, which was to "join the right of the army in Pennsylvania" on its march "toward the Susquehanna."

These observations receive support from the comment of an able and accomplished military critic, Captain Cecil

Battine. In his "Crisis of the Confederacy" (1905) he says, referring to General Stuart's raid:

"By the light of what happened, it may now be said that the raid was a mistake, and especially when Stuart found the Federal Army to be moving northward did he commit an error of judgment in attempting to traverse its lines of communication, thus severing his connection with Lee at the crisis of the campaign." (Page 156.)

"Balancing what might be gained against what was certain to be lost for the invading army by the absence of the best half of the cavalry with its distinguished chief, the same judgment must be made as Jackson pronounced on Stoneman's raid six weeks earlier." (Page 158.)

"Having acquired this knowledge (that the Federal Army was marching north), Stuart would certainly have done well to have marched up the right bank of the Potomac and so made sure of rejoining the army, but his character was not one to lightly abandon an enterprise which he had once undertaken." (Page 160.)

Colonel Henderson, the distinguished author of the "Life of Stonewall Jackson," is of the same opinion. He says: "Stuart forgot for once that to cover the march of the army and to send in timely information are services of far greater importance than cutting the enemy's communications and harassing his rear." ("The Science of War," p. 303.)

It must also be acknowledged, I think, that Stuart erred in judgment again in the course he took after he had brought his five thousand horsemen across the Potomac during the night of June 27th. Instead of proceeding "with all despatch" to join Ewell, he stopped to break up the canal, to intercept and capture boats (at least a dozen of them), and burn them. He also captured a great wagon train and "took it along." Some of the teamsters were chased into the suburbs of Washington. That was on the morning of the 28th. These proceedings consumed valuable time that should have been devoted to marching to Ewell. By that

time Lee was at Chambersburg and Ewell had already
been one day at Carlisle. Was it not Stuart's duty to
make all speed to overtake Ewell, as three precious days
had been lost? And could he do this encumbered by captured wagon trains? It is about seventy-five or eighty
miles from Seneca Ford to York, which could readily have
been covered by Stuart's horsemen in two marches if that
was his objective. He knew that Hooker had crossed the
Potomac and was marching northward. Then would it
not seem that his supreme purpose should have been to
march day and night and to place himself in communication
with Ewell, and be at hand for whatever service his cavalry
could render? He does not seem to have been of that
opinion, for he had only gone as far as Westminster by the
evening of the 29th. Now Westminster is about fifty miles
or less from Seneca Ford, where he had crossed. Had he
pressed on, the morning of the 28th, he could easily have
reported to General Early at York (thirty miles farther)
before nightfall of the 29th, not long after that officer
received orders to march to Cashtown, or certainly before
daybreak of the 30th. In either case he would not have
made the fruitless march to Carlisle on July the 1st, but
would have marched with Early on the 30th, and would
almost certainly have been interposed between the enemy
and the infantry of Early and Hill, and would thus probably
have prevented the battle from being precipitated by Hill
on the morning of July 1st. Since writing the above, I
find that Colonel Henderson reached the same conclusion.
(See his "Science of War," p. 289.)

There can be no doubt that the march of Stuart's horsemen was seriously impeded by the captured wagon train
which he "took along."[1] Colonel Mosby admits (page 191)

---

[1] This is also the judgment of Gen. E. P. Alexander, who says (page
375): "In saving a large number of wagons instead of burning them,
and in delaying twelve hours to parole his prisoners instead of bringing
along the officers and letting the men go, Stuart committed fatal

that he might have reached York on the 30th instead of July the 1st, if he had burned the wagons. He crossed the river the night of the 27th, and York is about eighty miles from the ford. More important is the statement of General Stuart himself in his report in more than one place. Thus, on page 695, "Rebellion Records," Vol. XVII, he says, speaking of the engagement at Hanover:

"If my command had been well closed now, this cavalry column would have been at our mercy; but, owing to the great elongation of the column, by reason of the 200 wagons and hilly roads, Hampton was a long way behind, and Lee was not yet heard from on the left."

Again, on page 696, he says:

"Our wagon train was now a subject of serious embarrassment, but I thought by making a détour of the right by Jefferson, I could save it."

Two possibilities were eliminated by the drag put on General Stuart's column by the captured wagon train: 1. But for the delay thus occasioned he might have marched from Westminster to Gettysburg by Littletown, as apparently he hoped to do, for he could have reached Westminster certainly by the morning of the 29th, instead of at sundown (for that place is only forty-five or fifty miles from Seneca ford), and at that earlier hour he probably would not have found the Federal cavalry on that road.[1] That cavalry reached Littletown during the night of the 29th.

blunders." And he adds, "The delay caused to subsequent marches by the long wagon train, and the embarrassment of protecting it, was responsible for the loss of time, which made, on the whole, a sad failure of the expedition."

[1] In his report General Stuart says he reached Westminster at five P.M. and camped at Union Mills, midway between Westminster and Littletown, on the Gettysburg road (page 695). Scouts reported that the Federal cavalry had reached Littletown during the night. But for this it would appear Stuart would have marched to Gettysburg. Instead he marched to Hanover. General Kilpatrick in his report says "Stuart was making for Littletown."

2. Had he decided instead to press on through Hanover to York he would have been able to effect a junction with General Early at York by the evening of the 29th, or the early morning of the 30th, and his superb leadership would then have been available in the march from York to Cashtown on the 30th, and in the operations on the fateful 1st of July.

Certainly it is not strange that General Lee should have been surprised that he had no intelligence from General Stuart between the 23d of June and the 2d of July; and the question is whether that long delay was unavoidable under the circumstances in which General Stuart found himself after he parted with General Lee. Colonel Mosby says General Lee had studied astronomy and knew the nature of an eclipse. Yes, but General Lee was not surprised at the eclipse, but at the length of its duration. He sent couriers in every direction to gain, if possible, news of General Stuart. Colonel Mosby insists it was no part of General Stuart's duty to report to General Lee the movements of Hooker's army. Yet Stuart himself writes in

Gen. E. P. Alexander, in his important work, page 375, says that had General Stuart's column "here followed the direct road *via* Littletown to Gettysburg, only about sixteen miles away, it could have occupied Gettysburg before 11 A. M. on the 30th, when it would have found itself in good position in front of Lee's army, then concentrated at Cashtown." And he adds that in that case "Lee's army would have occupied some strong position between Cashtown and Gettysburg, and the onus of attack would have been on the Federals, as had been the plan of the campaign."

It would have been natural for General Stuart to make Gettysburg his objective, for in his report he says he had been instructed that one column of our army would move "by Gettysburg." His language is not conclusive as to whether he had meant to march by Littletown and Gettysburg, but it is a natural inference from what he says that but for the news that during the night of the 29th the Federal cavalry had reached Littletown, he would have marched to that place and so on to Gettysburg. But for that unnecessary and fatal delay he would have been at Littletown before the Federals, and could have reached Gettysburg by the early morning of the 30th.

his report, "It was important for me to reach our column with as little delay as possible, to acquaint the commanding general with the nature of the enemy's movements, as well as to place with his column my cavalry force." (Page 695.)

Colonel Mosby tells us of Stuart's energetic action in Hooker's rear between the 27th of June and the 1st of July; but General Lee did not instruct him to destroy Hooker's trains, or to damage the canal, or to break Hooker's communication with Washington, or to burn the railroad bridge at Sykesville, but "after crossing the river (at Shepherdstown, or Seneca), you must move on and feel the right of Ewell's troops, collecting information, provisions, etc." It was a brilliant raid, executed with great skill and with marvellous endurance and intrepidity — but it was not ordered by General Lee, and the results were very unsatisfactory.

Does it not appear reasonable that General Stuart, having been, even if without fault of his own, delayed two days in crossing the Potomac, would then have felt, if he was to perform the service entrusted to him by General Lee on the 23d of June, he must march with all possible haste, by the shortest practicable route, to place himself in touch with General Ewell?

Did he do this? Or, did not his eager and aggressive nature lead him to undertake enterprises which greatly delayed his march? The infantry of the Fifth Corps of the Federal Army was only one day behind Stuart's column at Westminster, though when he began his movement that corps was in Virginia.

But there is a previous question. When Longstreet and Hill had crossed the Potomac, and Hooker, learning the fact, had followed, the plans of the Confederate commander were, as I have stated, revealed to General Hooker, and the reason given for Stuart's march being made in rear of the Federal Army, no longer existed. Should not that officer then have reverted to the other route and crossed at Shep-

herdstown so as to be able to carry out his instructions as
promptly as possible?   Was not this course also the more
important when he found that he could not cross the Potomac
on the 25th, because the Federal columns were moving
north?   His cavalry had been assigned a definite part in
the campaign then opened — that is, to guard Ewell's flank,
keep him informed of the enemy's movements, and collect
supplies for the army.   Everything should have been
subordinated to the accomplishment of this end.   Had it
been, General Stuart would have resisted the temptation
to break the Federal communications with Washington,
and to capture and carry off the enemy's wagon train, and
would have joined Ewell several days before he did.   However brilliant and daring his operations in Hooker's rear,
and however beneficial their results, it is not pertinent
to the question at issue, which is simply this: Did General
Stuart exert himself with whole-hearted energy to carry
out the instructions he received, and in the most expeditious
manner?   In so critical and fateful a movement as the
invasion of Pennsylvania, it was supremely important
that every officer should carry out the orders of the commander-in-chief with the strictest fidelity and exactness.
As a matter of fact, Ewell made his march to the Susquehanna (starting on June 23d from Hagerstown) without
receiving any aid from General Stuart.   That officer
was not able to accomplish any of the things he was charged
to do in connection with Ewell's advance.   And he was
not able to accomplish them because, *first*, he took the
course behind the Federal Army when the reason for that
line of march no longer existed and when the circumstances
under which he had received permission to do so had completely changed; and, *secondly*, because having crossed the
Potomac on the 27th, he did not then march as directly
and as expeditiously as possible, to effect a junction with
General Ewell.   It cannot be· supposed that when Lee
gave Stuart his instructions on June 22d, he had any idea

that that officer would not report to General Ewell until the 1st of July — the ninth day afterward.

Colonel Mosby says that Stuart's cavalry could not have been of any material service to Lee even had they been present at Gettysburg from the beginning of the battle, and yet he says (page 189) that "the withdrawal of Buford's cavalry left Sickles' flank in the peach orchard uncovered — 'in the air,'" "and that Longstreet took advantage of it and struck him a stunning blow." These two statements are inconsistent. Colonel Henderson is of opinion that the skilful handling of the Federal cavalry "practically decided the issue of the conflict." ("Science of War," p. 278.)

Colonel Mosby makes much of the alleged inconsistency of the statement in General Lee's report of Jan., 1864, that Stuart was instructed "to lose no time in placing his command on the right *of our column* as soon as he perceived the enemy moving northward," with the orders he actually received to accompany *the column of General Ewell*. But is there any inconsistency? In using this language, Lee was thinking of his army as a unit, and could not have meant that he expected Stuart to be with Longstreet when he had ordered him to be with Ewell, as is stated in the report which Mosby criticises. This is explicitly stated in the same report a sentence or two before the allusion to "the right of our column." "Our column," in the connection in which it stands, can only mean General Ewell's column. Such criticism is captious and unfair.

In analyzing Colonel Mosby's defence of General Stuart, and pointing out what I consider his mistakes, I have had no desire to associate myself with those who seek to cast the whole responsibility for the failure of the Gettysburg campaign on the shoulders of the commander-in-chief of the cavalry of the Army of Northern Virginia. General A. P. Hill, General Ewell, General Longstreet —especially the last — must all share it with him. I think it must be acknowledged that the battle was precipitated by the un-

authorized advance of General Hill on July 1st. I think
also that Colonel Mosby is right in the opinion that Lee
had no intention of fighting a general battle at Gettysburg:
he was dragged into it by his lieutenant. But on the other
hand, I think that if General Stuart had been with Early,
as he might and ought to have been, on the night of the
29th, or the morning of the 30th,[1] his cavalry would in all
probability have prevented the rash advance of General
Hill. Marching from York to Cashtown on the 30th, by
way of Heidlersburg, he would have felt the enemy, ascer-
tained his position and his strength and left no excuse for
that reconnoisance which prematurely brought on the battle
on a field Lee had not selected. . . . Colonel Mosby's book
involves very serious strictures on General Lee, which his
soldiers are loath to accept save on the most incontrovertible
evidence. He asks us to believe, as I have said, that the
report of the Gettysburg campaign which General Lee
signed in January, 1864, not only reflects gross injustice
on General Stuart, but bristles with inconsistencies and
grievous mistakes on points of capital importance. It is
incredible that these two reports of the battle were signed
by General Lee without reading them. It is inconsistent
with his habit in other cases. We know that he took time
to read General Pickett's report of the battle. Why not
then read his own reports? And if General Lee read them,
then certainly their salient statements, to say the least,
have the stamp of his authority. But Colonel Mosby
asserts that it was not Lee's purpose on the 28th of June to
advance against Harrisburg, though he says so in his report,
and though Colonel Marshall says he himself sent orders to
that effect to Hill and Longstreet on the night of the 28th.

[1] Colonel Mosby says, page 191, if Stuart had arrived on the
30th at York "he could not have communicated with Lee." No,
but he would have received the orders Lee had issued for concentration at Cashtown, and he would have marched that day with Early
toward Cashtown.

He insists also that the change of plan and the orders to concentrate at Cashtown were not the consequence of the intelligence brought by a scout on June 28th, although General Lee affirms it in his report. No matter: Colonel Mosby knows better; he is sure that Lee had ordered Ewell back from Carlisle on the 27th, and he is satisfied of this by the letter in Lee's letter book, not copied, but written from memory afterward by Colonel Venable. His whole argument on this point rests, as I have said, on the accuracy of the *date* of that letter. I have shown that, on the hypothesis of an error in date, the 28th instead of the 29th, the inconsistencies Colonel Mosby alleges disappear.[1]

---

[1] Colonel Mosby is of the opinion that the scout who came in at Chambersburg late on June 28th was as unreal as Cæsar's ghost at Philippi. "No spy came in at Chambersburg," he says. Yet General Longstreet positively affirmed it. General Lee's report states it as a fact and Colonel Marshall says that he was sent for to General Lee's tent after ten P.M., June 28th, and found him in conference with a man in citizen's dress, who proved to be General Longstreet's scout. This is a threefold cord of testimony not to be easily rent asunder by the *ipse dixit* of Colonel Mosby. What appears conclusive proof to Colonel Mosby that the story of the scout is a myth is the statement, in after years coupled with it, that the said scout also brought intelligence of the appointment of General Meade that very day to the command of the Army of the Potomac; but there is no mention of this in General Lee's report. It may be a later edition to the original story. But whether true or false, it does not concern the defenders of the accuracy of General Lee's statement in his report. It is not alluded to either in that report or in the report of General Longstreet. However, the fact is that General Hooker telegraphed his resignation on the evening of June 27th. Meade was at once appointed in his place, and the news of his appointment reached Frederick in the forenoon of June 28th. Colonel Mosby thinks it impossible that the alleged scout could have carried this news so soon from Frederick to Longstreet at Chambersburg. But if by some chance the said scout learned the news in the forenoon of the 28th, is it certain he could not have travelled fifty-five miles before eleven P.M.? President Roosevelt could have done it; perhaps he could. I do not think his quotation from Colonel Freemantle proves that the news of Hooker's being suspended was not received by Longstreet until the 30th of June. But, as I have said,

Now General Lee's report does reflect on General Stuart, so far as to intimate surprise that he did not report to Ewell or to Lee before the 2d of July, and it reflects the feeling of the commander-in-chief that he was greatly embarrassed by this absence. But it leaves it *an open question* whether that absence was unavoidable. Now, if there was one feature in Lee's character that was conspicuous and undeniable, it was his magnanimity. He showed it in a remarkable degree at Gettysburg, and when he states in his report the fact of Stuart's absence, and the embarrassment it caused him, his soldiers feel that the statement is to be accepted as absolutely true. Military critics at once recognize that the absence of the cavalry was the most serious drawback to the success of the campaign. We think Lee was a better judge than Colonel Mosby whether the cavalry of Stuart, under such a superb leader as he was, would have contributed to the success of the campaign, or would have, at least, prevented the precipitation of the battle when and where it occurred.

I do not think Colonel Mosby has shown that Stuart was without blame, and I therefore feel that *part* of the responsibility (I do not say the larger part) for the failure of the campaign must rest on him. And when I say this, I nevertheless yield to none in my admiration of that superb soldier whose military genius and magnificent intrepidity place him so high among the great leaders of the Confederate Army.

the question is of no importance in the argument on behalf of the accuracy of General Lee's statement in his report.

Gen. E. P. Alexander is another witness on both these points. He says (page 379), that on June 28th, General Lee still believed Hooker had not crossed the Potomac; that he issued orders for an advance of his whole army next day upon Harrisburg; but that his plan was changed by the arrival of General Longstreet's scout about midnight of the 28th, with news that Hooker had crossed into Maryland, and that he had been superseded.

It is greatly to be regretted that Colonel Mosby should have deemed it proper, in defending General Stuart against what he considers unjust criticism, to indulge in these strictures upon the conduct and the military judgment of General Lee. He declares, as we have seen, that General Lee was absolutely in error in several of the salient and most important points of his reports. Or, if we wish to save General Lee's reputation in these respects, he suggests an alternative, inconsistent with Lee's whole character and record, and dishonorable to him as a responsible officer; viz., that he signed his reports without reading them. Was Lee then an automaton to do the bidding of Colonel Marshall, his military secretary?

Again, in referring to General Lee's suggestion before he embarked on the Pennsylvania campaign, June 23d, that General Beauregard should be sent to Culpeper Court House with an army, however small, to threaten Washington, Colonel Mosby dismisses the subject lightly with the remark that "if it had been practicable to raise such an army, as the campaign closed the next week at Gettysburg, it could not have been assembled in time to render any assistance to General Lee in the Pennsylvania campaign." (Page 84.) Yet there were five brigades at Petersburg, Richmond, and Guinea Station, besides three brigades in North Carolina, and if General Beauregard and even two of these brigades had been at once sent forward to Culpeper, they could have reached there by rail in a few days, and the moral effect would have been such as probably to turn back some of Hooker's army for the defence of Washington — greatly to Lee's advantage in the approaching battle. Captain Battine, a military critic of ability, remarks that it would have been "worth incurring great risks" to have drawn four of these brigades — "to comply with this suggestion about Beauregard." (Page 166.)

Again, Colonel Mosby challenges General Lee's statement tha the was embarrassed by the absence of General Stuart with the larger part of the cavalry. Colonel Mosby knows better — Lee had all the cavalry that he needed. It does not appear to be necessary to ascribe infallibility to General Lee, in order to justify the conclusion that that great soldier probably knew better than the gallant partisan colonel whether or not the presence of Stuart and his horsemen could have been of great service to him in the campaign. General Lee doubtless was not infallible, but his judgment in military matters was, if we may say so without offence, much less fallible than that of Colonel Mosby.

The same able writer already referred to says (p. 195):

"Probably it was the want of information due to the lack of coöperating cavalry which lay at the root of the halting tactics of the Confederate leaders. Thus every move of the enemy took them by surprise and inspired them with unnecessary caution at the very moment when boldness would have gained so much." (See pp. 219 and 220.)

But the most painful thrust which Colonel Mosby makes at the reputation of General Lee is contained in the following paragraph:

"There is a floating legend that General Lee assumed all the blame of his defeat. He did not; his reports put all the blame on Stuart."

That General Lee said to his soldiers after the repulse of Pickett's charge that he was responsible for the failure is not a "floating legend" but a well-attested fact. That he refrained from reproaching his three lieutenants, Hill and Ewell and Longstreet, with their share in the defeat is another well-known fact. That he wrote to Jefferson Davis that touching and pathetic letter asking that a younger and better man be placed in command of the army, because of his lack of success, is yet another proof that he assumed the responsibility of the failure. And to say that in his report he "put all the blame on Stuart" is a grave inaccuracy. The first report states the simple fact, without any animadversion, that "the absence of the cavalry

rendered it impossible to obtain accurate information."
The second rehearsed the orders given General Stuart,
and added that it was expected that officer would "give
notice of the movements" of the Federal Army, but as
"nothing had been heard from him," it was "inferred that
the enemy had not yet left Virginia."[1] The report leaves
it an open question whether Stuart was, or was not, to
blame for his absence and for the lack of information.
General Fitz Lee, in his life of General Lee, with these reports
before him, states that General Lee and General Longstreet
were responsible for Stuart's absence, a statement with
which I cannot agree.

The untoward conclusion of the Pennsylvania campaign
— in a drawn battle which compelled him to retreat, instead
of in the decisive victory he had a right to expect — must
have been a crushing blow to the spirit of General Lee:
and it must forever remain a splendid illustration of the
magnanimity of that great soldier that he made no attempt
to shield his military reputation behind the shortcomings
of his lieutenants.   To state the consequence of the absence
of General Stuart was a part of the story — the *res gestæ* —
of the campaign, and could not have been omitted in any
intelligent account of the same.   But to refrain, as he did,
from stating that the absence of that officer and his command
was due to a failure to strictly observe the orders he had
received — was a generous and magnanimous act which
has few parallels in military history.   It is to be deeply
regretted that any officer who ever drew sword in Lee's
army should seek to tarnish the splendor of such noble
self-restraint.

On the whole I fear the careful critic will be constrained
to pass on Colonel Mosby's book the criticism that writer

---

[1] I have quoted on a previous page a passage from General Stuart's
report of his operations, in which he states that it was "important"
for him to "acquaint the commanding general with the movements
of the enemy."

has passed on Colonel Marshall's work in Lee's report:
"It is a fine example of special pleading, and the composition
shows that the author possessed far more of the qualities of
an advocate than of a judge."

Library of Congress Cataloguing in Publication Data

McKim, Randolph H. (Randolph Harrison), 1842-1920.
A soldier's recollections.
(Collector's library of the Civil War)
Reprint. Originally published: New York: Longmans, Green, 1910.
Includes index.
1. McKim, Randolph H. (Randolph Harrison), 1842-1920.
2. United States—History—Civil War, 1861-1865—Personal narratives, Confederate.
3. Confederate States of America. Army of Northern Virginia—Biography.
4. Gettysburg Campaign, 1863—Personal narratives, Confederate.
5. Soldiers—Virginia—Biography.
I. Title. II. Series.
E605.M47   1984   973.7'455   83-24215
ISBN 0-8094-4271-X (library)
ISBN 0-8094-4270-1 (retail)

Printed in the United States of America

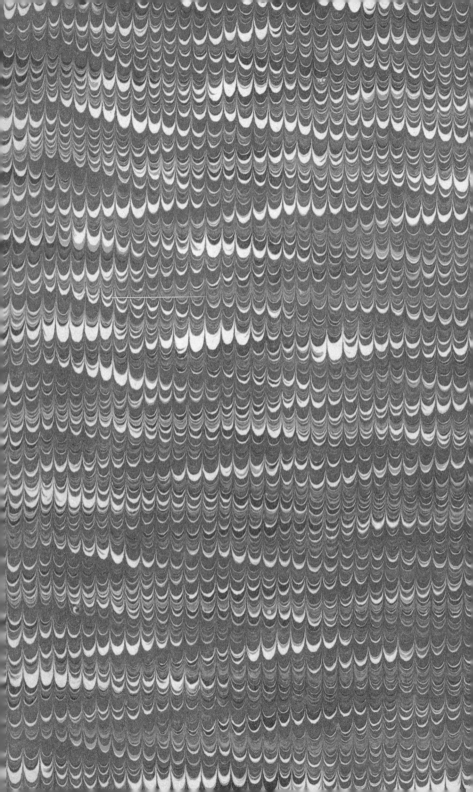